Metaphysical Sociology

This volume critically engages with the work of the acclaimed Australian sociologist John Carroll. It makes the argument for a metaphysical sociology, which Carroll has proposed should focus on the questions of fundamental existence that confront all humans: 'Where do I come from?', 'What should I do with my life?' and 'What happens to me when I die?'. These questions of meaning, in the secular modern West, have become difficult to answer. As contemporary individuals increasingly draw on their inner resources, or 'ontological qualities', to pursue quests for meaning, the key challenge for a metaphysical sociology concerns the cultural resources available to people and the manner in which they are cultivated. Through wide-ranging discussions which include, film, romantic love, terrorism and video games, *Metaphysical Sociology* takes up this challenge. The contributors include emerging and established sociologists, a philosopher, a renowned actor and a musician. As such, this collection will appeal to scholars of social theory and sociology, and to the general reader with interests in morality, art, culture and the fundamental questions of human existence.

Sara James is a Lecturer in the Department of Social Inquiry at La Trobe University, Australia. She is the author of *Making a Living, Making a Life: Work, Meaning and Self-Identity* (Routledge, 2017), a major study of the significance of work in contemporary lives. Sara is co-author of *Sociology in Today's World* (3rd edition), an introductory sociology text for first-year students, and in 2016 she co-edited a special issue of *M/C Journal on Authenticity*.

Morality, Society and Culture

www.routledge.com/Morality-Society-and-Culture/book-series/ASHSER1429

The Morality, Society and Culture series publishes rigorous scholarly work exploring how moral questioning and action have been transformed in contemporary social relationships and by contemporary culture. Can cultural texts such as films, television broadcasts and art be vehicles for moral demands? Do we learn what it means to be 'good' from soap opera and advertising? If cultural texts are forms of moral mimesis, then are the standards of the 'right' and 'good' dependent on external considerations of cultural visibility and social relevance – and if so, how are some moral issues made visible or invisible, relevant or irrelevant?

Now that morality has become cultural and is amenable to sociological and cultural study as well as philosophical investigation, this series explores how and to what effect moral questioning, action and debate are inextricably entwined with contemporary social and cultural forms, texts and institutions. The books in this series offer new understandings of the connection of morality, society and culture, analyse key contemporary events, and establish new methodologies.

Editor

Keith Tester is Professor at The Thesis Eleven Centre for Cultural Sociology at La Trobe University, Australia and Senior Fellow at the Centrum Myśli Jana Pawła II, Warsaw, Poland. He is the author of *Humanitarianism and Modern Culture, Panic, Eric Rohmer: Film as Theology, Moral Culture, The Social Thought of Zygmunt Bauman* and *Animals and Society*, co-author of *Conversations with Zygmunt Bauman* and *What Use is Sociology?*, and co-editor of *Utopia: Social Theory and the Future*.

Published

Making a Living, Making a Life: Work, Meaning and Self-Identity
Sara James

Sociological Noir: Irruptions and the Darkness of Modernity
Kieran Flanagan

Metaphysical Sociology
On the Work of John Carroll

Edited by Sara James

LONDON AND NEW YORK

First published 2018
by Routledge
2 Park Square, Milton Park, Abingdon, Oxon OX14 4RN

and by Routledge
711 Third Avenue, New York, NY 10017

Routledge is an imprint of the Taylor & Francis Group, an informa business

© 2018 selection and editorial matter, Sara James; individual chapters, the contributors

The right of Sara James to be identified as the author of the editorial material, and of the authors for their individual chapters, has been asserted in accordance with sections 77 and 78 of the Copyright, Designs and Patents Act 1988.

All rights reserved. No part of this book may be reprinted or reproduced or utilised in any form or by any electronic, mechanical, or other means, now known or hereafter invented, including photocopying and recording, or in any information storage or retrieval system, without permission in writing from the publishers.

Trademark notice: Product or corporate names may be trademarks or registered trademarks, and are used only for identification and explanation without intent to infringe.

British Library Cataloguing-in-Publication Data
A catalogue record for this book is available from the British Library

Library of Congress Cataloging-in-Publication Data
A catalog record has been requested for this book

ISBN: 978-1-138-09178-8 (hbk)
ISBN: 978-1-315-10783-7 (ebk)

Typeset in Times New Roman
by Swales & Willis Ltd, Exeter, Devon, UK

Contents

List of contributors vii
Acknowledgements ix

1 John Carroll's metaphysical sociology 1
SARA JAMES

2 What is metaphysical sociology? 13
JOHN CARROLL

3 *The Existential Jesus*: transcript of an interview with
Stephen Crittenden and John Carroll 25

4 John Carroll's Jesus 35
ROGER SCRUTON

5 John Carroll: towards a definition of culture 43
JOHN DICKSON

6 The Passion in Port Talbot 58
MICHAEL SHEEN

7 A Neo-Calvinist sociology: John Carroll's metaphysical
modernity 66
PETER MURPHY

8 The eclipse of metaphysics 80
KEITH TESTER

9 Digital Western dreaming 95
MARCUS MALONEY

10	Ego-terrorism: the benefit of an anarcho-psychological perspective of terrorism WAYNE BRADSHAW	111
11	Mortality, time and embodied finitude MARGARET GIBSON	125
12	Modern metaphysical romance SARA JAMES	139
13	Response JOHN CARROLL	156
	Index	168

Contributors

Wayne Bradshaw is a PhD candidate at James Cook University in Townsville with a Bachelor's degree in English and a Master's degree in Politics. His research focuses on the influence of the writings of Max Stirner and Friedrich Nietzsche on the radical politics of the literary avant-garde, using an analytical framework that draws upon John Carroll's *Break-Out from the Crystal Palace*. He has served as an editorial assistant for both *Literature in North Queensland* and *eTropic*.

John Carroll is Professor Emeritus of Sociology at La Trobe University in Melbourne, Australia. He has degrees in mathematics, economics and sociology from the universities of Melbourne and Cambridge. His work focuses on culture, and its crucial role in the human search for meaning, with particular reference to the modern Western society. His recent books include *The Existential Jesus* (2007), *Ego and Soul: The Modern West in Search of Meaning* (2008), *Greek Pilgrimage: In Search of the Foundations of the West* (2010) and *Land of the Golden Cities: Australia's Exceptional Prosperity and the Culture that Made It* (2017).

John Dickson's PhD is titled *Strange Gods: The Crisis of Meaning after Nietzsche*. He began this project at Yale University and completed it under the supervision of Professor John Carroll in 2014. He has contributed a chapter titled 'Philip Rieff and the Impossible Culture' to *The Anthem Companion to Philip Rieff* (2017). John is also a musician who records, among various projects, under the name Little John. His last solo recording was called 'Put Your Hands on Me'.

Margaret Gibson is a Senior Lecturer in Sociology in the School of Humanities, Languages and Social Science at Griffith University, Australia and a member of the Griffith Centre for Social and Cultural Research. She is author of numerous publications on death, mourning and material culture, including *Objects of the Dead: Mourning and Memory in Everyday Life* (MUP, 2008), and has a forthcoming book, *Living and Dying in a Virtual World: Digital Kinships, Nostalgia and Mourning in Second Life* (Palgrave). Her more recent research focuses on digital materiality and mourning, and the transnational, social interface of online mourning and memorialisation practices.

Sara James is a Lecturer at La Trobe University in Melbourne, Australia. Sara is a cultural sociologist whose research focuses on work, self-identity and meaning. She is the author of *Making a Living, Making a Life: Work, Meaning and Self-Identity* (Routledge, 2017), a major study of the significance of work in contemporary lives. In 2016, she co-edited a special issue of *M/C Journal* on the theme of authenticity. She is co-author of *Sociology in Today's World*, 3rd edition (2014), an introductory sociology text for first-year students, and *Key Concepts in the Humanities and Social Sciences* (2018).

Marcus Maloney is a Teaching Associate in Sociology at Monash University in Melbourne, Australia. His research focuses on media narratives/representations, games studies and digital culture. Marcus' first single-authored book, *The Search for Meaning in Film and Television: Disenchantment at the Turn of the Millennium*, was published in 2015 by Palgrave Macmillan.

Peter Murphy is Adjunct Professor in Humanities and Social Sciences at La Trobe University and Research Fellow in the Cairns Institute at James Cook University. He is the author of *The Collective Imagination: The Creative Spirit of Free Societies* (2012), *Universities and Innovation Economies: The Creative Wasteland of Post-Industrial Societies* (2015) and *Auto-Industrialism: DIY Capitalism and the Rise of the Auto-Industrial Society* (2017).

Sir Roger Scruton is a writer and philosopher who has published more than forty books in philosophy, aesthetics and politics. He is widely translated. He is a fellow of the British Academy and a Fellow of the Royal Society of Literature. He teaches in both England and America and is a Senior Fellow at the Ethics and Public Policy Center, Washington D.C. He was knighted in the 2016 Birthday Honours for 'services to philosophy, teaching and public education'.

Michael Sheen OBE is an acclaimed theatre and screen actor. His recent work includes the films *The Queen, Frost/Nixon, The Damned United* and the Showtime series *Masters of Sex*. He is a BAFTA, Emmy and Golden Globe winner. In 2011, he received the Theatre Award U.K. for Best Director for his production of *The Passion* in his home town of Port Talbot, Wales. It is this production that is the subject of his chapter in this book, as it was partly inspired by John Carroll's book *The Existential Jesus*. Sheen is an Honorary Fellow of the University of Wales, the Royal Welsh College of Music & Drama, Swansea University, Aberystwyth University and Swansea Metropolitan University. He has been awarded the James Joyce Award by University College Dublin.

Keith Tester is Visiting Professor at the Bauman Institute, Leeds University and Adjunct Professor at the Thesis Eleven Centre for Cultural Sociology at La Trobe University. He is a Fellow of the Academy of Social Sciences and his previous appointments include Professor of Cultural Sociology at the University of Portsmouth and Professor of Sociology at Kyung Hee University, Seoul. His publications include *Moral Culture* (1997), *The Social Thought of Zygmunt Bauman* (2004), *Eric Rohmer: Film as Theology* (2008) and *Humanitarianism and Modern Culture* (2010).

Acknowledgements

This book is a result of discussions with Eduardo de la Fuente and Keith Tester. I am grateful to Eduardo for envisaging and initiating the project and to Keith for his enthusiasm and assistance in developing it. I am indebted to the authors who contributed essays and to Stephen Crittenden for allowing us to reproduce the transcript of his interview with John Carroll. Neil Jordan and Alice Salt at Routledge provided timely and proficient support throughout the process. Special thanks to John Dickson, Scott Doidge, Marcus Maloney, Anne-Maree Sawyer and Melinda Turner for their perceptive comments and discerning advice. Finally, I would like to thank John Carroll for both contributing to the collection and inspiring it.

1 John Carroll's metaphysical sociology

Sara James

From anomie and alienation to liquidity and the reflexive project of the self, sociologists have been adept at articulating the difficulties – and occasionally the rewards – of the modern human experience. For John Carroll, the major problem of modernity is that it is 'metaphysically precarious' (2014: 565). Modernisation may have dealt with most of the material hardships that plagued previous eras, but it has not been able 'to neutralise the Old Testament wisdom that we do not live by bread alone' (Carroll, 2008: 4). The problem, for Carroll, is one of meaning; and the solution lies in the realm of culture.

This focus on meaning, on the metaphysical as opposed to the physical requirements of life, sets Carroll apart from much contemporary sociology. Carroll has proposed that a metaphysical sociology should focus on how societies grapple with the fundamental existential questions that confront all humans – 'Where do I come from, What should I do with my life, and What happens to me when I die' (2014: 1). In the modern West, with the declining influence of religion and other traditional signposts, these questions of meaning have become difficult to answer. Contemporary individuals increasingly pursue individual and experimental quests for meaning, drawing on their own inner resources, their 'ontological qualities' (Carroll, 2012: 221). The key question for a metaphysical sociology then is: 'What metaphysical resources are available to people and how do we cultivate them?'

John Carroll is the author of one of the most important and ambitious projects in contemporary cultural sociology. While Jeffrey Alexander describes him as a 'maverick' and 'one of the most interesting theoretical minds in sociology', others question whether he belongs within the discipline. This is partly because Carroll is an effective populariser of insights from classical sociology; his work transcends the narrow jargon-laden categories of contemporary academic sociology. This is reflected in the breadth of contributors in this collection, which includes a philosopher, a renowned actor and a musician.

Carroll's body of work spans four decades. He completed his PhD at Cambridge University, supervised by George Steiner and Anthony Giddens. Stimulated by Steiner, he moved away from political and economic concerns, towards culture, also citing Riesmans's *The Lonely Crowd* as a major influence (Campain, 2005: 7). His PhD thesis was published as *Break-Out from the Crystal Palace: The Anarcho-Psychological Critique: Stirner, Nietzsche, Dostoevsky,* in 1974. Carroll returned to Australia and was appointed as a lecturer at La Trobe University in Melbourne, where he taught for over forty years and is now Professor Emeritus. He has also held visiting appointments at Harvard, Yale and the London School of Economics.

Carroll is also a prominent public intellectual, bringing a sociological perspective to current affairs and introducing sociological thought to the general reader. He has been a frequent writer of essays for popular literary journals such as *Meanjin, Quadrant* and *The Salisbury Review*. Carroll also regularly publishes opinion-piece articles in broadsheet publications such as *The Age, The Australian* and *The Australian Financial Review* and appears frequently as a commentator on radio programmes. Many of his books have found an audience beyond academia. *Australian Book Review* said of *Ego and Soul*: 'A genuine attempt by an academic sociologist to deal with the crisis of meaning that is felt everywhere in the wider community, especially in youth culture.' Carroll's work strikes a chord with the public audience because it speaks to issues that are felt by many but seldom articulated in public discourse.

This collection of essays provides a critical survey of Carroll's metaphysical sociology,[1] while also expanding the project into new areas. My aim in this introductory chapter is to familiarise the reader with Carroll's approach, while outlining his major themes, in order to contextualise the chapters that follow. I do not provide a comprehensive survey of Carroll's body of work; I intend only to set the scene and explain the rationale for this collection. Later chapters, particularly those by Dickson and Murphy, provide more detailed accounts of Carroll's intellectual project.

Carroll's vision and approach

Taken as a whole, Carroll's published works and lectures present a distinctive vision of the history of the West and its cultural implications. Following Nietzsche and Weber, he argues that the major challenge faced by the modern West is a 'crisis of meaning' (1998: 1), brought about by the birth of humanism:

> We live amidst the ruins of the great, five-hundred-year epoch of humanism. Around us is that 'colossal wreck'. Our culture is a flat expanse of rubble. It hardly offers shelter from a mild cosmic breeze, never mind one of those icy gales that regularly return to rip us out of the cosy intimacy of our daily lives and confront us with oblivion.
> (Carroll, 1993: 1)

Emerging in the European Renaissance and articulated fully in the Enlightenment, humanism attempted to 'put humans at the centre of the universe' (Carroll, 2004: 2) and establish an order where human flourishing was a consequence of their own achievements, rather than by the grace of God. Reason was enshrined as the path to human maturity. This vision of progress as a consequence of human reason led to the questioning of religious and traditional authority, paving the way for the political, scientific and industrial revolutions that marked the beginning of the modern era. Carroll (2004: 7) makes it clear that modernity has brought extraordinary physical and material benefits, liberating people from the 'miserable struggle to survive'. His argument is that the concurrent *cultural* decline left the modern West psychologically and spiritually starved (Carroll, 1974).

For Carroll, a healthy culture provides a firm foundation, a secure 'place to stand' (2004: 2). Without this, the world is 'relativity and chaos, without direction, bearings or sense – a world in which humans cannot live and stay sane' (Carroll, 2004: 2). Only from a secure platform can people live confidently and be creative (Carroll, 1977).[2] Modern Western culture struggles to provide this rock. The forms that give order and security have been broken down, in an attempt to remove the 'limits to pleasure' (Carroll, 1977: 87). Carroll argues that this liberation has had serious consequences: 'individuals detached from community are prone to egoism, restlessness, rootlessness, and a sense that life is aimless and futile' (1986: 4). This line of argument is influenced by Durkheim – who argued that the individualism humanism encouraged in a society lacking a strong collective conscience would leave individuals vulnerable to anomie – and Dostoevsky, who saw that when everything is permitted, the consequences are chaos and lethargy. Human flourishing requires authority[3] (Carroll, 1977).

Carroll describes contemporary Western culture as remissive – a term derived from Phillip Rieff – meaning that it lacks energy and authority. In a remissive culture, guilt, which is ordinarily a necessary regulator of human action, is not successfully sublimated and can lead to paralysis. Christianity used to help reduce guilt by providing an explanation for it and telling the individual how to reduce it, but Western culture has not been able to find a replacement for this (Carroll, 1986). Guilt, for Carroll, is not only psychological but spiritual. It is triggered when we violate the sacred order, thus performing the important function of making us aware of this order. Healthy cultures allow individuals to sublimate guilt through activity that connects them to the sacred order. Myths play a vital role here in guiding human action. These stories express the universal, '"capital T"' truths (Carroll, 2007: 2) that can guide human lives, offering a perspective that reminds individuals they are subject to the forces of fate: 'There are eternal laws – moral and metaphysical – and at its deepest level, the human consciousness is born understanding them . . . however much a particular period may distort and repress true conscience, it will not eliminate it' (Carroll, 2004: 267). In sum, humanism, in attempting to replace myth with reason, has not been able to provide answers to the big questions of how to live. As Carroll memorably puts it: the Western world is 'dying for want of Story' (2001: 7).

So far, this is a bleak assessment. In the prologue to the revised edition of *Humanism: The Wreck of Western Culture* (first edition 1993, second edition 2004), Carroll notes that the question he was asked most often in response to the first edition of the book was 'What is the remedy? Where do we go now?' (2004: vii). In his later works – beginning with the first edition of *Ego and Soul: The Modern West in Search of Meaning* (1998) – Carroll takes on this task. His critique of Western culture, set forth in *Humanism*, was levelled at the realm of high culture, which he argues failed in its key task of retelling the archetypal stories in a way that speaks to the times. He is more optimistic, however, about popular culture.

In *The Western Dreaming* (2001) Carroll shows how popular music, film and television have retold archetypal stories (including 'The Hero' and 'Soul Mate Love') so that they continue to provide guidance for the conduct of a meaningful life. In *Ego and Soul* (first edition 1998, second edition 2008) he demonstrates this through an analysis of everyday activity in areas as diverse as tourism, DIY cultures, sport and work. Carroll takes this project of reviving foundational stories even further in *The Existential Jesus* (2007) and *Greek Pilgrimage* (2010). In these two books, Carroll attempts to reconnect Western culture with its roots, which, he suggests, are to be found in ancient Greece (particularly the works of Homer and the tragedies) and in the Jesus story: 'We cut ourselves off from our sacred origins at our own peril: it is they that anchor us, that give us a sense of home and belonging, of past and future that are meaningfully continuous' (1986: 10). Written as a journey through the great sites and cultural works of ancient Greece, *Greek Pilgrimage* is both travel guide and meditation on its pivotal role in Western culture.

The Existential Jesus is much more daring. In this book Carroll attempts to retell Mark's gospel, recovering it from the churches' version, to revitalise the story of Jesus. The resulting narrative portrays a Jesus who is angry, solitary and enigmatic. As a work of sociology, it is strikingly unorthodox; as John Dickson suggests in a later chapter – drawing on a review by Peter Jensen – it is 'something like an old-fashioned sermon'. Unsurprisingly, it is a divisive book. While social theorist Zygmunt Bauman called it an 'awe-inspiring . . . work of genius', academic theologian Roland Boer described it as 'pretentious and arrogant', the first part of the book merely 'a paraphrase of Mark with a thin veneer of existential thought' (2008: 243–244). Carroll does not set out to shock or to generate controversy; his aim in this book is simply to retell the story. As the sociologist of religion Gary Bouma (2007) has commented:

> He appears to have no agenda other than retelling Mark's story as he has encountered and understood it. The book has no audience, no desire to convert, just to recount an authentic encounter with Mark's story of the Jesus who said 'I am' and demanded of others, 'Who am I?'

As early as 1980, Carroll argued that 'The art of story-telling is essential to sociology' (1980: 39). In *Sceptical Sociology* (1980) – his intellectual manifesto – he puts forward his vision for how sociologists should proceed. He argues that the discipline must return to its roots. The great classical works of sociology, 'like great works of literature or art', were able to 'reveal important things about the human condition that had not been seen before' (Carroll, 1980: 18). The discipline has become too idealistic and is preoccupied with a need to appear sufficiently scientific and socially relevant. In its use of 'barbaric jargon', 'legalistic syntax' and 'statistical tables' and in its 'obsession with the humdrum' (Carroll, 1980: 5) sociology has veered off course from its primary task. In the Preface, he writes:

I have been stirred by the belief that sociology since 1918 has tended to make the world as dull as it is at its worst, and that this tendency needs reversing. My second animating belief is that sociology lost contact with the great metaphysical questions that elevate men's lives, that precipitate crisis and that underlie feelings of success or failure – Tolstoy's questions of how to live and what to do.

This identification of Tolstoy's questions comes from Weber's vocation lectures. Carroll chooses 1918 as his cutoff point as this was the year Weber delivered the lectures, two years before he died. Durkheim had died in 1917 and Marx and Tocqueville were long departed. In later works Carroll refers to more contemporary sociologists who have kept this tradition alive, but his point here is to emphasise that the vast majority of sociological work no longer engages with the 'great metaphysical questions'. The best social theory, Carroll argues, teases out meaning from everyday life; it is a 'process of making intelligible' that which was previously inchoate. It is not a literal description of the routines of everyday life but rather 'the getting behind that everyday life to reflect in terms of the metaphysical questions of how to live and what to do, or alternatively the questions of where we are and where we might be going' (Carroll, 1980: 18). If sociology is to succeed, Carroll argues, then it must return to 'first principles' (1980: 3) and wrestle with the key metaphysical questions faced by us all.

I have sketched an outline of Carroll's approach and the major themes of his metaphysical sociology; this will be filled out in greater depth in the chapters that follow. Carroll has written two pieces for this book: an introductory essay and a response to the other contributors. There is also the transcript of a radio interview with Carroll and Stephen Crittenden. The other contributors to this volume were asked to write an essay that engages with Carroll's metaphysical sociology. While some provide critical discussions of his work, others use his ideas as a jumping-off point for new investigations. As such, this is a diverse collection in terms of subject matter, but thematically, all chapters return to the key concerns of culture, story and the question of how to live in modernity.

Metaphysical sociology

In the book's lead essay, 'What is metaphysical sociology?', Carroll puts forward his argument for a sociology that tackles the key questions of meaning faced by every individual: Where do I come from? What should I do with my life? And what happens to me when I die? The sociological 'parentage' of this approach, Carroll argues, can be found in Weber, Nietzsche and Durkheim. He also points to some later examples including David Riesman, Philip Rieff and Zygmunt Bauman. These accounts of culture and the contemporary Western condition, he argues, are too pessimistic. In the era following World War Two 'cultural despair' is not appropriate. Metaphysical sociology today should focus on the ways that people succeed in finding meaning in everyday activity and practices. Carroll gives an example of this in an analysis of the layers of meaning in the modern wedding, employing Weber's *verstehende* method of rich description and interpretation. Crucial to this approach, Carroll suggests, is narrative. Every culture has a body of sacred stories or myths that contain truths that guide lives and answer the meaning questions. Culture must retell these stories so that they speak to the times and provide the narratives individuals can draw on to 'give shape to what they experience'. Carroll proceeds by giving an overview of some of the key stories in Western culture (including *The Iliad, Hamlet* and *Pride and Prejudice*) and demonstrating that their central themes are metaphysical. Included in this is a discussion of Poussin's *Testament of Eudamidas*, the painting chosen as the cover image for this book. Close engagement with these 'archetypal stories', Carroll concludes, is critical for any discipline intent on making sense of its own era. For too long sociology has 'bracketed out' the metaphysical; if it is serious in its task of understanding the way people live, it must include in its consideration that which 'animates the human world'.

The following four chapters each engage with arguably the most ambitious of Carroll's works, *The Existential Jesus* (2007): a retelling or 'restoring' of Mark's gospel. This book seeks to recapture the story of Jesus from the churches' version of him as a meek comforter: The Good Shepherd. Carroll's reading of Mark in the original Greek reveals Jesus as existential hero, dark and enigmatic, uninterested in sin or the afterlife, instead concerned with the nature of being: the 'I am'. This Jesus, Carroll argues, speaks to current times that are largely post-church and plagued by crises of meaning, times where there are a plethora of 'theories and therapies that promise the self more understanding of its own nature' (2007: 4). Beginning this volume with discussions of this challenging text might seem an odd choice, but I would argue that the best way into Carroll's work is to begin with immersion in his reading of a key narrative. This kind of close reading is at the heart of Carroll's approach and the Jesus story is, for Carroll, 'the great story' of Western culture: 'Jesus is the man who made the West'. In addition, focusing on what many consider to be the most 'original' of Carroll's works demonstrates the distinctiveness of his metaphysical sociology.

The sequence of chapters begins with '*The Existential Jesus*': a transcript of a 2007 Australian Broadcasting Company radio interview with Carroll and interviewer Stephen Crittenden. Crittenden describes Carroll's book as 'daring'. It is an attempt, in Crittenden's words, to 'give Jesus back to non-believers'. Over the course of the interview Crittenden prompts Carroll to retell certain crucial moments – or as Carroll would describe them, 'impression points' – from the story. This gives the reader both a summary of the story and an insight into Carroll's approach and purpose. He explains that, while the surface narrative is simple, it is 'a story that works in its subtext . . . through a strange series of tactics where the subtext keeps undermining any understanding readers think they gain'. The interview proceeds by showing how this subtext is drawn out through examples of Carroll's interpretive work. Carroll also summarises the key argument of the book: that Jesus's key teaching is the 'I am' or the 'enigma of being'. This is a response to the central question facing all humans: 'Who am I?' The answer, the story shows, lies not in family, occupation or virtue, but in a knowledge of the inner essence of the self: 'Mark's Jesus is concerned with the righting of being, or the restoring of a character that is out of balance' (2007: 9).

In Chapter 4, 'John Carroll's Jesus', Roger Scruton delves further into Carroll's reading of Mark's Jesus and explains what, in his view, makes it such an 'original' work. Scruton states that the approach taken by Carroll in this 'highly unorthodox' reading is to interpret Mark's gospel as myth; he reads the story as a work of art that contains universal Truths. Scruton highlights the distinction Carroll draws between two experiences of time: *chronos* and *kairos*. *Chronos* is our everyday understanding of time, measured in seconds, minutes and hours. *Kairos*, however, cannot be measured in this way; it is composed of significant moments, or 'cruxes', points at which 'the world takes a new turn'. All myths, Scruton explains, are 'attempts to narrate human life as though it takes place in kairos time' and this is how Carroll reads Mark's gospel. In doing so, Carroll interprets particular episodes by referring to other great works of art in Western culture. Scruton suggests that Carroll is one of few contemporary expositors of a 'humane' sociology – incorporating art history, philosophy, anthropology and cultural criticism – practised by the early sociologists, including Weber, Durkheim and Parsons. Scruton's chapter provides an overview of Carroll's reading of the Jesus myth, highlighting his interpretations of the disciple John and Mary Magdalene that further the argument that the story's key message, the 'one existential testimony that matters', is the 'I am'. While the Jesus of the Christian tradition affirms the other, Carroll's Jesus affirms the self. Scruton concludes by suggesting that while Carroll's Jesus of self-affirmation is vital, the Jesus of other-affirmation has been just as important to Western civilisation: the 'riddle of existence' is situated as much in the 'you are' as the 'I am'.

In the next chapter, 'John Carroll: towards a definition of culture', John Dickson also responds to Carroll's reading of Jesus and raises related issues. He argues that Carroll's retelling is selective and leaves out two crucial elements of the story: the notion of love 'whether relational or universal' and the resurrection. Carroll's retelling, Dickson argues, is deeply subjective, 'more akin to inspiration than analysis'. This line of critique is raised at the end of Dickson's chapter, the bulk of which is devoted to tracing Carroll's broader intellectual project – which Dickson argues culminates in *The Existential Jesus* – and in so doing attempting to 'untangle' what Carroll means by culture. Dickson shows how, in Carroll's schema, the problem of religion becomes the problem of unbelief, which in turn becomes the problem of culture. He discusses the influence of Nietzsche, Dostoevsky, Rieff and Kierkegaard on Carroll's development of a theory of culture, which stresses the vital importance of archetypal myths in communicating the truths that guide lives and provide faith.

What is perhaps most unusual about *The Existential Jesus*, Dickson suggests, is Carroll's 'passionate absorption' in the story. He displays none of the detachment of the typical sociological approach. This is something Carroll admits in the epilogue, writing that he has been 'captured' by the story, that he is 'there, down inside . . . a long and complete dark saying' (2007: 237–238). When the reader immerses themselves in the story of Mark's Jesus, Carroll argues, when they 'walk in his shoes', it can be transformative. This was the experience of a reading group at La Trobe University that Carroll convened for a decade. As Carroll describes it in his interview with Crittenden, on the two occasions the group read Mark,

> An extraordinary thing happened . . . it was like becoming absorbed in this extraordinary, completely encompassing, cryptic narrative which possessed us . . . and without anything binding the group together apart from this sort of perplexed euphoria that came from struggling through this extremely enigmatic text.

In Chapter 6, 'The Passion in Port Talbot', actor Michael Sheen recounts a similar experience. In 2011, at Easter, Sheen re-enacted Christ's passion in the Welsh village of Port Talbot, using Mark's gospel as the reference, and with *The Existential Jesus* as a key inspiration. The performance ran continuously for 72 hours, drawing a crowd of thousands. It was set in a contemporary context, focusing on the story of Port Talbot, but with the story of the passion as the blueprint. As Sheen describes it: 'This created a sort of double story with the story/myth of the town being the surface or conscious version and the story/ritual of the events leading up to and around the crucifixion of Jesus being the deep currents/unconscious version'. This deep engagement with the story captured Sheen, like it did Carroll and his reading group:

> It's impossible to describe the events of those three days. I truly believe something else took over . . . I understood faith and what it could do . . . Life and art totally blurred . . . ultimately something mysterious and bigger than all of us that were there walked the streets that weekend, and we all knew it.

After full immersion in the Jesus story, we resurface and take a broader view of Carroll's metaphysical sociology. In Chapter 7, 'A Neo-Calvinist sociology: John Carroll's metaphysical modernity', Peter Murphy provides a survey of the major themes of Carroll's work, focusing particularly on the argument put forward in *Guilt: The Grey Eminence Behind Character, History and Culture* (1985), and drawing links between this and Carroll's later works. Murphy begins by charting Carroll's explanation of the emergence and development of modern guilt culture, bringing constructive order to Western European societies. Guilt channelled in the right way, Carroll argues, is constructive. Calvinism, through the notions of vocation and the companionate marriage, successfully channels guilt through hard work and productive fellowship. In Carroll's schema, this redirecting of innate aggression into dedication to 'serious worldly activity' was at the heart of 'successful modernity'. Murphy goes on to show how in Carroll's Neo-Calvinism – by which he means secular, post-Christian Calvinism that is embedded in everyday life and culture in the West – sublimation is extended beyond love and work to a range of everyday activities including sport and DIY. These activities can connect individuals to the sacred if they are pursued with concentration, inwardness, balance and grace. In culturally vibrant 'metaphysical modernity' – as Murphy describes it – musing about destiny and fate continues. These questions are addressed in archetypal stories that provide access to sacred truths. The counter to this is an 'anti-metaphysical modernity', characterised by 'repeated loss of nerve, depressiveness and hysteria', without sublimations or sacred myths. This insight, that without sacred order life is miserable and devoid of meaning, permeates Carroll's sociology.

The question of whether we exist in 'metaphysical' or 'anti-metaphysical' modernity is further investigated in Chapter 8, in an essay by Keith Tester titled 'The eclipse of metaphysics'. Tester questions whether it is possible – as Carroll suggests it is – to successfully answer the meaning questions confronting all humans through the existential assertion 'I am'. The 'I am' is a 'sort of personal spirit' that is discovered through adherence to the two Delphic principles: 'Know Thyself' and 'Nothing Too Much'. But, Tester asks,

> Is it possible to know thyself when there is no reason to assume we shall die naturally or in circumstances making any sense, and when the moment of our death is possibly also the *terminally too much* moment of the death of everyone and everything?

In our current 'unchosen circumstances', an era described by Gunther Anders as the 'Last Age', it can no longer be assumed that an individual death will be meaningful. Tester draws here on Adorno, who argues that Auschwitz has 'paralyzed' metaphysics. In the concentration camps, people died not as individuals but as specimens; every victim was treated the same, regardless of their 'personal spirit'. This possibility of a meaningless death hangs like a 'shadow' over us all. Beyond this, as Anders argues, after Hiroshima and Nagasaki the shadow is extended by the possibility that humanity itself might be exterminated. The circumstances of the Last Age pose a 'drastic challenge' to metaphysics; how are we to live under this shadow? Tester explores this further through a discussion of Michelangelo Antonioni's 1962 film *L'Eclisse* (The Eclipse). Tester selects the film because it arguably belongs in Carroll's category of cultural works that 'rattle their times, imposing on them a commanding turmoil'; these are the works, he argues, that can effectively speak to the 'Last Age'. *L'Eclisse* raises the 'anti-metaphysical' question: 'What does it matter?'

This question is addressed in the following four chapters, through investigation of seemingly disparate areas: video games, terrorism, death and romantic love. In Chapter 9, 'Digital Western dreaming', Marcus Maloney extends Carroll's ideas about the necessity of cultures retelling archetypal stories in a way that speaks to the times, into the arena of video games. Maloney provides a close analysis of four recent games: *Bioshock, The Last of Us, Red Dead Redemption* and *That Dragon, Cancer*. These case studies suggest that a new and interactive narrative form is emerging that engages with the key metaphysical questions outlined by Carroll. Countering claims that video games merely provide escapism, or are an inherently antisocial pursuit, Maloney argues that the medium is an increasingly diverse 'emergent cultural sphere', with many games telling stories of cultural significance. Maloney concludes by considering whether the interactivity of video games potentially leads to greater immersion in the narrative, drawing parallels to Nietzsche's reading of the feeling of 'oneness' experienced by the audience, chorus and actors in a Greek tragedy.

Wayne Bradshaw's chapter, 'Ego-terrorism: the benefit of an anarcho-psychological perspective of terrorism', argues for the importance of taking a metaphysical approach in trying to answer the question of what motivates terrorists. This approach focuses on 'what violence means to terrorists' and their sense of self, as opposed to searching for the source in the ideologies of terrorist movements. The chapter engages with two of Carroll's books: *Terror: A Meditation on the Meaning of September 11* (2002) and *Break-Out from the Crystal Palace* (1974). In *Break-Out* Carroll identifies an 'anarcho-psychological tradition' of critique in the ideas of Max Stirner, Friedrich Nietzsche and Fyodor Dostoevsky. Bradshaw draws on this perspective, which portrays terrorism as an attempt to overcome metaphysical doubt about the meaning of one's life by 'imposing structure on the flux of modernity'. He applies this perspective to an analysis of terrorist manifestos and polemics of different ideological waves of terror. This reveals a persistent 'terrorist persona': a persona that seeks self-realisation through violent overthrow of alienating moral and political institutions.

Chapter 11, 'Mortality, time and embodied finitude', is an essay by Margaret Gibson about our struggle with the question of mortality. Following Carroll's methods and employing a close reading of Michael Haneke's 2012 film *Amour*, Gibson interrogates the question of 'How should we die?' This question, she argues, is the 'Janus face' of 'How should we live?', which is at the centre of Carroll's metaphysical sociology. Death, Gibson argues, 'puts the meaning question most potently'. In an era when the influence of religion has waned in the West, and ageing and death have been increasingly medicalised and institutionalised, the idea of a 'natural death' is contested, creating what Gibson describes as a 'moral crisis' in hospitals and law courts across the globe. The question of how to die is one many are wrestling with. Gibson's chapter does not attempt to provide proscriptive answers to this question; instead, she uses Haneke's film to explore the idea of a 'beautiful death' that brings a meaningful life to its fulfilment. In doing so she discusses the role of art, beauty and love in imbuing life with meaning, all of which are key themes of Carroll's.

In Chapter 12, 'Modern metaphysical romance', I also undertake a close reading of a film about love: Spike Jonze's 2013 film *Her*, in which a man falls in love with his computer's operating system. This chapter aims to connect Carroll's arguments about the ongoing significance of the soul-mate archetype and the companionate marriage to contemporary concerns about the impact of Internet dating and mobile technology on relationships. It considers whether Carroll is correct in arguing that romantic love continues to be one of the key areas of life in which the search for meaning takes place, or if, as other sociologists argue, romantic relationships are increasingly fragmented, insecure and primarily a means to temporary gratification as opposed to ongoing fulfilment. The analysis of the film *Her* draws out the tensions and ambivalences present in our attempts to connect with the other in an individualised society.

In the final chapter John Carroll responds to each of the arguments put forward in the preceding chapters, reflecting also on comments made about his approach and the key influences on his work. I am grateful to John for his enthusiasm and close engagement with this project, which has been made much richer for his considered responses to the contributions and his opening essay.

Two other people were instrumental in conceiving of and facilitating this volume: Eduardo de la Fuente and Keith Tester. They, along with the other contributors to this book, recognise the significance of Carroll's work to contemporary sociology in reviving engagement with metaphysical questions through close readings of key cultural texts.

Notes

1 Not all of Carroll's intellectual output is discussed in this volume. Work that is not directly or only partially relevant to the central theme of metaphysical sociology – for example, his scholarship on nationalism – is not examined. This is in order to maintain the thematic clarity of the collection.
2 Carroll also applies this principle to the classroom. He argues that students require a structured and orderly environment if intellectual creativity is to flourish (Carroll, 1980).
3 This belief in the human need for order and authority underpins Carroll's political conservatism. For more on this, see 'How I became a political conservative' in *Quadrant*, May 2015.

References

Boer R (2008) Review of *The Existential Jesus* by John Carroll. *Journal for the Academic Study of Religion* 21(2): 243–244.
Bouma G (2007) The Existential Jesus. *The Age*. Available at: www.theage.com.au/news/book-reviews/the-existential-jesus/2007/03/30/1174761732548.html.
Campain R (2005) *The Decaying Foundations: A Comparative Study of the Work of Zygmunt Bauman and John Carroll*. PhD Thesis, La Trobe University, Bundoora.
Carroll J (1974) *Break-Out from the Crystal Palace: The Anarcho-Psychological Critique: Stirner, Nietzsche, Dostoevsky*. London: Routledge & Kegan Paul.
Carroll J (1977) *Puritan, Paranoid, Remissive: A Sociology of Modern Culture*. London: Routledge & Kegan Paul.
Carroll J (1980) *Sceptical Sociology*. London: Routledge & Kegan Paul.
Carroll J (1985) *Guilt: The Grey Eminence behind Character, History and Culture*. London: Routledge & Kegan Paul.
Carroll J (1986) *'Where Ignorant Armies Clash by Night': On the Retreat of Faith and its Consequences*. Bundoora: La Trobe University.
Carroll J (1993) *Humanism: The Wreck of Western Culture*. London: Fontana Press.
Carroll J (1998) *Ego and Soul: The Modern West in Search of Meaning*. Sydney: HarperCollins.
Carroll J (2001) *The Western Dreaming: The Western World is Dying for Want of a Story*. Pymble, NSW: HarperCollins.
Carroll J (2002) *Terror: A Meditation on the Meaning of September 11*. Melbourne: Scribe.

Carroll J (2004) *The Wreck of Western Culture: Humanism Revisited*. Melbourne: Scribe.
Carroll J (2007) *The Existential Jesus*. Melbourne: Scribe.
Carroll J (2008) *Ego and Soul: The Modern West in Search of Meaning*. Berkeley, CA: Counterpoint.
Carroll J (2010) *Greek Pilgrimage: In Search of the Foundations of the West*. Melbourne: Scribe.
Carroll J (2012) Beauty contra God: Has aesthetics replaced religion in modernity? *Journal of Sociology* 48(2): 206–223.
Carroll J (2014) Death and the modern imagination. *Society* 51(5): 562–566.
Carroll J (2015) How I became a political conservative. *Quadrant*. May 2015.

2 What is metaphysical sociology?

John Carroll

We humans live metaphysically. Our bodies depend on air, food, and water—the material. But everything that engages the mind and spirit, and gives sense to a life, has its source in the metaphysical.

True, there are material facts about us—today I had muesli for breakfast, at 7–30. Or, more seriously, I was born to those parents; I have a large Roman nose; and a susceptibility to chest infection. Modern Western science is limited to the material, which it has investigated, needless to say, with prodigious brilliance, and to such an effect that it has, over five hundred years, revolutionised the way humans live. Its power has disguised the severe limits of its perspective. Comfort is not happiness.

Without metaphysics we wither. We lose the sense to our lives that we only gain through stories. They shape everything, from day-to-day vignettes to grander trajectories of meaning—themselves gossamer entities no more substantial than air. As the greatest diagnostician of the modern condition, Friedrich Nietzsche, put it, in his first book, *The Birth of Tragedy*: every culture is founded on a primordial sacred site. That site is not a physical place. It is the culture's mythos: a body of mythic stories created in the beginning. Without enduring faith in the truths embedded in those stories, humans are condemned to contrived meanings and artificial values—what Nietzsche termed 'redemptive illusions'.

Literature and art of distinction focuses on the ways characters struggle to find a meaning in the midst of everyday routine; through storms of passion; or in the shock that follows tragedy. *The Iliad* becomes deep after the warrior hero, the 'godlike, man-slaughtering' Achilles, is deranged by grief and rage at the killing of his intimate companion. Always a big man, once his need for vengeance is sated, and his grief has softened, he undergoes a transformation, gaining a quite different charisma, that of mellow and selfless graciousness. *Oedipus the King* is strung to the eternal conflict between predetermined fate and human ego—in its case, that of a man who is as confident, intelligent, and powerfully successful as is humanly imaginable, a man who stands as a paradigm of worldly excellence. Oedipus' fate is famously diabolical, its determinism inviolable. The play observes the way the man struggles to make sense of what has happened to him; and the way he strives to restore order, in the world and for himself. The driving themes of *The Iliad* and *Oedipus the King* are metaphysical.

Jane Austen's *Pride and Prejudice*, which stands as arguably the perfect novel, operates in another key. While the surface genre appears that of romantic comedy, the story centres on qualities of character in its two principals, Elizabeth Bennet and Mr Darcy, and the evolution of a stormy and intense emotional chemistry that is generated between them. At stake is the elusive and airy notion of personal affinity. Likewise, Henry James' masterpiece, *The Ambassadors*, pivots on the reflections of its principal character, as he finds himself cast into an alien world in Paris. The novel observes his own slow illumination as he discerns competing cultures that wrestle for his attention, and even for his soul. Each culture is anchored in different ultimate values, ones that he is finally forced to choose between. James' novel is woven through the tapestry of consciousness and self-understanding.

Modernity's founding literary work, *Hamlet*, has its tragedy triggered by a loss of metaphysics. Hamlet's leading character trait is introspection, which has him conducting his life through mournful, self-reflective monologues—with two obsessive, recurring themes, his own lack of passion (code for lifelessness) and death itself, which he describes as 'felicity'. For him, existence has been reduced to a 'quintessence of dust'—that is, the profane and dismal material plane. Hamlet's celebrated attempt at metaphysics, in the 'to be or not to be' speech, is not a philosophical questioning of the meaning of being, but a simple disquisition on suicide, on whether he should kill himself.

The vast edifice of Tolstoy's finest work, *War and Peace*, has its most intense impression point, or climax, in the death of Prince Andrei. In Western culture, as in every other culture, death puts the central meaning question most potently. Is the material plane all there is, the plane on which death is merely death, the person gone, and the body left to its own oblivion of rot and stench? Or is there a higher, metaphysical order?

Tolstoy's death scene is free from any formal religion or conventional religious belief—Andrei is typical of the Russian writer's principal characters in finding himself entirely left to his own resources in seeking meaning in the course of his life. Dying brings on confrontation with whatever truth might be lurking in the shadows, if any.

Andrei knows he is dying and in his final days swings between clinging on to life, because of his beloved, Natasha, who nurses him, and feeling an exhilarated liberation, with himself lost in a euphoria of benevolence and love. Death comes easily in the end. His mood transmits itself to the two women who love him and who are close by, his sister Marya and Natasha. The women do not weep. Their feelings are so strong that they are not affected by the dreadful surface manifestation of death; they don't speak of him to each other, because words would not convey their feelings, and in any case, towards the end, he is not really with them anymore.

Proximity to death for each of Andrei, Natasha, and Marya, but in different ways, infuses them with a sense of the beyond. They are transported out of normal life, and into a sort of cosmic sacred chamber—a chamber in which no explicit god is present. Tolstoy has judged that what is of most profound interest to humans lies around the bed of the dying Prince Andrei.

The same is true for the neo-classical painter Nicolas Poussin. He depicted numerous death scenes in his work, as, for instance, in the painting reproduced on the cover of this book, *The Testament of Eudamidas* (hanging in Copenhagen). Eudamidas, who is poor, lies on his deathbed, dictating his will. The surface story celebrates the ethic of friendship, a Stoic ideal: Eudamidas' last testament requests two of his friends to take care, one of his wife, the other his daughter. Yet the metaphysical truth is displaced into the presence of the man who writes the will—the scribe. He sits in the foreground, absorbed in his task, head bowed as if in prayer, an exemplar of animate life—in contrast with a doctor, who represents the profane, standing by the dying man, idle and bored, as he takes the pulse. The scribe shows that he is more than mortal matter, and, as the subtext of the painting suggests, he writes the true story. That story, incarnate in the presence of its writer, anchors the world, providing a radiant still-point that transforms the gloomy death governing the scene. The dying man, who is virtually a corpse, uses his last energy to tune in to the scribe, sensing he holds the key to redemption; while the two grief-stricken women, staring into a hellish future empty of sense, are arrested in their downward slump.

Here is a parallel to the dying words of Hamlet to Horatio: 'Tell my story!' Poussin draws on the archetype, familiar in Renaissance art, of the young disciple John meditating in awe and dread, close to the corpse of Jesus, after it has been brought down from the cross. John will, decades later, write the story of his Master.

Continuing on chronologically, there is the domain of supposedly modern works, wrestling in the dark shadows of Nietzsche. But they do no more than continue the fundamental questioning of existential meaning that is staked out at the genesis of Western culture by Homer, Aeschylus, and Sophocles, and continued in Mark and John's Lives of Jesus. Joseph Conrad's *Heart of Darkness* explores what a Hamlet-like character of prodigious talents and confidence—artist, musician, orator, idealistic pamphleteer, explorer, entrepreneur, lover, leader—one who experiences the full range of human possibility, who incarnates that modern maxim 'Live your life!', or *carpe diem* (Seize the day!), what conclusion he comes to about the significance of it all. His dying words are: 'The Horror, the Horror!' His vast and imposing metaphysical exploration has collapsed into a void of terror, with the narrator concluding that, with nothing left to bow down before, he had kicked the world to pieces. His soul had gone mad.

F. Scott Fitzgerald continued Conrad's reflections in his 1925 novella *The Great Gatsby*. His thirty-year-old narrator searches for something to give sense to an aimless life, and discovers a man who is splendid and gorgeous, a man who had created himself out of nothing, and strung his life to a glittering fantasy love-affair. But the fantasy is crushed on the rock of reality, and Gatsby returns to being Mr Nobody from Nowhere. By the way, *Gatsby* was little more than a beautifully written reworking of Hamlet's metaphysical companion, Cervantes' masterpiece from three hundred years earlier, *Don Quixote*—its own hero the original colossal dreamer. The Don's maxim was: 'I dream, therefore I am.' Without a dream, however illusory, there is nothing. Dreams are beautiful; reality is sordid. Cervantes had attempted the most radical attempt at projecting a metaphysical canopy over human existence—one extreme end of the spectrum of higher meaning.

The life-meaning questions that drive the classics of literature, art, and film play the same role for metaphysical sociology. While the method and the costuming may be different—likewise they differ between a novel and a painting—the interest is the same.

Metaphysical sociology centres on questions of culture; more concretely, it focuses on the narratives people draw upon, and construct, to give shape to what they experience. As to its sociological parentage, the cue was provided by Max Weber's grand theory of the rise of the modern world as being dependent on an epochal change of consciousness—the Protestant ethic. One of the pillars supporting Weber's argument is that even 'capitalism' is defined by its spirit—its *Geist*—in contrast with the prevailing material definition of capitalism, sourced in Marx. *Geist*, translating into English as mind or spirit, is unambiguously a metaphysical entity. With *Geist* and 'ethic', Weber had positioned metaphysics at the centre of the discipline, as he saw it.

Further, Weber advocated *verstehen* as the method to be employed in sociology. *Verstehende* sociology was to be interpretive, or hermeneutical, with practitioners placing themselves as empathetically as possible in the shoes of those whom they were studying, in order to understand motivations and actions. In the mode of an art, not a science, there are parallels with what came later to be called 'method acting', whereby actors attempt to conjure up from within their own past experience equivalences to the disposition of the characters they were performing.

The second major tradition in sociology has focused on community—its founding father Emile Durkheim. Durkheim's central focus was on social pathology; that is, sickness in society. What makes a society 'healthy'? The ultimate aim of his study of suicide, for example, was to illustrate how individual well-being is dependent on a mental state, or consciousness, one generated by the communities into which that individual had been born. The 'collective conscience' is a kind of social glue that binds individuals together and provides frameworks of meaning, and attachment, that gives their lives purpose and motivation. For Durkheim, the principal threat to modern societies is not economic or political—not to do with inequality or domination. It is cultural.

Durkheim uses empirical data, and in particular social statistics, to buttress his argument. In reality, they serve as little more than costuming and make-up to render the theory more convincing. In other words, they function as rhetorical devices.

The third major tradition in sociology has been Marxist, with its interest largely confined to questions of power, domination, and inequality. This tradition can claim that it is predicated on an ultimate value: it assumes that in the ideal society all humans are equal, and there are no hierarchies of power. This is a metaphysical postulate, if a feeble one. The Hamlet riposte would counter that a world reduced to power, or equally the absence of power, becomes empty of meaning. Even Hamlet's uncle Claudius, whom the mournful prince accuses of the lowest power and ambition motives, is actually in love with Hamlet's mother. That is, Claudius is inspired by something ethereal.

Weber went on to argue that the emerging, secular Western world, in the later nineteenth century, having lost its higher beliefs, was in danger of becoming disenchanted, and withering into aimless materialism. He had come under Nietzsche's reading of the times as being overcast by the death of God, and by the threatening metaphysical void of nihilism, according to which those who were honest would accept the one fundamental truth about human life, that it is meaningless—more precisely, it is reduced to a dualism, that of the horrible or the absurd.

Metaphysical sociology, post-Weber, has moved in several directions. Some works have continued the disenchantment theme. Of special note are David Riesman's *The Lonely Crowd*, Philip Rieff's *The Triumph of the Therapeutic* and *Fellow Teachers*, Christopher Lasch's *The Culture of Narcissism*, the 'liquid modernity' books of Zygmunt Bauman, and more ambiguously, Daniel Bell's *The Cultural Contradictions of Capitalism* and Erving Goffman's *The Presentation of Self in Everyday Life*.

In my view, these works, like the later ones of Max Weber—notably his vocation lectures of 1918—are too pessimistic. Post-World War Two, the Western world has stabilised, and shed the horrors of millenarian nationalism, communism, and economic depression that had defined and afflicted the first half of the twentieth century. Apocalyptic pessimism has lost its cogency. The mission of metaphysical sociology has accordingly shifted, directed to showing the ways people continue to tease meaning out of what seems fleeting and ephemeral in their lives. This may be a less dramatic enterprise than the epics of cultural despair that came before, but it is truer to how people actually live.

I should add that one of my own works, *The Wreck of Western Culture: Humanism Revisited*, sounds apocalyptic, but in fact restricts itself to the domain of High Culture, and its modern mainstream, which the book argued had abandoned its metaphysical mission. The book has little to say about culture in the broad, and especially Popular Culture. I have engaged with popular culture in another work, *Ego and Soul: The Modern West in Search of Meaning*, which finds much to be optimistic about.

Let me consider a vignette from everyday life. Duchamp, painting contemporaneously with Weber's fears of disenchantment, titled one of his works *The Passage from Virgin to Bride* (1912). It is telling that the artistic master of messianic nihilism should have targeted what is, for many women, the most significant rite of passage in their lives, and turned it into a cubist absurdity. Duchamp, in his quest to reduce the human world to interpretative ruins, would five years later, in his *Urinal*, put the challenge that, once God is dead, there are no absolute standards left whereby his piece of profane porcelain might be judged less beautiful, truthful, or good than, say, a Poussin masterpiece.

In response to Duchamp, I want here to reconsider the wedding, and its multiple layers of motivation. I shall sketch an ideal-type.

The modern wedding is about the hope of transfiguration: casting a shining light across the couple, and especially the bride, so that the day be *not-ordinary*. The effort and expense needed to bring this off shows the seriousness of the enterprise. This is to be the day to remember.

At the same time, in a fateful either-or, the wedding is shadowed by the fear that it is no more substantial than a Gatsby illusion, of absurd and doomed rebirth into a different life. The extravagant staging points the way not to the dream, but a morning after of sagging tinsel and two dishevelled mortals crushed on the rock of reality.

On the day, the bride is prepared by a coterie of excited women—a chattering fuss of bridesmaids and family. Hair stylists and make-up professionals visit to work their magic. When the hour has sounded, she will be escorted by her father to a waiting limousine—the door opened by a chauffeur in livery. The drive of her dreams awaits her.

It is at this moment in the ritual, with uniformed chauffeur opening the luxury-car door, that the credibility gap is in danger of widening to a yawning chasm. She is not English aristocracy, nonchalantly at home in Rolls Royce, Bentley, or Jaguar; nor is she Los Angeles celebrity or casino high-roller used to the pretentious kitsch of a stretch limousine. She is a suburban girl normally slouching round at weekends in tracksuit pants. The wedding stage-set risks being too grand for her to pull the occasion off, its pageantry showing up the clumsiness and shabbiness of the petty actors. The day requires ugly duckling to turn into swan.

The bride's arrival for the ceremony is signalled by live music as she steps onto the red carpet, stops, and is prepared by her bridesmaids to begin the slow procession down the aisle. The audience stands, on cue to the music, and turns to the rear. There she is, a shimmering apparition, resplendent in dazzling white, her head veiled in gossamer. A gasp of wonder eddies through the throng, itself a gathering of two family tribes and friends. People smile and nod with benevolent approval, some remembering their own great day, or anticipating theirs to come, reflecting that this is how it is, how it should be, and all is worth it for this moment.

The walk down the aisle is at a slow and measured pace, formal and almost grave, her face veiled. The bride is being presented to the world, and to her betrothed, who awaits her. The father drifts away once he has delivered her to the dais. The two stand before God and before those present—the supernatural and the natural witnesses. They swear an elaborate oath of faithfulness to each other. Rings are placed by each on the other's ring finger—binding them in hoops of incorrodible metal. A life without an oath is at risk of losing its bearings, and its sense. This oath gains its authority from the trust they have in each other, from the presence of the gathered witnesses—all of whom have, in effect, countersigned the pledge—and from the ritual itself.

After a pause, and standing beside her life companion, she is unveiled—revealing to him, and to those assembled, not just ordinary old her, but an archetype, an archetype of transcendent beauty etched with her features. An image of immortal fineness is imprinted on the groom's imagination, with the hope that the radiance of this moment will defy time and its ravages, time and its vicissitudes, and time and its tedium, serving to reconnect him, when necessary, to his wedding dream.

Ambivalence shadows today's wedding ritual. In part, the day is aesthetic. It is about showing off, tapping into the vanity of celebrity performance. The photographer is more important than the minister or celebrant. The climax is less the oath—'I do!'—than the overall brilliance of the occasion, and especially that of the bride.

On the other side of this ambivalence sits an old wisdom, that all of life is a show. It is the substance rounded out by the fantasy that counts—or rather, the dynamic interchange and balance between the two, the substance and the fantasy. The wedding is not different from other major life dramas, aspiring to elevate the substance and increase the potency of the fantasy. Bride and groom bring to the day a range of motives, as they always have; some couples are better suited, as they always have been; and oaths are taken more seriously by some individuals, as they always have been. The greater likelihood today of divorce is more due to economic prosperity, and the weakness of communal sanctions, than to any greater inauthenticity in the wedding ritual itself.

The dream that inspires the wedding as the preeminent social ritual today is itself two-layered. There is the fairy-tale fantasy, glamorised in the royal wedding. *This occasion brings both of our separate, earlier lives to a climax, conjoining us: we shall live together from this moment on, as one, happily ever after.* The fairy-tale motif is reinforced by the enduring presence of the soulmate archetype: *we have been eternally chosen for each other, uniquely, with our union inscribed in the heavens, witnessed by the stars.* She is the only one whom the glass slipper fits.

At the same time, a quite different metaphysical longing complements the fairy tale, one that is more maturely adult, and is thereby tinged with a potentially tragic mood. The wedding is a mode of tuning in. She attracts the radiance, bathing in splendour, becoming herself demi-godly in form. Shining, the bride glides down the aisle, accompanied by the music of angels, delivering her to her spouse, and to the admiring universe. She takes the oath, swaps rings, lifts the veil, and finishes it all with a kiss. The dress, coiffure, and make-up disguise the individual woman, the mega-role she has assumed a masque, crowned by awesome beauty. This is her Transfiguration, drawing upon the archetype of Jesus, at the midpoint of his story, going up a mountain and being bathed in iridescent white light, before descending to meet the crowds below, 'shining'.

Paradoxically, she is alone at this moment, in an accentuated solitariness which reduces all the others in the room, including the groom, to a background chorus. This bright light on her life-path is hers to tend. The responsibility weighs heavily, given the volume of inflated mythology she has to carry to keep the show moving. It helps that she is buoyed up by the glamour of the moment. In this, the test-case for over-dreaming, she may consummate the glittering fantasy as reality. It is hers to bring off; or not. To bring it off, she will need maturity, the full arsenal of her character virtues, the aid of good fortune, and an empathetic husband.

In this, my wedding example, I have tried to illustrate the method of *verstehende* sociology: by choosing an important contemporary practice, and aiming to understand it through rich description, combined with interpretation.

Let me consider a second example of the centrality of metaphysics to sociology. There is the unanswered big question: what are the causal factors that combine together to generate a dynamic modern economy? In the language of economists: what is the secret to growth? Modern economies are centred in cities—the metropolis is the key to their dynamism. The literature on the subject, led by the most encyclopaedic recent book on cities, Peter Hall's *Cities in Civilization* (1998), stresses that what makes a prosperous contemporary city is buzz, fizz, and, in the language of John Maynard Keynes, 'animal spirits'. In other words, the key is not concrete and steel, technological hubs and finance conglomerates, broad economies and creative industries, as important as they all are. It is a special energy, as intangible as Shakespeare's 'airy nothing', to which poetry gives a local habitation and a name.

In parallel, the HBO television series *Treme*, set in New Orleans, imagined how that city, after Hurricane Katrina, was dependent on the spirit of the inhabitants to keep it alive. In spite of a stagnant economy, festering in ruins, and pervasive political and police corruption, New Orleans continued to enchant locals and visitors alike, in part because of its music. Its flamboyant jazz rhythms had not been silenced. The message is reminiscent of Prospero's reflection: 'We are such stuff as dreams are made on'. The *Geist* of Max Weber recurs in many guises.

To return to the first principles governing this essay, every culture has, at its core, a body of archetypal stories, created a long time ago. Each generation is driven to retell these stories in adaptations that speak to it, providing a timeless lens through which individuals can view themselves. I have devoted several of my own books to this regenerative task, notably *The Western Dreaming, The Existential Jesus*, and *Greek Pilgrimage*.

Weber's theory of the Protestant ethic taps into the Western archetype of 'vocation'—that of a central life activity bestowing a meaning beyond the prosaic facts, work that is more than a job. The vocation motif is to be found in Homer and Greek tragedy, as it is in the Jesus cycle.

In effect, the quest is always for ultimate meaning, articulated through narratives that tap into timeless themes, and yet illuminate the particular life here and now. In modernity, the message has been commonly transmitted by negation. Duchamp set himself up as the High Priest of negation, proclaiming nothing endures, nothing beyond animalistic antics on the human plane. Hamlet had reached the same conclusion, but in his case it drove him to despair. Having met the ghost of his murdered father, and lost trust in the most important person in his life, his mother, he felt he was left with nothing, apart from the blank gaze of the long-dead court jester's skull.

The most recent, revealing figure in this tradition, teetering on the precipice of there being no higher truth, is Tony Soprano. When the metaphysical flies out of his life—in the form of a flock of wild ducks that had settled in his swimming pool—he collapses unconscious. This panic attack, which occurs in the first episode of the 86-part HBO television series *The Sopranos*, is symbolic death. Tony's next panic attack occurs when his mother mocks that a retirement home is where people come to die. That mother, who is a caricature of rancorous dispiritedness, describes death to Tony's son as 'the big nothing'. Tony spends the entire story striving to find something to engage him more than fleetingly, something to believe in. Journeying through his own heart of darkness, he tries family, gang leadership, womanising, rampant sadism, nostalgia for the old mafia, nostalgia for the old America, and love of animals, but everything fails. Like Hamlet, he is terminally melancholic for want of metaphysics.

The Sopranos makes explicit that metaphysics needs to come in the form of a life narrative, described by one of its characters as an *arc*. A life without an arc—a given trajectory, directed towards a set end—is pointless.

Hamlet and *The Sopranos* illustrate that without metaphysics there can be no tragedy, only melodrama. Tragedy, in the high Greek sense, depended on belief in the existence of a higher order, which is violated, and then, by means of the story, restored, if in a different form. The modern nihilist anti-heroes find their lives stalled, motionless, drowned in a melancholy fog. By contrast, the work of neo-classicists like Poussin and Tolstoy strives to resist the existential negation; as does the performance of the contemporary bride.

Death has been prominent in this essay. For many, the other central meaning question might appear primary: 'Why am I here, and what should I do to make sense of my life?' Indeed, one might plausibly assume that once the 'How should I live?' question has been successfully addressed, then death, when it knocks, will take care of itself. But maybe not. Tolstoy's inference is that a kind of ease of individual being emanates from the internalised sense of the numinous, which itself derives from a commanding intuition that death is meaningful—that death is more than death. Once death is empty of meaning, Tolstoy asserts elsewhere, then the preceding life is condemned to absurdity. Hamlet would have agreed.

Any intellectual tradition, including sociology, that takes seriously the mission of interpreting its own era must engage with archetypal stories. How can a serious discipline that aims to understand the way people live, and the dynamics of the communities and societies they build—one with the 'logic of society' as its name—bracket out what animates the human world?

Much of sociology has done just such a bracketing, on the grounds that *meaning* is not susceptible to scientific analysis—which is true, given that science, in the strict sense, is limited to material phenomena. Several disciplines that belong in the Humanities—most strikingly economics, psychology, and sociology—have perpetrated a sleight of hand in pretending to be scientific in the manner of the Natural Sciences. An insecurity in relation to metaphysics has triggered this illusory quest for legitimacy. The result is either banal or phony. On the one front, it is possible to study 'scientifically' what time Warnambool fishermen have breakfast, but who cares.

On the other front, it is not possible to reach clear, confident, and distinct conclusions about what possesses the consciousness of the two women tending to the dying Prince Andrei—that requires the art of a Tolstoy. Those sociological theories that draw upon empirical data—including case-studies, diaries, eye-witness reports, opinion surveys, and demography—as does Weber's Protestant Ethic thesis, may well employ this data as their own rich description, in an equivalent manner to Tolstoy painting Prince Andrei's death. But the theory will only resonate if it rises above the material plane. It must, further, if it is to endure, achieve the insight and judgement which are the preserve of art.

Metaphysical sociology, at the heart of its enterprise, has to tap into one of the big truths. In my experience, university students only become seriously absorbed in their study of sociology when a course links itself to timelessly significant life-questions. An aspect of Weber's achievement was to combine profound meaning themes (theological, philosophical, and psychological) with a theory of both the historical rise of the modern West and the driving logic of capitalism.

Such a sociology needs to be brave, even wild, in what it takes on. Often the territory of the most potentially edifying questions will remain opaque to understanding, and it will demand tentative steps, wily conjecture, and artful interpretation. If it succeeds, what it produces may resemble, in one of its aspects, a parable. The best-known component of Weber's Protestant Ethic thesis comes as a metaphor—the *iron cage*—a metaphor with the inner complexity of a parable, which is the main reason it has retained its evocativeness (oddly enough, it was the invention of Weber's English translator, Talcott Parsons).

The elusiveness of the possible mysteries at the heart of the human story was caught by Luke, in the story with which he ends his Gospel. I have reflected on the Road to Emmaus before in my work, but as it seems to hold some essential clue to the mystery, I shall revisit it. Karl Kraus quipped he would prefer to be read twice, or not at all.

Two men set forth on the most fateful journey of their lives. Clueless as to what is happening, it is the Sunday two days after the crucifixion, resurrection Sunday, and their instinct is to flee Jerusalem, north-west along the road to the village of Emmaus, twelve kilometres away.

On the open road, a stranger is with them. How can this be? Where has he come from? Some nobody, they hastily suppose, some intrusive vagabond going nowhere. Failing to read their own fear, and forgetting the significant events pressing upon them, they make the normal human assumption. This moment, the here and now they inhabit and look out upon through blurred minds, is nothing, just another arbitrary speck in time, another indistinct smudge on the scratchy meandering line of their bit-part scripts. Irritated by this further jolt to the fracturing order of their lives, they note with disgust that his cloak is fouled with grime and age, his long hair unkempt. He is ordinary.

The third man queries their conversation. They stop in their tracks, gloomy, amazed that the stranger does not know what has just come to pass in Jerusalem. They tell him, ending with the tomb that had been found empty that very morning. He lectures them.

At last they draw near the village of Emmaus. As it is towards evening, they persuade the stranger to rest. So what is to be just happens, in the tiny public room of a local roadside inn where he joins them at a rough-hewn table set for three. They watch with mounting apprehension, by the wildly flickering light of an oil-lamp, as he takes the bread. Suddenly his presence shimmers, filling the shadowy room. Bathing them in a pained and knowing look, he breaks the bread and gives it to them. As in a spell, they become their vision, hovering at a remove out in front of their physical selves, and dissolve into the broken bread. Now they think they see clearly. It is Jesus himself, who on the instant disappears.

The darkness of this night is in keeping with recent events, and they are left alone and bewildered, hunched over the table. In fact, the story tells us that the two around the flickering oil-lamp soon reconstruct: 'Did not our heart burn within us, while he talked with us by the way.' Within the hour they set off back to Jerusalem.

It is left open whether these two seemingly incidental characters have understood anything whatsoever, in their unwilling confrontation with the archetype of resurrection. Here is the surprise encounter among thousands that might cross any human path, and, if recognised, might change a life; an encounter that may come in other forms than that of a man—maybe an intuition, or an experience. Presumably, fear now possesses the two men. But it still remains unclear why they are returning to the scene of tragedy; and to what, indeed, they return, apart from a ghostly, ghastly city.

From the Emmaus inn back to today's world might seem a long stretch. Yet, the bride seeks to find, in her moment, the enchantment of the breaking of the bread; and those present at the death of Prince Andrei do experience a mysterious transfiguration. Max Weber, in his central work, demonstrates that the office, the business, the school, and the multitude of other organisations and activities that orchestrate the modern world depend on an ethic, and a spirit, driving those who inhabit them. He warned, in effect, that the sullen anguish of the pair fleeing Jerusalem, on resurrection Sunday, awaits one and all, once the West's sacred myth has lost its binding hold. In other words, the journey that begins on the Emmaus road and stretches to modern individuals, and what they do, is where a metaphysical sociology must ply its trade.

References

Austen J (2003) *Pride and Prejudice*. London: Penguin.
Bauman Z (2000) *Liquid Modernity*. Cambridge: Polity Press.
Bell D (1976) *The Cultural Contradictions of Capitalism*. London: Heinemann.
Carroll J (2001) *The Western Dreaming: The Western World is Dying for Want of a Story*. Pymble, NSW: HarperCollins.
Carroll J (2004) *The Wreck of Western Culture: Humanism Revisited*. Melbourne: Scribe.
Carroll J (2007) *The Existential Jesus*. Melbourne: Scribe.
Carroll J (2008) *Ego and Soul: The Modern West in Search of Meaning*. Berkeley, CA: Counterpoint.
Carroll J (2010) *Greek Pilgrimage: In Search of the Foundation of the West*. Melbourne: Scribe.
Conrad J (2007) *Heart of Darkness*. London: Penguin.
de Cervantes M (2005) *Don Quixote*. London: Vintage.
Durkheim E (2006) *On Suicide*. London: Penguin Books.
Fitzgerald F (2004) *The Great Gatsby*. New York: Simon & Schuster.
Goffman E (1971) *The Presentation of Self in Everyday Life*. Harmondsworth: Penguin.

Hall P (1998) *Cities in Civilization: Culture, Innovation and Urban Order*. London: Weidenfeld & Nicolson.
Homer (1951) *The Iliad*, trans. Lattimore R. Chicago: University of Chicago Press.
James H (2002) *The Ambassadors*. New York: Dover Publications.
Lasch C (1980) *The Culture of Narcissism: American Life in an Age of Diminishing Expectations*. London: Abacus.
Nietzsche F (2003) *The Birth of Tragedy*. London: Penguin Classics.
Rieff P (1968) *The Triumph of the Therapeutic: Uses of Faith after Freud*. New York: Harper & Row.
Riesman D (1961) *The Lonely Crowd: A Study of the Changing American Character*. New Haven, CT: Yale University Press.
Shakespeare W (2016) *Hamlet*. London: HarperCollins.
Sophocles (2010) *Oedipus the King*, trans. Greene D. Chicago, IL: University of Chicago Press.
Tolstoy L (1993) *War and Peace*. New York: Random House.
Weber M (1958) *From Max Weber: Essays in Sociology*, trans. Gerth HH and Wright Mills C (eds). London: Routledge & Kegan Paul.
Weber M (2002) *The Protestant Ethic and the 'Spirit' of Capitalism*, trans. Baehr P and Wells GC. London: Penguin Books.

3 *The Existential Jesus*

Transcript of an interview with Stephen Crittenden and John Carroll

The following interview on the Australian Broadcasting Company's Radio National Religion Report took place on Wednesday 7 March 2007 at 8:30AM: Stephen Crittenden speaking with sociologist John Carroll on his new book about Jesus in the Gospel of Mark.

Transcript

Stephen Crittenden: Today, as promised, we're reading Mark's Gospel, the earliest of the four Gospels and arguably the darkest and most cryptic. Mark's is the angry Jesus who casts out demons, curses fig trees, gives up trying to teach his disciples anything and dies completely alone.

Oscar Wilde wrote about Jesus that his entire life is also the most wonderful of poems: 'For pity and terror there is nothing in the entire cycle of Greek tragedy to touch it'.

Sociologist John Carroll certainly captures that in his new book about Jesus, *The Existential Jesus*, where he argues that Mark is one of the pinnacles of Western literature; that Mark's Jesus is the great Western teacher on the nature of Being; and that his real tragedy is that he ends up as his only student.

John, welcome back to the programme; it takes a certain kind of daring to write a book about Jesus, let alone a book in which you basically ignore two of the four Gospels, Matthew and Luke, because they're not very interesting!

John Carroll: Jesus is a creation of four stories. We know virtually nothing about him apart from the four Gospels. There are snippets in later supposed Gospels; the letters of Paul tell us next to nothing; and there's virtually no independent historical or archaeological evidence. So he's a creation of four stories. The overwhelming consensus today is Mark is the first Gospel that was written. To me, and great literary critics like Harold Bloom in the United States, and Frank Kermode in England, Mark's is the pungent, powerful great narrative of the four in any literary or narrative sense. And next to it, Matthew repeats about 80% of Mark, and adds a lot more. Compared to Mark, he's long-winded, the narrative is jumbled and often incoherent, and it lacks subtlety and any of the depths and charge of the grand metaphysics that you become embroiled in once you get into Mark.

I think Luke is a lot more interesting; there are pieces of great literary flair in Luke, and he adds the parables of the Good Samaritan and the Prodigal Son, which no-one else does. But overall, it's got similar weaknesses to Matthew, and in my reading John is the one of the three – they're all writing with Mark in front of them – he's the one of the three who really understood Mark. What he does, at his best, is provide a series of brilliant narratives to elaborate and extend things that are too cryptic or undeveloped in Mark.

SC: Oscar Wilde described the four Gospels as four prose poems about Jesus. You're arguing there's really only one prose poem, Mark, and the rest are footnotes, and the best footnotes are by John.
JC: That's exactly what I'm saying.
SC: John, you mentioned the English literary critic, Frank Kermode. His book on Mark, *The Genesis of Secrecy*, is one of my favourite books; in fact I think it propelled me into the Religion Department at the ABC. Mark used to be seen as a pretty clumsy and unsophisticated Gospel written in poor Greek. Kermode shows that it's very sophisticated indeed, especially in the way the narrative is structured. It's not meant to be understood naturalistically, but as a kind of puzzle.
JC: Kermode's book has been more useful to me than all the Biblical commentary and New Testament interpretation that I've read, and I've read a lot of that. And it is so for the simple reason that, as you say, the surface text is in common or very simple Greek. But this is a story that works in its subtext. And it works through a very strange series of tactics where the subtext keeps undermining any understanding readers think they gain, as they proceed through the text.

Now the fall guys for the reader are the twelve followers, or disciples, who learn nothing. I mean, this Jesus finds out very early on that it's a waste of time trying to teach them anything. Now a narrative that works through enigma and dramatic paradox –

SC: And allegory too, John.
JC: And allegory, and keeps ripping your feet out from under you, so to speak, as you progress, has to be read in terms of its own logic, and what Kermode is great at is the technique of this unique type of storytelling. I don't think there's anything else like it in Western culture.

[Music]

Reader: He made the twelve take a boat and precede him to the other side of the Sea of Galilee, to Bethsaida. He sent the crowd away, and when they had all gone, he left the wilderness and went up the mountain. It was evening, and he was alone. From on high he saw the boat in the middle of the sea with the twelve struggling to row into a rising headwind. At about the fourth watch of the night, he approached, walking on the water. He wanted to pass them by but seeing him, and taking him for a phantasm, they all screamed out in terror. He spoke to them, 'Courage, I am; don't fear'. He approached and got into the boat. The wind abated.

JC: Jesus goes up on the mountain by himself. He's fed up with teaching the multitudes because he's starting to realise that, at that level, he's acting as a type of vaudeville magician, carrying out miracles, but no-one's learning anything. He's fed up with his disciples. He sends them across the Sea of Galilee. It's night; he goes up the mountain to be alone by himself. As the twelve are rowing across the Sea of Galilee, in the middle of the night, the wind starts to rise. Jesus, all alone, is looking down and sees them becoming more and more fearful. That's a bit odd in itself, in that they're fishermen who've spent their lives on this very Sea of Galilee, and there's no indication in the text that their boat is threatened with sinking.

After a while, he charges down the mountain and comes across the sea, walks, the famous walking on water scene. He is in some sort of supernatural state; it's probably not very interesting to press what that actually means. These disciples don't recognise him, they think he's a ghost and they're terrified. Plus the fact that right from the beginning in Mark, *pneuma*, or what's usually translated as Holy Spirit, sacred *pneuma*, the charged breath, the wind, the sacred essence, is what breathes through this story. Pretty much replacing God, but that's another issue.

So, in this scene on the Sea of Galilee, in the middle of the night, there is also the sacred wind or the spectral breath flowing down. No wonder the poor old twelve followers are beside themselves with fear. And the better they know him, the less they recognise him. In this scene you get the feeling that he's some sort of supernatural monster in their eyes, coming across the water towards them. He utters, at this point, what becomes his central teaching. He says, 'Courage, I am. Don't fear'. Now the 'Courage, don't fear' provokes the most extreme fear in them – it's a sort of negation. And this often happens in Mark. If there's a charged saying on the surface, it will have exactly the opposite effect on those who take it in.

SC: A very good example of that is in the empty tomb at the end. The young boy says, 'Don't be afraid', and the last line of the Gospel is, 'And they ran away terrified'.

JC: Exactly. And in fact this is set up, I think, in the dancing across the Sea of Galilee in the middle of the night.

28   The Existential Jesus

SC: Now let's come back to the question of 'I am'. The book's called 'The Existential Jesus', the central teaching you say is 'I am'. What does 'I am' mean?

JC: One of my arguments is that Jesus is the great teacher in the West on the nature of Being.

SC: Why is 'Being' the problem?

JC: Well, he basically says *Being* is the problem. And I think a lot of the contemporary world today would agree. For instance, there are all of those books and therapies, and everything else, that asks the question: 'Who am I?' 'What is the nature of the self?' 'What is the nature of identity?' If there is a meaning in why I'm here and what I have to do with my life, it's got something to do with finding out who I am. And Mark's Jesus would answer: 'Yes, that's correct'.

Now of course once you've said that all you need to know is 'I am', you ask the question: 'Well what in the hell does he mean by that?' The first half of the story spends a fair bit of its time stripping away what the 'I am' is not. If you want to ask who I am, it's not my family, it's not that I'm from Nazareth, it's not that I'm a carpenter or a carpenter's son. It's not even, to go further, and this is harsher, it's not even that I'm a particularly good man, or a bad man. It's not to do with one's virtue or ethical character.

SC: You say in fact, quite specifically, Mark's Jesus is not a teacher of morals and ethics.

JC: And this makes him particularly problematic, I think, for church religion. He's not an ethical teacher at all; he's just simply not interested in morals. What he is interested in is *Being*, the nature of the 'I'.

SC: And when Peter says to him 'You are the Christ', he sort of snorts as though that's the wrong answer.

JC: Exactly, and he goes even further and says: 'The Devil's in you, Peter'. This is an astonishing charge, because in what Peter is doing there, in saying 'You are the Christ', he is parroting Jewish belief from the time, which was looking forward to a Messiah, or in Greek Christ (*Christos*), who would come to save the Jews from the Romans. So, when Jesus asks the followers, 'Who do you think I am?' or 'Who do you say I am?' and Peter blurts out, 'You are the Christ', Peter is providing a formula, he's giving a sort of doctrinal reaction, and this is precisely what the I is not to do with. In fact, Mark's Jesus attacks that impulse in all of us, especially when we're agitated or anxious, and we want something concrete, we want something secure, we want to be able to say, 'Well I am X, Y or Z'. He's constantly cutting that out from under the reader.

SC: John, in your translations in the book, in various passages you leave individual words in the Greek text, untranslated. They're just left there in Greek so that we notice how often they appear, and also so they don't lose the power that's been taken away from them by the official translations that they've been given.

JC: That's true with a number of key words. I don't translate *pneuma*, 'sacred *pneuma*', which has usually come down as 'Holy Ghost' or 'Holy Spirit' with capital letters. That translation into English loses the range of Greek meanings of 'wind', 'breath' and 'spirit'.

Probably of equal importance from my point of view, the original Greek for the word translated as 'sin' is *hamartia*. I think this is really where the Christian churches and the translators have distorted Mark's text. Now *hamartia*, in its origins, means a loss of direction, a bit like a spear throw that's gone wrong. Aristotle uses it in his theory of tragedy, which was well known in the time and place in which the Gospels were written, to mean 'character flaw'. Now, translating *hamartia* as 'sin' moralises the text. It's as if Jesus is constantly concentrating, as the Old Testament does, on transgression, sin and, in other words, a moral language. My argument is this is not what's going on in the text at all. No, Jesus is much more interested in *Being* that's lost its way.

SC: OK, now your careful attention to the Greek text results in two brilliant interpretations involving Peter. The first relates to his name, Peter from *Petros*, meaning 'rock' or 'stone'. And as we know, the entire Catholic Papacy is built on a single line from Matthew's Gospel: 'You are Peter, and on this rock I will build my church'.

But you show how the greater storyteller, Mark, links Peter's name to the parable of the seed sown on stony ground. The name 'Peter' is a put-down.

JC: Yes. Mark is very harsh towards Peter. I mean poor old Peter has done everything right and he gets everything wrong. The first time the word appears in the text is when Jesus gives him – his name is Simon – Jesus gives him the nickname, *Petros*, or Peter translated into English. *Petros* in Greek means 'stone' or 'rock'. When we come to the first big parable, that of the Sower, a pivotal parable, the part of the parable that Jesus is most interested in is seed sown on stony ground. And what's characteristic of seed sown on stony ground is that there's not much soil, so it rises with joy the moment it's sown, but the moment, because it hasn't got any roots, the moment the sun comes out, it withers. Now stony ground in the Greek is *Petrodes*; in other words, it's the matter out of which Peter, *Petros*, is formed. So, Peter is of his own nature, stony ground, and in fact here is a perfect caricature of his nature. He rushes in with joy and enthusiasm, but the moment any pressure or heat comes on, he collapses, he withers.

Further, in this series of associations, Jesus has already healed a man with a withered hand; we've already been told what the metaphor of withering is to do with. The healing takes place inside the synagogue; or church; or temple.

SC: This is one of these juxtaposition episodes that indicate to you how to read the story.

JC: Exactly. And I think, in effect, in reading that episode carefully, Jesus chooses this particular affliction, the withered hand, and he draws the man with the withered hand out of the church in order to heal him. I think he sets up this sort of two-way momentum: there are people who are withered, but they need to be drawn outside churches to be healed. On the other hand, there are embryonic beings, i.e. Peter, who the moment there is any pressure on them, wither, and they actually belong inside the church. Soon after, Peter is given the role of church-building, even by Mark's Jesus, not just by Matthew's Jesus.

SC: This is at the Transfiguration, his response to the Transfiguration is: Quick, let's build some churches.

JC: This is precisely at the mid-point of Mark's text. Jesus is losing his powers, he's completely fed up, there's a suggestion even that he's almost going blind. He goes up the mountain, and what follows is a kind of baptism by fire. Suddenly he's shining in bright light. He has taken Peter, James and John with him, and Jesus, up there, meets big-man ancestors – Moses and Elias. Peter says, 'Let's put up tents for Jesus, Moses, and Elias'. The Greek word for 'tent' equally means 'temple' or 'tabernacle'.

There's a black cloud overhead out of which speaks the voice of God. Now I think the subtext here is that Peter, in his profane blindness, reads the divinity as rain, and thinks it's about to rain. So he wants to build tents to protect the three holy men from getting wet. Linked is the sense, of course, that he doesn't want to look on the shining. He wants to get inside, to protect himself from Jesus. The moment he becomes anxious, Peter's reflex is to build a church. But 'church' generalises here into any cosy communal environment in which I am protected from the truths that I suspect – that this man who increasingly terrifies me – the truths that he is confronting me with. Peter does not want to look on the shining.

SC: John, I said before that there were two fine readings in your book that relate to Peter. The second one is of a passage in St John's Gospel where Jesus says, 'Simon Peter, do you love me?' And, of course, there are three different words for 'love' in Greek. But because we don't have the original Greek text in front of us we tend to overlook the real drama in this scene.

JC: This is the last chapter of John. But he's drawing out what is in Mark, and Jesus questions Peter three times: 'Do you love me?' Peter gets pretty irritated by the way he has to be questioned three times. The first two times the Greek 'Do you love me?' is *agape*, meaning 'selfless' or 'sacred' love.

SC: Do you like me, *agape*?

JC: And Peter responds, 'Of course I love you', but he uses *philos*, brotherly or friendly love, or mateship love. So Jesus repeats it: 'Do you love me, *agape*?' Peter answers again, a bit agitated, 'Of course I love you, *philos*', brotherly love. The third time, Jesus switches to *philos*: 'Do you love me?' In effect, he's shrugging his shoulders that Peter's not capable of selfless or sacred, or higher love, or whatever you want to call it.

The Existential Jesus 31

SC: So he downgrades it.

JC: He downgrades it to 'brotherly love', and in fact that becomes, in John's reworking, Peter's way. John is kinder to churches than Mark. It's as if John sees how uncompromisingly hostile Mark's Jesus is to all churches. John provides a role for churches; it's a role of service, and Peter is told to follow and serve, in combination with brotherly love. This is a very important shift, I think, from Mark to John.

SC: Let's come back to Mark. On your reading, Mark almost blows the whole canon apart, and it makes you wonder why it's even there. It is so subversive.

JC: I believe it was almost lost in the early years. I recently have come to suspect that the reason it was tucked in as No. 2 behind Matthew – Matthew almost certainly comes later – was to hide it. The church Gospels are Matthew and Luke. Matthew restores continuity with the Old Testament, and he provides a whole series of lessons for building churches, a sort of a handbook for building churches. Luke produces the good shepherd Jesus, the children's Little Lord Jesus who lays down his sweet head. The Good Samaritan Jesus is Luke's Jesus. Mark's Jesus is not at all like that.

SC: Angry Jesus.

JC: And solitary. It's hard to think of a text in the Western canon in which the principal figure is so alone. There's virtually no God present in the second half of Mark's story. If we go from the Thursday night of the last week through to the crucifixion, he dies at 3 o'clock the following afternoon . . . he speaks only two words between the Jewish trial sometime the night before and 3 o'clock the following afternoon. Two words: 'You say', to Pilate.

SC: 'Are you the King of the Jews?', Pilate says to him.

JC: Yes, and it's, of course, a question about the nature of the I. Mark's Jesus always responds to 'Who am I' questions.

SC: And so Pilate says: 'Are you the King of the Jews?', and the response is?

JC: 'You say'. It's very difficult to know how to read that. I think in effect by the end of the crucifixion scene, that's what he says to God, with a shrug of the shoulders: 'You say'. And the next words after 'You say' are on the cross just as he's about to die, 'My God, my God, why have you forsaken me?' This underlines the fact that forsakenness is the condition of this crucifixion. There are no followers around the cross; there's no family; there's no-one familiar. And there's a strong sense that God's gone from the story too, so this, 'My God, my God, why hast thou forsaken me?' I think is a sort of existential cry of despair. It's followed, we assume soon afterwards, by a great scream, and he dies. And then, straight out of the silence a wind tears through the Jerusalem temple, and rips the veil from top to bottom. This is the last manifestation of the power of *pneuma*.

SC: I suspect Jewish readers aren't going to like this book, even though this Jesus isn't really the Messiah; he denies in a way that he's the Messiah. This seems to me to be a reading of Mark that says the Jewish Old Testament, if you like, is just irrelevant, it's superseded.

JC: There are two sides to that. The first side is, Yes, Mark starts with the single word *arche* meaning 'foundation' or 'in the beginning', and he very deliberately cancels Genesis in the Old Testament, which has God creating everything. The real creation is the story that I'm about to tell, that of Jesus. And this Jesus basically ditches ethical religion, the Ten Commandments, ritual religion, virtually all the elements of the Jewish tradition.

SC: And of course frowned very much on the Temple.

JC: Yes, and late in the story, in the last week as they're walking up from the village of Bethany, up the hill to Jerusalem above, he says: 'And if you trust, you will be able to pick up this mountain and throw it into the sea'. Well, that's usually been taken metaphorically, but this mountain, the one explicitly there above them – I think this is even more than subtext – is the Jewish Temple. He's basically saying that what I'm doing is going to throw the culture of the Jews into the sea.

On the other side, however, there are two distinctions in Mark's text, and notably one between insiders and outsiders. There's no distinction between Jews and non-Jews. The people who respond to this Jesus, some are Jews, and some are not. Perhaps even more importantly, Jewish religion, and its synagogue, is taken by Mark as a prototype for all religion. The text is against all institutional religion, but it's not anti-Jewish.

SC: Just one other thing about the Temple. I must get you to tell – this is one of those absolutely pivotal allegorical moments where Jesus comes into Jerusalem and visits the Temple and walks around and walks out again, and then you get the story of the withering of the fig tree – we're back to withering again.

JC: One of the most powerful and enigmatic moments in any of the Gospels occurs the following morning after Jesus' entry into Jerusalem. They are going up the hill and he sees a fig tree. The implication is that he's hungry. But there isn't any fruit because it's the wrong season. The fig tree's got green leaves, but it doesn't have any figs. Jesus curses it. The next morning, as they're going past it again, it is withered from the roots upwards. Predictably enough, it's Peter who says: 'Oh look, look Master, the tree has withered'.

I think the symbolism is over-determined. The most obvious reading is that the fig represents the Jewish Temple, which is in fact about to empty. The Temple is the withered tree, and it's never going to fruit again.

The second reading is that it's the followers we've had withering throughout this text, an affliction particularly identified with Peter. Peter is the withered fig.

But the third and principal reading is that the fig represents the cross, and poignantly so. In three or four days' time, this is the black stump onto which Jesus is about to be nailed.

In the 20th century, we've had similar imagery from the First World War, used by T. S. Eliot in *The Wasteland*. Mark's Jesus is someone who lays waste to everything. Here is an image of laying waste to nature. From laying waste to nature, he's about to go up the mountain and lay waste to culture, and basically leave nothing apart from three hours of darkness with him nailed to a black stump.

SC: John, let's talk about some of the other peripheral characters in the Gospels. Pontius Pilate is someone you have a very positive reading of.

JC: Mark's account of Pilate is very brief, but it's clear that Pilate is intrigued by Jesus, he knows the Jewish charges are trumped up, and by the end of the story he's actually starting to know something. Now this is a case where John, I suggest, in a brilliant piece of narrative, develops Pilate into a major figure, uttering the famous question: 'What is truth?' Pilate follows up, as he stands before the Jewish crowd screaming to crucify Jesus, with a kind of proclamation: 'Behold, the man!' – the Greek, by the way, could just as easily be translated, 'Know the man!' Actually, Pilate is on the edge of becoming an insider. He's a borderline 'I am'; he's in transition to getting it, ending the episode with a very strong statement: 'What I have written, I have written'. It's almost as if Pilate is writing the Gospel himself.

SC: Judas is anti-*pneuma* in your reading.

JC: Judas is the one of the twelve in Mark's story who understands Jesus, and understands principally that he does not have the 'I am' essence. He understands basically that 'I am not', to use that language.

Mark develops a theory of evil, one which is quite different to most of Western theories of evil, including church ones, which postulate excessive desires, or rampant passions, as the sources of malevolent action. Mark's theory of evil centres on *Being*, and I think it's a far more profound –

SC: And Judas is anti-being.

JC: He is anti-being, and Judas, unfortunately for himself, understands too much. He wants to be Jesus, whom he is irrevocably not. Obviously, his is an envy condition.

SC: OK John, you've given Jesus back to non-believers, but what can the churches possibly be expected to make of this book?

JC: I would hope, given the fact that they're struggling, and the times, in most senses sociologically speaking, are post-church or anti-church, that they'll take seriously an argument that says that why you have failed is that you have failed to re-tell the great story that you've been given. If you manage to start re-telling this story, then you will engage with people today. Because, for the modern West, this is the great story, I think. Even more so than the magisterial Greek tragedies.

SC: Well, let's come back to the reason you wrote the book. I imagine one of the things you're hoping people who read your book will do is go back and read Mark. But what are you hoping they'll do then? Are you hoping they'll go back to church? That sounds like a stupid question after this conversation, but what are you hoping they'll do?

JC: I don't know. I've been, as best as I can, a servant of this text, trying to re-tell it and interpret it in a way that will speak today. What happens then, I don't know, in fact I don't even know if my – I'm still sort of submerged in the text . . .

SC: Tell me about the reading group that you are part of at La Trobe University, that's been reading over several years now St John's Gospel and St Mark's Gospel. What effect has it had there?

JC: Well actually this book started from the reading group which has been running for – or ran, it's now finished – ran for ten years, which read a book from the Old Testament and the New Testament alternately, a chapter a week. The group had seven members, changing over time. In ten years, we twice read Mark and we twice read John. An extraordinary thing happened on both occasions with Mark and with a largely different group. It was like becoming absorbed in this extraordinary, completely encompassing, cryptic narrative, which possessed us – most of the members of the group are secular, by the way, maybe there was one practising Christian or two practising Christians, so it was a pretty irreverent group. But after Mark, and this happened both times, everything else would disappoint. It was like joining some sort of sect but without any doctrine, and without anything binding the group together apart from this sort of perplexed euphoria that came from struggling through this extremely enigmatic text.

SC: John Carroll is Professor of Sociology at La Trobe University, and his new book, *The Existential Jesus*, is published by Scribe.

The audio version of this interview may be heard via ABC.net.au, Radio National Archive; or via John Carroll's website, johncarrollsociologist.wordpress.com.

4   John Carroll's Jesus

Roger Scruton

The early sociologists, such as Durkheim, Weber and Parsons, did not distinguish their discipline from anthropology, regarded modern societies as composed from the same raw material as the tribes studied by their Victorian predecessors, and acknowledged that a large part of sociology consists in philosophical speculation on the human condition, with a view to making sense of our distinctiveness. For a thinker like Weber, the writings of Kant and Nietzsche are every bit as relevant as the polls and surveys conducted by empirically minded colleagues. The real task of the sociologist, for Weber, was not just to ponder the data but to find the theory that made sense of them. Sociology needed an account of the human person, which would show what distinguishes us from the other animals and what makes us simultaneously so easy to relate to and so hard to explain.

That old idea of sociology as a humane discipline, a synthesis of philosophy, anthropology and cultural criticism, which would explore our human distinctiveness and make sense of it, has few remaining expositors. One, however, stands out, not only for his breadth of learning and capacity for synthesis, but also for the originality—indeed, the shocking originality—of his mind, and that is John Carroll. If I were to say in a brief compass what is so distinctive of Carroll's writing it would be this: he believes that human nature is most fully revealed in the art and religion of a people, since these embody the self-consciousness of the social organism. Statistical surveys won't tell us the deep truth about humanity; instead we need a critical study of what inspired and intelligent people, in their most urgent creative endeavours, have tried to say and what others have preserved in the way of sacred texts and monuments. Works of art and literature, liturgies, hymns and the lonely speculations of hermits and philosophers are therefore the true data of a realistic sociology. And this means that the sociologist must also be a writer and a critic—in short, a seriously cultivated person—if he is to fulfil the aims of his profession. It is in this way that John Carroll has made his mark, as representative of a humane sociology, in which philosophy, anthropology, history of art and literary criticism are all integral to the argument.

No book of Carroll's exemplifies this characteristic to greater or more shocking extent than *The Existential Jesus* (2007). To present a work of sociology as a commentary on St Mark's Gospel is original enough; to draw on the most advanced New Testament scholarship in establishing the argument is an even more unexpected departure. Most remarkable of all is the resulting portrait of Jesus, as a martyr to the truth about being—the truth that we all have reason to avoid, but better reason to confront and affirm. In *The Existential Jesus* Carroll has produced an imaginative portrait of the most extraordinary individual in Western history, as well as a work that is provocative and illuminating beyond the normal register of his subject.

Carroll accepts the now orthodox view that Mark's gospel is the earliest of the four, put together anonymously from material that included eye-witness accounts. It is written in Greek for readers largely unfamiliar with Jewish religion and traditions—hence the translation of Aramaic words. Although it makes no mention of other literature, the text reveals a familiarity with Greek literary culture. It is notably disparaging of the disciples, in a way that suggests a familiarity with at least some of them, and presents Jesus and his mission in mysterious terms that repeatedly raise the question of who this person really is.

That is the question that interests Carroll, but in an entirely new way: so as to shift attention from the "who" to the "is". Mark's gospel, Carroll insists, is an "enigma", a "dark saying", in which an individual who enters the world as a stranger enacts his solitary being to the end. God gets a mention here and there, but only at the edge of things, when the narrative abuts on the wondrous, the inexplicable and the "great fear" that invades us in the face of nothingness. Jesus should be understood as replacing the creator God, not representing him. The "pneuma" that descends at the moment of his baptism is, for Carroll, not the Holy Spirit, as the orthodox translation insists, but "the charged wind, the cosmic breath, the driving spectral force". This primeval force blows through the deranged individuals that Jesus encounters and through Jesus himself: it is a summons to being to reveal itself, to make itself known in the affirmative "I am".

In approaching that highly unorthodox reading, Carroll interprets the gospel of Mark as myth. Even if the episodes that it records were largely factual, and even if Jesus said, did and suffered the things that Mark attributes to him, we should not understand the gospel merely as a record of those events. It has the force and unity of a work of art, is clearly influenced by the Greek tragedies that would have been well known in Hellenised circles, and has a sparse, searing logic that forces a symbolic meaning onto every detail. Myths are not about the accidents of history, but about human universals, and when a human being steps into the space of myth he leaves his historical particularity behind, to be reborn as a symbol. Such was Jesus's fate, and Mark conscientiously sets out to record it, producing in consequence one of the most remarkable narratives in the whole canon of Western literature. Carroll quotes approvingly the remark of Harold Bloom, that "whoever composed Mark is a genius still too original for us to absorb" (cited by Carroll, 2007: 17).

The Jesus described by Mark has a mission. But it is not, in Carroll's view, the mission attributed to him by subsequent Christian commentators. The Jesus of Mark's gospel is the "archetypal stranger". There is no birth narrative, no attempt to portray Jesus as the messenger from another realm or to attribute to him either a special origin or indeed any origin at all. He appears from nowhere, solitary, uprooted, with neither occupation nor any form of worldly power. He lives without the comforting illusions that enable others to turn away from the question of being—without family, career, nation, city or daily routine. He chooses his followers, but is exasperated at their failure to understand him, and finds comfort only in those who seek nothing from him, save the opportunity to acknowledge his being—notably the woman who anoints him with precious ointment, for no apparent reason than the cost of it. Jesus lives with the truth of his own being. But what is that truth, the Truth about which Pilate asked his immortal question? What is contained in the words (only one word in Greek) "I am", which Carroll regards as the summary of Jesus's teaching?

The Jesus of St Paul, glossed also in the other gospels, is the founder of a church, who wishes to lead his followers to salvation, by providing them with rules for a godly life. He is the Good Shepherd, meek, mild and oozing with holiness. For Carroll, however,

> Mark's Jesus is not remotely like any of this—and he is not interested in ethical teaching. Worse, he identifies all churches with the withered and the stony-hearted. He exposes their nature as innately driven to suppress Truth . . . Mark's Jesus is concerned with the righting of being, or the restoring of a character that is out of balance. This is an issue of *being*, not of *morals*.
>
> (2007: 9)

But how do you convey a message about being? Not in a list of maxims. In the end the message about being is contained within the life of Jesus itself. Truth is *muthos*, myth in the Greek sense of an exemplary story, which serves as a focus for other stories, for other lives, for the insight into one's own being that comes from reflecting on a life lived in full consciousness of itself. The story told by Mark consists of a sequence of "impression points", as Carroll describes them, highly charged events or climaxes which anchor the story in the deep subjectivity of Jesus. These impression points "provide entry into the subtext in which the *mystery* lies buried" (Carroll, 2007: 39). Other characters in the story are, as it were, interrogated by those impression points, brought into relation with the Truth, which is the being of Jesus. The story itself is "a self-contained numinous object" (Carroll, 2007: 19), an archetypal account of a man who lived his own being to the full, and showed us what it would be to do the same. If we read with understanding Jesus's life becomes a "shining", an example that shows us what it is to exist in this world in full consciousness of the "I".

This interpretation is spelled out at length and in remarkable prose that works in the way Mark's gospel works—not by expounding thoughts but by crystallising them in images. One of the most valuable features of Carroll's narrative is its *allusive* quality. Jesus himself alludes to things, and all symbols work through allusion. In a way, allusion is the true counter to illusion—the way in which we connect to a truth instead of denying it. And Carroll is acutely aware, from his wide acquaintance with Western art and literature, of the ways in which the life of Jesus has been used by painters, sculptors, poets and novelists as the source of allusions of their own. Carroll may illuminate an impression point in Mark's narrative through a sculpture by Donatello, a painting by Poussin or a narrative of Herman Melville's. For the story told by Mark is the foundation myth of our civilisation—so Carroll would have us believe—the Western "Dreaming", to which we return in order to know who we are. All the real art of our civilisation makes room for this story, which must be interpreted anew for each generation in order to be repossessed by each of us as *mine*.

This way of approaching Mark's Jesus illuminates all the incidental characters and actions. The people whom Jesus encounters divide at first into the insiders, those who understand his world-changing message, and the outsiders, who grasp only the external signs. The Jesus of Mark's gospel is frequently exasperated by those around him, since they fail to respond to his call to live in another way. They are prone to the "great fear"; they lack faith or "trust", and are constantly hoping to be raised out of this life, rather than rubbed into it. Simon Peter comes in for some particularly fierce reproaches, and his character, put to the test by the servant girl at the crucifixion, is as though expressly conceived as a foil for Jesus, who even in the death to which his will has inexorably led him continues to affirm "I am". Clearly Peter is not the "rock" on which a new church can be built, or if he is, then so much for churches. Carroll dislikes institutions, which are the vehicles of Heidegger's "inauthenticity", encouraging the desire to slip out of one's life as the young man in the garden of Gethsemane at the moment of Jesus's arrest slips from his clothes. The significance of Jesus is precisely that he stands aloof from all such compromised ways of being, answerable to pneuma, to the Spirit, alone.

The insiders form a dwindling class as the narrative unfolds. Let down by the disciples, Jesus has gathered only misfits and drop-outs: those whose disordered pneuma he has cured, such as the lunatic whose many warring spirits call themselves "Legion", and which escape from him into a herd of swine, and the Magdalene, who may or may not be identical with the woman who anoints the feet of Jesus. These insiders have, like Jesus, wrestled with the Spirit, but until encountering the Teacher have been unsuccessful in the struggle. Carroll goes so far as to identify Legion as "the Master's other self ... Both beings are governed by pneuma, and so belong together. Both are dynamos of mighty passion—roaming among the tombs, withdrawing up the mountain, crossing the *daimôn*-infested waters" (Carroll, 2007: 47).

The most important of the insiders is Judas, a character portrayed with masterly concision by Mark. Judas is to Jesus as "I am not" to "I am". He might have led an ordinary and uneventful life. But encountering the Master, he is forced to recognise that this person is what he wants to be and cannot be. It is not envy that compels him, but a sense of existential failure. He "wants to undo his own creation", so that "his *doing* is no more than the howl of wounded *being*" (Carroll, 2007: 194). Carroll's description of Judas is worth quoting, since it touches more nearly than any other passage on what the message of Jesus (or at least of Carroll's Jesus) really is:

> The primal source of evil is existential lack. It is the hopeless and inescapable inner vacuum of *I am not*. Excessive and illicit appetites only grow if there is chaos at the centre. They are a sort of pandemonium of character.

>Judas is different from most of his kind in that he is conscious of his condition. He is not blind. He is not in denial. He is cursed to know, and to know that *I am not*. The light shineth in the darkness, but Judas comprehended it. For this he is a big man.
>
> (Carroll, 2007: 194)

As the allusion to St John's gospel suggests, Carroll is putting Judas in the context of a metaphysic of creation. He is interpreting the distinction between good and evil as that between affirmation and negation. Goethe's Mephistopheles—the "spirit who always negates"—is the descendant of Mark's Judas, and in treating the opposition between Judas and Jesus as he does, Carroll is placing the story at the centre of his own Nietzschean view of what is at stake in human life. This indeed is the message that Jesus strives to impart to us, through his words, through his extraordinary silences, and through his being there, at the centre of this hallucinatory narrative. Carroll summarizes the message thus:

> Everything orbits around living *being*—that of the individual. It is the nucleus that determines all. It is both creator and creation. It is the source and the shaper of the constellation of energies that will drive a life—every human life.
>
> (2007: 195)

The message is a mystery. Hence in addition to the outsiders and the insiders there are the watchers, those who know that the mystery is before them, and are waiting for the revelation that will explain it. Watchers know that they stand in the presence of the "shining"—the mortal "I" that has replaced the old God of Israel. For Carroll, the episode of the transfiguration on the mountain is the old God's "exit blessing": "in this moment the great Jewish founding fathers and spiritual leaders have been superseded, and so has their God" (2007: 75).

The watchers sometimes have little else to do except watch, like the young man who is found in the vacated tomb. But sometimes they give voice to the mystery. The most important of them is Pilate, whose sparse but penetrating utterances place a frame around the crucified Jesus that is an integral part of our civilisation's holiest icon. Through Pilate we witness Jesus in the stunned consciousness of someone with the highest political power, who recognises the power of something vastly higher. "What is Truth?" "Behold the man", "The King of the Jews"—all these sayings, recorded without embellishment or redundancy, are ways in which the troubled Pilate acknowledges the presence of "I am".

But what exactly happened at the crucifixion, and what was its aftermath? Carroll's answer depends on a metaphysical distinction between two experiences of time, which the Greeks name *chronos* and *kairos*. The first is time in its regular character, measured by the moments as they tick away. *Kairos* time is not measured in that way: it is composed of cruxes, of which the cross (crux) is one. At these cruxes the world takes a new turn: the arrow finds its target, the shuttle leaves the hand, the kiss touches the cheek. Mark expressly draws on this ancient distinction. *Chronos* time is drawn like a veil over a great abyss, in the bottom of which huge landscapes are dimly perceivable. At the *kairos* moments the veil is lifted and another dimension of being is revealed to us. All true myths are attempts to narrate human life as though it takes place in *kairos* time rather than *chronos* time, and Mark's gospel is no exception. The *kairos* moments are also those in which the Spirit, pneuma, makes itself known. The great cry that issues from Jesus at the moment of his death is pneuma's doing, as is the whirlwind that follows, tearing the sacred veil of the temple. This is the moment at which another of the watchers—the Roman centurion charged with overseeing the crucifixion—witnesses *I am*, knows that there is a mystery of being and knows that this man was it (Carroll, 2007: 124).

Was or is? Did he "go before them into Galilee", or is that only a saying that must be interpreted in another way, in the pure language of being, whose fundamental utterance is "I am"? The astonishing ending to Mark's gospel in what is now taken to be its original version leaves the matter there. The three women come to the tomb and encounter a young man in a white robe who tells them not to be afraid, that the crucified Nazarene has arisen and gone before them into Galilee. "They fled from the tomb quivering in ecstatic fear. They said nothing to no one, for they were terrified." And so the gospel ends, leaving us to strive to understand that last *kairos* moment from its discarded wrapping. The question of Jesus's resurrection is left without a clear answer.

That, in very broad outline, is Carroll's reading of the story, and it serves as a frame with which to explore not only the character of Jesus—a domineering and in many ways desperate character—but also the fundamental loneliness of all the people who cling to him. Carroll brings to bear on each episode of Mark's gospel not only the retellings in the other gospels, but also the great works of art through which our civilisation has tried to make sense of it, so that *The Existential Jesus* is also an unusually penetrating study in art history. Carroll does not see societies as purely biological formations of creatures burdened by their evolutionary origins. He sees them as collective spiritual enterprises, which can expand in every direction to embrace all the ways of thinking and doing that we comprehend as "civilisation". Jesus, for him, is not simply the founder of Western civilisation, but the model, the pattern to which we return in every attempt to make sense of our social being. Even atheists and sceptics must, if they are truly to inherit the collective soul that waits for them, take into themselves the truth of Jesus, and in describing that truth in existential terms—as the affirmation of being in the face of the great fear—Carroll is consciously remaking it for the use of his modern readers.

Reflecting on the two greatest of the subsidiary characters—the "beloved follower" of John's gospel, usually assumed to be John himself, and St Mary Magdalene—Carroll invites us to look on our own lives in a moment of "metaphysical judgement". And then we must

> forget all such life-questions as: *What have I achieved? What have I learnt? Who have I become? What do I believe?* Answers to such questions are without significance. There is only one existential testimony that matters: *I know*

that I am! Anyone who can truthfully speak their own ease of *being*, with surety, as the single and essential knowing, says enough. They verify an island of calm within the ocean of eternity.

(2007: 231)

Yet Jesus, as Mark and Carroll describe him, was surely only incidentally "an island of calm". He was a trouble to himself and to all whom he encountered. He was often angry and exasperated; he wilfully offended the priests and scribes (whom Carroll calls "intellectuals"); he challenged the existing order while responding with silence to those who asked him why. And he died a horrible death that, with a bit of wriggling, he might have avoided. All this reinforces the paradoxical nature of Jesus, and also of Carroll's interpretation of him. The traditional reading of the gospels resolves the paradox by transcending it. Jesus does not, in this reading, replace the old God, but comes down from Heaven as God's incarnation. His mission is one of redemption. He is to redeem us from our psychic burdens by taking them upon himself, replacing the realm of guilt with the realm of forgiveness and offering himself up as a sacrifice for the remission of our sins. *That* is why he is an island of calm—namely, that he offers to cleanse us of our self-inflicted pollution, to bring us back into the fold of the saved.

Carroll will have none of that. He is seeking in the life of Jesus for an imminent, not a transcendent, meaning. And he is of course aware that he belongs to a tradition of powerful writers, from Nietzsche to Heidegger, Sartre and beyond, who have sought the answer to the riddle of existence in the fact of existence itself. Writers in that tradition are not merely writing against religion, as traditionally conceived, but also against the condition of those who have believed in it. Ordinary people, in their attempts to find refuge and comfort in worship and prayer, in churches and families, in the "little platoons" of civil society, are adopting a "slave morality" (Nietzsche), are living inauthentically (Heidegger), are guilty of *mauvaise foi* (Sartre). In fact, Sartre goes further. Just about everything you and I do by way of finding comfort in the actual world—owning things, joining things, creating families, schools, hospitals, clubs and teams—consigns us to the class of *salauds*, who turn out to be the majority. The merely "bourgeois" existence of these people, Sartre's fellow citizens, condemns them to nothingness in the eyes of a supercilious intellectual released by his self-affirmation from the demands of ordinary morality.

Carroll does not want to go down that line, aware as he is of its abuse by both left and right in the world of political extremism. His Jesus is a challenge to the followers and watchers who surround him. His message is that we must exist fully as individuals. But Carroll, as a sociologist, is profoundly aware that "existing as an individual" is a social achievement. Individuals do not exist in the state of nature; they are outgrowths of social traditions and institutions, indeed the embodiment in a single organism of the vast achievements of our civilisation. The individual is, to a great extent, a post-Enlightenment creation, an offshoot of institution-building and constitutional government. That is why the beloved disciple and Mary Magdalene are so important: for they do not see the call to affirm their own being as a summons to a greater loneliness, but as an invitation to *agape*—to the "love to which we are commanded", as Kant beautifully put it. Whatever is to be gained from understanding the full impact of "I am", it is, for such beings, inseparable from the humility that acknowledges the other as more important than the self. John and the Magdalene are also proto-individuals, avatars of Enlightenment, who stand at the beginning of the long process that leads to a society based on critical reflection and the rule of law.

I suspect that, in those thoughts, I am pointing to the real distinction between Carroll's Jesus and the Jesus of Christian tradition. The first affirms the self; the second affirms the other. And there is a modern philosophical tradition, from Hegel to Wittgenstein, Levinas and beyond, which situates the riddle of existence in "you are" rather than "I am". The other is the one whose recognition I seek, and in whose face my own face is reflected as in a mirror. That is the Jesus of John's Gospel. I value Carroll's commentary for having shown the Jesus of self-affirmation in all his stark and nightmarish integrity. But when it comes to Western civilisation, and its expression in the soul of you and me, I am certain that the Jesus of other-affirmation is just as important.

Reference

Carroll J (2007) *The Existential Jesus*. Melbourne: Scribe.

5 John Carroll
Towards a definition of culture

John Dickson

When I first met John Carroll as a young post-graduate student in 2004, I arrived at the door of his office in the Social Sciences building at La Trobe University five minutes after our arranged meeting time. This was customary for me, and a practice that was largely free of guilt, living as I was by an internal clock that was Mediterranean in temperament. A tall, forbidding figure with straight posture rose from behind a large desk and stated tersely: "Punctuality is important to me". The directness earned my respect. Professor Carroll's reputation, though, had preceded him. I had heard conspiratorial whispers in the corridors that were tinged with reproach. "He's the only right-winger in the department", another post-graduate warned me gravely. As if that explained anything. Better, anyway, I thought, to be talked about than not talked about at all. We were evidently on different sides of what has unproductively been called the "culture wars". But I had no intention of staying in the same position my whole life; I was eager to learn, and awaited hearing a lecture with intrigue.

The course I attended was the ominously titled "Disintegration and Dread in Modern Society". While the students settled, Professor Carroll removed an elegant silver time-piece from his jacket pocket and placed it on the table in front of him. A small, antique touch but one that communicated seriousness and order. The students soon settled. Later I would reflect that his insistence on punctuality was an offshoot of a carefully considered ethical outlook, and one in which "order" took high importance. "Human beings like order" was a consistent refrain during his supervision of my thesis. Morality is in fact closely tied to order in the John Carroll schema. In fact, order in the Greek (*nomos*) gives way to the French antonym *anomie*, Durkheim's sociological shorthand for the loosening hold of a common morality. Order, however, only takes such significance because of the power of its chaotic counterpoint, the Dionysian—a central category to which I will return later.

The first lecture was titled "Dostoyevsky: The Problem of Religion". I was thrilled. Having finished my undergraduate degree in religion and theology at the University of Melbourne, I remained intellectually underwhelmed. The study of ancient texts was interesting yet unsatisfying. I had done a three-year survey of the major religions: Judaism, Islam, Christianity, Hinduism and Buddhism. It all felt quite superficial and distant from my experience. My knowledge amounted to something like a thorough reading of Karen Armstrong's *History of God*: a synthesis, contained and admirable, but hardly a compendium that bubbled over with ideas, experience and passion. I was not a believer but religion remained a problem for me. This was not only a personal problem, but also, I believed, a problem for contemporary societies, and I wanted to get to the heart of it.

The best way into the "problem of religion", from John Carroll's point of view, was through specific works of art and theory. In this instance, the work in question was Dostoyevsky's novel *The Possessed* (1962, originally 1872). His presentation of the problem in fact pivoted on the fate of a concrete individual: the predicament of the central character, Stavrogin—a brilliant, troubled and charismatic young aristocrat. Stavrogin has lived life to the full; he is well educated, well travelled, intelligent and superior. All the other characters of the novel fall for him in one way or another, orbiting involuntarily around his stronger presence, looking vainly for guidance and love. But Stavrogin is numb; having done everything and found no limits, even in acts of depravity and evil, he is impotent, half-hearted and suicidal:

> I tried my strength everywhere . . . But what to apply my strength to—that's what I have never seen and don't see now . . . I can still wish to do something good, as I always could, and that gives me a feeling of pleasure. I can still wish to do something evil and that gives me pleasure too . . .
>
> (1962: 305)

The world seems to him a "sterile promontory"; he finds it "weary, stale, flat and unprofitable". For, as students of John Carroll would recognise, Stavrogin is a Hamlet archetype. If ancient philosophers such as Socrates found virtue through reflection, or discovered the truth and purpose of life through the faculty of reason, Hamlet and Stavrogin found its horrifying flip-side. The contrast is instructive. For Carroll, culture is born out of the lives of charismatic individuals who offer a version of the ideal human being. Traditionally, for the core of Western culture, these exemplars have been Socrates, representing Athens, and Jesus, representing Jerusalem. Stavrogin and Hamlet are their modern counterparts—or their modern reversals. They reflect in their achievements and, more importantly, in their *despair* and their lack of *commitment*, the furthest reaches of individualist and humanist philosophy. These are the dark truths of modern literature and they express, in Carroll's view, the cultural failure of humanism. The problem of religion can then actually be stated in a contemporary sense as the problem of unbelief: it is that of atheism and nihilism, which are the logical conclusion of humanism's failure to answer metaphysical questions. Nihilism is the uncanny guest haunting Stavrogin's table—telling him that we are floating in space, that human passions are just a way of warming up the universe, and that nothing is really worth doing.

The lecture was powerful. The approach seemed to align with at least a couple of my own naïve intuitions, still firmly held: that ideas are real and books are sacred. That life is not a joke—that the metaphysical questions about the value and destiny of human life remain the same across time, space and cultures. Amid the proliferation of jargon that I was accustomed to in universities about dead books, amid the pedantry of academic specialisation, and amid the hotchpotch, trivializing and directionless mental fog of post-modernism, Stavrogin came alive for me. Carroll's interests reflected a consciousness that seemed to belong more properly in the 19th century: the type for which art was a matter of life and death, a seriousness about culture shared by one of his early mentors, Philip Rieff, and incidentally, though with less affinity, Rieff's first wife, Susan Sontag. He also shared their breadth; making detours through psychoanalytic theory, art history, film, classical sociology, political philosophy, literature and biblical exegesis in any given undergraduate course. And like a 19th-century intellectual, he made wide-ranging generalizations and judgements; he was provocatively magisterial and absolute—the antithesis of the relativism and faddishness that plague contemporary study of the humanities.

Regardless, though, of what century it came from, somebody had cut through, and seemed to say something related to life and its meaning. Carroll made use in these preliminary lectures of the Greek word *aletheia*—a word Heidegger revived and understood alternately as "disclosure" or "truth". Its opposite is *lethe* or "forgetfulness", associated in classical mythology with the river Lethe, a river which wipes away memory, which helps people forget and remain unconscious. The human condition is essentially a state of unconsciousness to fundamental truths—in particular to the truth of our mortality. This is the way we live our lives, mostly in forgetful oblivion; then occasionally, in moments of extremity, or moments of insight or inspiration, we get woken up. In such moments, we feel that we can see more clearly, more wholly, more deeply into our human lot. We do not stay there very long—"humankind cannot bear much reality", as T.S. Eliot put it in *Four Quartets* (1979: 14). This "waking up", though, is one of the higher functions of the teacher. Peter Jensen, the former Archbishop of Sydney, understood something of this when, in a review, he called Carroll's later work *The Existential Jesus* (2007) "a sermon". It is a fitting epithet for his lectures too. And even if it was not entirely good news being offered, I signed up.

The last man

For Carroll—as indeed for T.S. Eliot, whose controversial 1948 book *Notes towards the Definition of Culture* gives the name to my subtitle—the problem of religion is the problem of culture. For Carroll, stories are crucial; culture is made up of that series of vital and animating stories and myths upon which faith, and therefore individual well-being, are dependent. The solution, then—and in this respect, Carroll is also a traditionalist or perhaps a "foundationalist"—is to re-work and re-tell the archetypal stories that make up the life-blood of a culture. It is this "mythical" quest that ultimately provides the direction for the second half of Carroll's career and his more ambitious later works including *Ego and Soul* (1998), *Western Dreaming* (2001), *The Existential Jesus* (2007) and *Greek*

Pilgrimage (2010). The background locus of these works, elusive yet pervasive, is a notion of "true culture", from which true myth and individual faith derive.

To untangle these terms—"culture", "myth" and "faith"—let us return, then, to employ one of Carroll's rhetorical moves, to "first principles". The central theorist here is Nietzsche, an interest traceable to the beginning of Carroll's written work, a reworking of the PhD Thesis he completed at Cambridge University, *Breakout from the Crystal Palace: The Anarcho-Psychological Critique: Stirner, Nietzsche and Dostoyevsky* (1974). His fascination with Nietzsche and Dostoyevsky (his interest in Stirner did not prove so enduring)—is the first thread. In some ways, Carroll, perhaps under the guidance of his European supervisor, the polyglot classicist George Steiner, helped bring the more tormented "soul" of the Slavic Empire and a metaphysics more typical of the Continent to the shallower philosophic soil of the Anglosphere.[1] For Carroll, the "death of God" is a historical and cultural fact of immense magnitude, one whose impact still reverberates today yet whose importance remains misunderstood, ignored or even repressed. To evangelise precisely this point was Nietzsche's *raison d'être*. *Breakout* delineates three separate key modern intellectual traditions; first, the liberal, rationalist model exemplified among others by the British philosopher John Stuart Mill; second, the Marxist-socialist tradition; and lastly, the final stream, and one largely neglected by intellectual history, is what Carroll calls the "anarcho-psychological" and is represented by the eponymous figures of the book. The first two materialist philosophies helped provide the modern West with economic and technological abundance; but they have also created the conditions of spiritual complacency out of which grows Nietzsche's caricature of the "last man", the bourgeois shorn of higher ideals. The third stream is the deepest response: that of an intuitive and literary "depth psychology" that appeals almost purely to the "spirit" in its most radical, individualistic and unconscious forms. This stream detects a gaping chasm underlying notions of "rationalist" economic and cultural progress. The "death of God", for Nietzsche and Dostoyevsky, threatens life, however prosperous and comfortable, with a hollow insignificance.

Nietzsche was *incensed* that people did not realise God was dead, that their entire moral structure had been removed. His demented madman cries that we have "drunk up the sea" and "wiped away the horizon" (1960: 167). There is no longer any up or down. There is no way to prove this—it is prophecy, and prophecy is really a matter for those who have the eyes to see. There was, however, a taken-for-grantedness of morality, particularly in the English utilitarian guise, that disgusted and maddened both Nietzsche and Dostoyevsky—and drove them to some of their finest and most incisive condemnations.[2] For both, the pursuit of pleasure and avoidance of pain advocated by utilitarian philosophy is farcical. "Mankind does not strive for happiness", Nietzsche famously quipped, "only the Englishman does that" (1990: 80–81). What then could save the world from conformity to the superficial materialism of Western ideals? What could redeem staid material progress and "enlightened self-interest"? For Dostoyevsky, it was a messianic and Russian Christianity—only this sort of purity, and perhaps not even this, could save a Stavrogin or a Raskolnikov; for Nietzsche it was something he regarded as Dionysian, an ethic of instinct and tragic beauty. Carroll inherits and grapples with both metaphysics, and finds his own in the tension between the two, a point I will return to in the conclusion.

First, though, what Carroll wants to show in *Breakout* is how Nietzsche and Dostoyevsky deliberately attack the barriers of rationality. They confront and experience, to use a phrase that comes partly from Nietzsche and partly from Thomas Mann, all that is strange and questionable in human existence. Nietzsche considers himself the prophet of dangerous knowledge: "my truth is dreadful", he claims at the beginning of *Ecce Homo* (1992: 96). Nietzsche unveiled his theory of truth and knowledge through Hamlet himself in *The Birth of Tragedy*, Carroll's urtext for teaching his own theory of culture:

> Knowledge kills action; action requires the veils of illusion: that is the doctrine of Hamlet, not that cheap wisdom of Jack the Dreamer who reflects too much and, as it were, from an excess of possibilities does not get around to action. Not reflection, no true knowledge, an insight into the horrible truth, outweighs any motive for action, both in Hamlet, and in the Dionysian man.
> (1968: 60)

The Dionysian—that nightmare realm of instinctual drives, fears and cruelties—is the actual basis of reality. Nietzsche destroys the naïve optimism of utilitarians and scientific positivists alike that reason, or knowledge alone, can lead us towards a life worth living. Reason is rather the "Devil's whore", as Martin Luther put it, a snake that bites its own tail, something that ultimately inspires horror, absurdity or nausea at existence (Carroll, 2004: 55).

Welcome, it might be said, to the dark side. Indeed, one could well reverse William James' famous title and rename Professor Carroll's undergraduate course: "The Varieties of Irreligious Experience". What we seem to have is, rather, extended meditations on our "lack of religion": nausea, horror, dread, fear and trembling, and symbolic violence, either of a chaotic or a primordial, Old Testament variety. This is not too far from the truth; Carroll was, after all, exploring the *experience* of the dark side of religion.[3] This may represent something like what Jung called the "other side of the God-image" (1995: 38). There are parallels to Jungian psychology: For Jung, too, the Christian God was dead; it had been reduced to a benevolent, moralising projection of a father figure; the reality was a divinity that existed beyond the narrow moral realm. To return to Nietzsche's categories, however, the question Carroll asked here was: what is there on the other side of the "last man"? What is there apart from pleasure, comfort and digestion? Well, it is something that apparently resembles Nietzsche's "Dionysian man".

Dionysian man

Carroll's primary example of the "Dionysian man" is Kurtz from Joseph Conrad's *Heart of Darkness*. Kurtz too, like Stavrogin and Hamlet before him, approximates the Renaissance ideal of humanity. However, exposed to the solitude and lawlessness of the jungles of the Congo, the scrawled footnote at the end of his humanitarian manifesto, "Exterminate the Brutes!", and his final words, "The horror! The horror!" to Marlow, are his true epitaph; his version of Dionysian knowledge. Marlow, in his own disgust with the empty veneer of civilisation, becomes a sort of missionary for the personal truth of Kurtz's revelations. This is crucial, for Marlow is a defender of Kurtz and his dying words, in some ways; if not as a sort of affirmation, at least as a form of honesty. This is to concur with Lionel Trilling's theory of modern culture and literature when he calls Kurtz a "hero of the spirit". Trilling expands further on this theme, in a way that is illuminating for reading both Nietzsche and Dostoyevsky:

> Wherever in modern literature we find violence, whether of represented act or of expression, and an insistence upon the sordid and the disgusting, and an insult offered to the prevailing morality or habit of life, we may assume . . . that we are being confronted by that spirituality, or the aspiration towards it, which subsists upon violence against the specious good.
>
> (1965: 67)

Promises of the spiritual life made in terms of pleasure, in terms resembling the "last man"—of comfort and rest—have little power over us. In this way, Kurtz's life is a type of affirmation of spiritual freedom. This may well be our *real* spiritual condition; this is, unfortunately, one form of "depth".

Kurtz is only the first, although primary, representative of a litany of Dionysian "heroes of the spirit" that exert a fascination for Professor Carroll. Others employed in his teaching include Tyler Durden from *Fight Club* (1999) and Ethan Edwards in *The Searchers* (1956). And more recently in his writing, the Joker from *The Dark Knight* (2008) and Al Swearengen from *Deadwood* (2004–7) have come to the fore. The worlds inhabited here are in one way or another Hobbesian and lawless; human nature is stripped back to its elemental, brutal core. There are other commonalities too, though granted the personalities and contexts are extremely diverse: all the characters here have more "life", more psychic energy; they are leaders, certainly more violent, but also more powerful and passionate; they are "bigger" than the other characters around them; they have, to use a word that arises more than once in Professor Carroll's teaching, "vitality". Or, to employ other language typical of Carroll's writing, in these characters there is no romantic haze, no wishy-washy utopian thinking, no hypocritical cant about noble causes—there is only a return to the bare facts, the essence, however hard to swallow.

The other thing, I suspect, that elicits Carroll's interest, and in the case of Swearengen his admiration, is their *honesty*; a cardinal virtue in his pantheon of values. They live—and this is Carroll's paraphrase of Kierkegaard—in the categories in which they think. So there is no God, therefore there is no moral code (with complex exceptions in the case of Ethan Edwards and Swearengen), and as a consequence of our deepest impulses, there is cruelty, violence and chaos; but there is, within these parameters, and through charismatic action in the world, some sort of integrity, if not, particularly with Swearengen, a little artistry. That is not to say they are not dangerous, or even deadly. Vitality, after all, is hardly a reliable ethical touchstone. The Nazis, for instance, had their own ample quota of the "life-force". In this context, it should be noted that at least two of these characters (Durden and the Joker), like Kurtz, are ultimately purely destructive and psychopathic—even if they are playful and charming. But this is the metaphysical territory of the Dionysian, of operating by id and instinct, and for the most part without reference to conventional morality or what we understand as conscience. On the other side of the last man lie the perils of the unrestrained Dionysian. Carroll seems to potentially align here with a Freudian-Rieffian conception of culture as primarily a mode of instinctual renunciation; the power of the Dionysian is such that the human being needs curbing.

The politics of re-enchantment

These are the dangers of renewal and this, for Carroll, is the challenge. They may be heroes of a type—but restraint is lacking. Where Carroll posits limits is in his conservative political philosophy, which at this point calls for explanation. It is partly, as I implied at the beginning of this piece, a source of order and civility; and on a deeper level, an ethical brake on the power of the Dionysian. One caricature of the political conservative is that of the unthinking defender of their own interests, protecting the status quo out of selfishness because the current social arrangement suits them. Even the apparent arch-conservative T.S. Eliot called the political conservatism of his time a "mental vacuum" (in Kirk, 2014: 23). There is truth to this shallowness but in Carroll's case, his conservatism is more foundational. To give a broad first principle, Western civilisation is in a stage of decline. In his early theoretical "manifesto" *Sceptical Sociology*, Carroll, following Nietzsche, refers to a decadent civilisation (1980: 3). The "decadent" was Nietzsche's sworn enemy—the enemy within, perhaps, given that Nietzsche also identified as a decadent himself. Decadence is a combination of many elements: at once a loosening of moral standards, no longer being sure of one's instincts, a loss of cultural self-confidence, and accompanying that, a dwindling belief in the guiding principles and beliefs of that culture. The danger is that the individual decadent may then in desperation jump from introspection—from the morbid reflections of psychology—to a redeeming and active moralism and utopianism.

Re-enchantment in such cases is sometimes achieved by total immersion in revolutionary ideology. One explicit and illuminating example is the decision of the Hungarian aesthete and cultural critic, Georg Lukács, to join the Communist Party in 1918. He would eventually move to Russia and become an apologist for Stalin. A central motif for Lukács was the "escape from decadence". A keen, almost fanatical reader of Dostoyevsky, upon reading *The Possessed*, Lukács claimed that Stavrogin had three choices insofar as he was sincere: "suicide, decadence, or revolution" (1983: 48). Stavrogin was typical of the Russian intellectual: the person who, possessing strength and brilliance, but finding only an abyss of aimlessness, turns to depravity and, eventually, suicide. Lukács found the conditions of his life and culture intolerable; he could not live in the categories in which he thought. Trying to avoid the fate of Stavrogin, he joined the Communist Party, a decision inspired not by love of the dispossessed, but rather by the need for a leap of faith to belief and purpose. The danger here is a "malign" sort of moralism, to quote Carroll, a morality that fulfils an independent and pre-existing emotional need (1980: 29). Or otherwise, the idealism is founded in an escape from reality; particularly true in the case of those intellectuals who proclaim an abstract love for mankind, but who have little capacity for it when faced with the varying dispositions and talents of concrete individuals.

Utopian hopes, however, turn to terror; a phenomenon so universal in the 20th century as to form a grotesque social-psychological law. The ethical certainty that derives from a broad intellectual blueprint for society legitimises repression, justified by reference to an ideal that with each escalation of violence recedes further from view. If as, Dostoyevsky warned, "everything is permitted", then it is possible to remake the human being according to the dictates of ideological belief. And if the vision is sustained by a millennial picture of a "new man", the willingness to sacrifice or experiment on others deepens. These are the lures and contradictions of serious revolutionary purpose. If nothing is sacred, the metaphysical line separating absolute commitment from deadly nihilism is very thin. Two competing value systems, or entire moral worlds even, seem to be in operation here, particularly in exemplary cases like Lukács.[4] The first morality is Nietzschean. For Nietzsche, the world is only justified as an aesthetic phenomenon. So the Nietzschean morality is one of aesthetic self-affirmation, and of a morality, or more precisely an authenticity, beyond good and evil. It is the atmosphere we recognise from Kurtz in *Heart of Darkness*, Dostoyevsky's *Notes from Underground* and *Crime and Punishment*, Thomas Mann's *Death in Venice*, to mention only a few, and in more recent writers like Norman Mailer. This is a sort of perverse "heroism of the spirit" more common to the artist: it is the oscillation between superhuman and subhuman, of the desperate creative-destructive search for a "place to stand". These adventures in consciousness, however, appear to have little or nothing to do with the second morality: the political pursuit of utopian justice. This morality, on the other hand, is usually hygienic; it makes overbearing, puritanical and strict moral demands on adherents. Yet both these contradictory moralities frequently come together in the breast of political actors espousing what Weber called "ultimate ends" or "ethics of conviction" (1958: 128). For Carroll, this is a sign that our idealism is either spent or intellectually incoherent.

The key question here in politics is: who has the right to carry out their morality on behalf of others? If we regard politics as our common life, it is also a life that is borne along by inherited culture and slowly developing institutions of hundreds if not thousands of years. Conservatism, in this respect, is dependent on culture as custom and convention, not necessarily as metaphysics. But it is these deep cultural roots that also, more than anything, guarantee the operation of morality. Therefore, it is the tenuous moral certainty that is the key failure of those who are all too willing to act on behalf of others and on behalf of radical change. Weber is right in this respect to emphasise "responsibility" over "conviction"; politics in the deepest ethical sense is responsibility for consequences. Convictions like those of Lukács come and go like pollen in the wind.

Mythical home

Political conservatism acts as ethical restraint, a bulwark against the potential tide of nihilism, or as depicted earlier, the dangerous metaphysics of the Dionysian. Conservatism, then, is the answer on the practical, ethical plane. Yet it is a flimsy answer, as Carroll himself admits. Conservative-minded critics revert to bemoaning the loss of community and traditional notions of morality, and loudly proclaim the "need for roots", to use Simone Weil's term, in ways that ultimately are implausible, unrealistic and empty on a cultural level.[5] The problem for Carroll, however, and this is where he is more interesting and audacious than most cultural conservatives, is that he attacks the problem not on the level of community or morality, but precisely on the level of culture and meaning.

I

The other thing that Carroll shares with Nietzsche and Dostoyevsky (to return to his PhD thesis) is a mental obsession with or a sort of hammering away at the mystery doctrine of Christianity. Whereas what Dostoyevsky sought was its restoration in a purer form, what Nietzsche sought was its overcoming, particularly in his strident and hyperbolic later works such as *Ecce Homo* in which he made the terms of his spiritual struggle most explicit, signing off: "—Have I been understood?—Dionysus against the Crucified" (1992: 104). Carroll, however, turns Nietzsche on his head and in *The Existential Jesus* attempts a returns to the heart of the Christian myth—in a manner, it should be noted, unlike Dostoyevsky. This is the culminating point of Carroll's later period, and his deepest inferred exploration of the meaning of "culture", informed by the dual pillars "faith" and "myth". *The Existential Jesus* is the clearest point at which these notions converge, hence its significance.

Before we proceed to *The Existential Jesus*, let us at least try to untangle what Carroll is pointing to when he uses these three difficult and amorphous words. First, culture. Some notion of "true culture" is certainly posited as the first principle of recovery. Carroll, like other culturalists including Steiner and perhaps going back to figures like Jacob Burckhardt, has an honorific sense of what culture is. The task of the teacher here is that of esteem and reverence: he helps students to recover the past, stand outside the limitations of their own self and culture and give a freshness to classic works of art and intelligence. Carroll would interpose an idealised past to reveal and redeem the inadequacies of the present moment. Ultimately, his interest here, like that of the great culturalists of the past, is to track the process by which we seem to have lost the ancient art of transcendence. Second, culture is also based in a physical locale, to use the Nietzschean phrase, a "sacred site"; Carroll returns to try to find whatever is alive in the oldest forms of dreams and myths of the classic and Judeo-Christian culture.

Theology may, as Thomas Mann noted, spark thirst, but it fails to sate it; the vital need of the age is for a myth that provides a foundation for cultural health—Carroll's diagnosis is that "the Western world is dying for want of a story". The ground for this diagnosis is evidently Nietzschean but its most famous proponent has been Jung—this despite Carroll's temperamental preference for and affinity with Jung's cooler, more stoical counterpart, Freud. Jung asked himself in 1912, after his break with Freud, "what myth do I live in?" (1995: 40). With the currency of his father's Christian myth exhausted, he decided honestly that he had none. However, what Jung understood was that without something to direct them beyond the self, individuals without belief will get lost in psycho-pathology. The gods thereby are reborn as diseases. It is ultimately this self-absorption, the spread of neurosis and half-hearted depression combined with low levels of commitment to anything beyond the self, that may well lead to the "going under of the West", Carroll contends in *Ego and Soul*, using Spengler's title (1998: 225). This is not to say that there are no values; rather it is that no values really impress us anymore. To paraphrase Eliot again, the world dies with a whimper, not a bang.

Carroll, like Jung, and following Nietzsche, posits the cure of myth against reason. This quest for a mythical home is, to invert Yeats' famous phrase, for that deepest centre that can hold. It is, like all quests of course, deeply utopian. However, as Steiner put it in his extrapolation of T.S. Eliot, culture has a "utopian core" (1971: 8); it is a sort of stretching out of hope beyond all reason. Perhaps "culture" in this sense is simply the name for that impossible longing. Facts fail us at a certain point, Matthew Arnold claimed, and his accompanying insight that "the strongest part of our religion today is its unconscious poetry" is suggestive in this context (1880: 1442). Arnold's prophecy here is that the facts of religion would be replaced by the language of poetry. Poetry, and perhaps the poetry of religious emotion, represents a "finer spirit of knowledge" (1880: 1442). *The Existential Jesus* belongs to this tradition, if there is one: it is a semi-poetic, semi-interpretative enterprise that seeks out the enduring centre of the religious story, and perhaps from there the "primal centre" beyond culture, and out of which culture is formed. For Rieff—Carroll's main theoretical shadow—culture is basically law: a series of "Thou Shalt Nots" that put a civilising and repressive cork in the dike of insatiable human instinct. For Carroll, however, culture is not moral; it is the deep symbolic expression of the nature of "being", and thus the importance of the figure of Jesus who is the central representative of what "being" is in our culture.

There may be something to this, but it is just one of the many points of fracture between Carroll's poetic study and conventional Christian readings of Jesus as "saviour". In this unique book, Carroll returns to a sort of narrative foundationalism so pure that it escapes not only traditional Christian metaphysics, but perhaps also the categories of our rationality and morality. Let me be clear: this is not to say there is no ethics in *The Existential Jesus*; it is to say that "faith", the "one thing needful", lies beyond the ethical. This is to note the correspondence between Carroll's theory of culture and one of his key predecessors, the Danish theologian Soren Kierkegaard. Indeed, insofar as Carroll's interpretation can be analysed—which, to be honest, is not very far—it is best to approach it through Kierkegaard and his hierarchy of the three spheres: at the bottom, the aesthetic; above that, the ethical sphere; and the highest, the religious. Kierkegaard takes as his starting point the father of faith, Abraham, and of particular importance is his tortuous account of Abraham's attempted sacrifice of Isaac in *Fear and Trembling* (1843). Systematic philosophers such as Hegel mistakenly seek to understand the God of Abraham within the categories of human reason. However, it is precisely in its absurd and quite horrible unreason that Kierkegaard identifies the divine request for sacrifice. Such faith as Abraham must have had is total, uncompromising and beyond good and evil; faith—unlike ethics—is personal, paradoxical and dreadful.

This is the background atmosphere of *The Existential Jesus*. What we have in Carroll's re-telling of Mark's Life of Jesus is something approaching a notion of *sola fide* (faith alone). I suspect this is what liberal-minded reviewers intuit when they call John Carroll's books "dangerous"—an assertion that has been made about books as varied as *Guilt* and *Humanism*. Mark's Life of Jesus is an "enigma"; Carroll uses the Greek word *ainigma* which in modern English translates to something like "riddle", or even more pertinently, "dark saying". *The Existential Jesus* heaps on the mystery of solitude, darkness and doubt in order to push towards the precipice of a leap of faith. Stripping Mark's story of the later added, but doctrinally standard, account of the resurrection, the Jesus story comes to resemble more a Greek tragedy than a Christian tale of salvation. The denouement rather becomes God's abandonment of Jesus: "My God, my God, why have you forsaken me?" (15:34). And then an empty tomb, and then fleeing in terror and fear (16:8).

Is faith possible in the modern world, Carroll asks through Kierkegaard (2004: 187–191)? Faith seems to require the miracle of revelation; however, in the modern world, we no longer believe in miracles; we no longer believe in the death of deaths. Kierkegaard has faith that faith exists—but no true faith himself. He wants to make a complete choice on behalf of God in the form of Jesus. His solution, in his search for the consolations of ancient faith, is to heap darkness, guilt and dread onto his overburdened soul in order to try to make an impossible leap of faith. What Luther had, on the other hand, in a parallel to Mark's "dark saying", is the "darkness of faith". The darkness of faith forces human beings to make an either/or choice—of either death or a place where Luther claims "death killeth death". This is the place at the pit of reason, where, to use Carroll's words, "the light of reason does not shine, and there are bewildering contradictions" (2004: 56). At the very least, the intention here is to escape or supersede our familiar rational understanding, and at the deepest level to imagine, like Kierkegaard, something of the origin of religious passion.

In Carroll's imaginative re-telling, there is no scepticism or detachment, only passionate absorption in a sacred story. Clearly, this is an unusual work for a sociological author. Carroll admits as much himself. In a surprising epilogue, he writes that, having climbed inside Mark's narrative of the Jesus story:

> I have little idea what I have done as an author—whether it has worked, or even what that might mean. I am in there, down inside, with only the dim sense that I have been captured by a long and complete dark saying.
> (2007: 237–238)

There is little certainty here but also little of the objectivity recommended for the social scientist. Carroll, though, while sceptical, never held much stock in the value-free distinction. The method is more akin to inspiration than analysis. I would move, however, one step further: *The Existential Jesus*, to use Peter Jensen's term again, is something like an old-fashioned sermon. Erudition finally begets simplicity. Carroll finds a living myth—Jesus' enigmatic "I am"—and, like Kierkegaard, will deliver this message over and over again to a distracted public. Carroll perhaps here moves, in the tradition of Nietzsche's ideal of the philosopher, from teacher and cultural custodian to something like value-creator or myth-maker.

II

There is a timeliness in this return to the "foundations" of Western culture, even if the method is unconventional and idiosyncratic. However, occasionally the retelling feels like a return to the essentials of the story without the actual essence. First, the Jesus of Carroll's narrative is angry and remote, trapped and isolated by his charisma. *The Existential Jesus* is selective in that it does not have at its centre any notion of "love", whether relational or universal. The Christian imperative, after all, is "to love thy neighbour as thyself". But our familiarity with this command betrays its radical nature; in Steiner's words, it is a "call to anarchic love" (1971: 43). This "call" for a "change of heart" is meant to reveal a deep disjuncture between our everyday life, its institutions, customs and moralities, and that of some other, better world—but also perhaps a world more real. Only by answering this call, and in a way that its demands completely consume the spirit—think, for example, of Dostoyevsky's Idiot—does one enter and know the "Kingdom of God". Perhaps this claim for Carroll—that is, for someone so firmly anti-utopian in all aspects of character and outlook, someone convinced of the truth of many of Nietzsche's psychological propositions related to pity and *ressentiment* in *The Genealogy of Morality*, and someone who abhors the unrealities and excesses of compassionate, mythical politics—is simply untenable.

Second, *The Existential Jesus* fails, deliberately, to explicitly incorporate the resurrection. While there are justifiable historical reasons for omitting it from the earliest telling of the story in Mark, it remains the foundational event of Christian theology. Carroll's major impression point is not the crucifixion or the Sermon on the Mount, but rather unusually, Jesus' attempted reassurance of his disciples when they see him walking on water. Terrified and shaken, Jesus says to them:

"*I am*. Do not fear" (Mark 6:50). This is a gnomic gesture, but one upon which Carroll places considerable metaphysical weight. The concept of the resurrection is, however, more crucial and more concrete: it is what Christianity throughout history stands or falls by. To use a Freudian line, the appeal of Christianity is based on the psychological foundations of the human "wish" for eternal life. While Carroll does employ the motif of the "empty tomb" and the absence of a corpse as highly suggestive, this is the realm of paradox and ambiguity which is now our only avenue of access to the noumenal or unsayable. It is, however, precisely the extent to which the resurrection is literally true, and not poetic, that accounts for the power of Christianity in actual history. It is this that accounts for the massive historical promise and success of Christendom. Poetry, as Goethe put it, cannot act as a guide for life and nor can it fulfil the demands of religion. This is what I believe Flannery O'Connor meant in a famous exchange with Mary McCarthy at a dinner party in New York in 1955. McCarthy was rhapsodising about the "beautiful symbolism" of the Eucharist, to which the backwoods Southerner O'Connor angrily replied: "Well, if it's a symbol, to hell with it!" (in Kazin, 1997). This, I believe, is probably what faith, to the extent that it has the texture of ancient faith that is the animus of the story, looks like—unpleasant, impolite and fundamentalist.

I agree that the development of something like true inwardness is not an intellectual endeavour, and requires some reference to what we understand as the mythical. In this sense, *The Existential Jesus* is of great interest, particularly for those of us whose imaginations are haunted by the figure of Jesus or for whom, like Carroll, "Jesus is a central but obscure presence" (2007: 5). But this is ground of the deepest subjectivity; Carroll's re-telling of the Jesus story is a personal intermingling of the objects of his passionate interest: faith, myth and culture. That is indeed precisely its power. For Carroll, the mystery is in the story itself; truth, or "truth with a capital T", is *mythos* itself. Story and myth are true culture—or perhaps better said, the principles operating behind the constitutive myths of culture are mysterious and transcendent. At some point in Western history, people thought of themselves in relation to God and that made up the heart of culture. However, culture no longer guarantees a sense of purpose higher than the self in the way it used to. Can we contrive its return? Do we even want it back? Carroll is not so prescriptive; his method is indirect and he is smart enough to be modest in his explicit claims. At the very least, he is interested in the nature of the self, and of the right relation of that self to its culture. But he also seems to ask for some return to cultural origins, and in the work under investigation, to Christianity—that most compelling and mysterious of our cultural myths. The diagnosis is perhaps right, but as is so often the case—as for Nietzsche, as for Jung—the therapy is more difficult to execute. Perhaps such a retrieval of such a culture is impossible. His own intellectual project, though, brings a depth and sincerity to the grappling with metaphysical questions, in a time when the urgency of the questions seems to have receded from cultural view. The endeavour is real, and that is enough. After all, for us, there is only the trying.

Notes

1 Steiner is, along with Frank Kermode and Harold Bloom, perhaps the last of the great magisterial literary critics in the tradition of F.R. Leavis. John Carroll told me, in conversation, that Steiner has a soft spot for Oswald Spengler's quaint and dated prophetic work *The Decline of the West* (1918). Steiner's works are in this vein; immensely broad, erudite reflections on the fate of literary-philosophic Western culture; his great theme is the failure of the teaching of the humanities to humanise—particularly in that repository of civilisation, Germany. It is understandable that reflections of this magnitude and depth often fall to the ethical Jewish teacher in secular mode; for those, if not for being one step removed generationally, may well have been sacrificed for the sake of that apparent cultural "decline" or its attempted "renewal" in Nazi Germany. This is true in the American university in the case of Lionel Trilling and Philip Rieff. A similar trend can be observed in Australia in the careers of two of our most prominent ethical-public intellectuals, Robert Manne and Peter Singer. Carroll perhaps inherited some of his breadth of judgement, among other things, from Steiner.

2 Here is Nietzsche's devastating critique of the British utilitarians. Arguably, this is just as accurate today of the sort of "meta-Christian" thinking typical of the "new Atheists", for whom morality is certainly *not* a problem: "They have got rid of the Christian God, and now feel obliged to cling all the more firmly to Christian morality . . . In England, in response to every little emancipation from theology one has to reassert one's position in a fear inspiring manner as a moral fanatic . . . If they consequently think they no longer have need of Christianity as a guarantee of morality; that is merely the *consequence* of the ascendancy of Christian evaluation and an expression of the *strength* and *depth* of this ascendancy: so that the origin of English morality has been forgotten, so that the highly conditional nature of its right to exist is no longer felt. For the Englishman morality is not yet a problem" (1990: 80–81).

3 This probably comes close to answering the question of why Professor Carroll did not pursue a career in philosophy, when, after all, the three figures from his PhD are of a type: literary-philosophers. The answer is that philosophy is experiential, a matter of the passions as much as it is of the mind. Philosophy cannot be—nor should it be—divorced from affect or, indeed, inspiration. Academic philosophy is too removed or "abstract"—a favourite term of disparagement. He had little patience for byzantine sentences and thought experiments. How, rather, does the philosophy fit the actual life? He would also agree with Nietzsche that a philosophy is an "unconscious memoir" of the philosopher themselves. What character does it represent, what integrity does it show? Philosophers, from this point of view, are law-givers; they present or "create" values, or overturn the tables of the previous laws.

4 I owe the substance of this interpretation to Carroll's contemporary and fellow conservative Roger Scruton, whose devastating outline can be found in his piece "The Philosopher on Dover Beach" (1990: 4–8).

5 This is true for Rieff's later hand-wringing in *My Life among the Deathworks* (2006), the semi-prophecy scattered through Daniel Bell's *Cultural Contradictions of Capitalism* (1976) and Scruton's quixotic nostalgia for *England: An Elegy* (2000). Much the same can be said for Alisdair MacIntyre's designs on Aristotelian community in *After Virtue* (1981).

References

Arnold M (1880) The Study of Poetry. In: Abrams MH (ed) *The Norton Anthology of English Literature*. New York: Norton & Co.

Bell D (1976) *The Cultural Contradictions of Capitalism*. New York: Basic Books.

Carroll J (1974) *Breakout from the Crystal Palace: The Anarcho-Psychological Critique: Stirner, Nietzsche and Dostoyevsky*. London: Routledge & Kegan Paul.

Carroll J (1980) *Sceptical Sociology*. London: Routledge & Kegan Paul.
Carroll J (1998) *Ego and Soul: The Modern West in Search of Meaning*. Melbourne: HarperCollins.
Carroll J (2001) *The Western Dreaming: The Western World is Dying for Want of a Story*. Pymble, NSW: HarperCollins.
Carroll J (2004) *The Wreck of Western Culture: Humanism Revisited*. Melbourne: Scribe Publications.
Carroll J (2007) *The Existential Jesus*. Melbourne: Scribe Publications.
Carroll J (2010) *Greek Pilgrimage: In Search of the Foundations of the West*. Melbourne: Scribe.
Dostoyevsky F (1962) *The Possessed*, trans. Andrew MacAndrew. London: Penguin.
Eliot TS (1979) *Four Quartets*. London: Faber & Faber.
Jensen P (2007) He Would Have Disappeared Years Ago. *The Monthly*, May 2007.
Jung CG (1995) *Memories, Dreams, Reflections*. London: Routledge Classics.
Kazin A (1997) God and the American Writer. *The New York Times*, October 12.
Kierkegaard S (1843) *Fear and Trembling*. London: Penguin.
Kirk R (2014) *Eliot and his Age: T.S. Eliot's Moral Imagination in the Twentieth Century*. Washington, DC: ISI.
Lukács G (1983) Stavrogin's Confession. *Lukács: Reviews and Articles*. London: Merlin Press.
MacIntyre A (1981) *After Virtue*. Notre Dame, IN: University of Notre Dame.
Nietzsche F (1960) *The Gay Science*. New York: Frederick Ungar Publishing.
Nietzsche F (1968) *The Birth of Tragedy*, trans. Walter Kaufmann. New York: Modern Library.
Nietzsche F (1990) *The Twilight of the Idols and the Anti-Christ*, trans. RJ Hollingdale. London: Penguin.
Nietzsche F (1992) *Ecce Homo: How One Becomes What One is*, trans. RJ Hollingdale. London: Penguin.
Rieff P (2006) *My Life among the Deathworks*. Charlottesville, VA: University of Virginia Press.
Rieff P (2008) *Charisma: The Gift of Grace and How It Has Been Taken Away from Us*. New York: Random House.
Scruton R (1990) *The Philosopher on Dover Beach: Essays*. London: Palgrave Macmillan.
Scruton R (2000) *England: An Elegy*. London: Sinclair-Stevenson.
Spengler O (1918) *The Decline of the West*. New York: Alfred A. Knopf.
Steiner G (1971) *In Bluebeard's Castle: Some Notes towards the Redefinition of Culture*. New Haven, CT: Yale University Press.
Trilling L (1965) *Beyond Culture*. New York: Harcourt Brace Jovanich.
Weber M (1958) *From Max Weber: Essays in Sociology*, trans. HH Gerth and C Wright Mills (eds). London: Routledge & Kegan Paul.

6   The Passion in Port Talbot

Michael Sheen

I was asked by John Carroll to write a piece about a theatrical project I worked on in my hometown of Port Talbot that became known as *The Passion*. There was one single performance that lasted for seventy-two hours. It began at dawn on Friday, April 22, 2011 and ended at approximately 10:30 pm the following Sunday. In the creation of it, John's book *The Existential Jesus* (2007) was of great inspiration. It is difficult to describe the process of working on it and the experience of performing it. I have decided to do it by using extracts from three emails I wrote. The first is to John himself after we first started corresponding almost five years after the performance had taken place. The second is to the Welsh rock band Manic Street Preachers about eight weeks before the performance took place, asking if they would be a part of it—they agreed. The third is to my friend Lily and was written just a few weeks after it happened. They are each preceded by a quote that was meaningful to me at the time of working on it. This way of trying to describe my experience seems to have a little of the spirit of the original piece about it.

> The wise one . . . wanders like a bird and leaves no trace behind him . . . pursues no intention. And he is not going anywhere. He goes without direction. He melds completely with the path which, as of itself, leads nowhere.
> (Laozi)

Extract from email to John Carroll dated February 3, 2016: almost five years after the performance

It began with me being asked if I was interested in doing a production of some kind for the newly formed National Theatre Wales. They said they were looking to work with local communities more and in non-traditional theatre spaces. I immediately thought of the local Passion play I'd seen a few times when I was growing up. It was performed by a mix of local amateur performers and members of the community and took place in a local park with the crucifixion happening at sunset. It affected me in a very powerful way for all kinds of reasons. And so that was my starting point in thinking about what I was going to do.

Over the next two years it developed into something that had the biblical story of the Passion as the blueprint but was set in a contemporary context and with the specific story of my hometown—Port Talbot—as its focus. This created a sort of double story with the story/myth of the town being the surface or conscious version and the story/ritual of the events leading up to and around the crucifixion of Jesus being the deep currents/unconscious version.

Port Talbot is a town with a lot of socio-economic challenges and a complicated relationship with industry. The local steelworks, and before that the local coal and tin mines, have provided a livelihood for the people of the town for generations but they've also taken a toll on its health. It's also created a form of dependency, which at this very moment is transforming from what has been, for many years, a constantly impending threat into what is now becoming a potentially devastating reality. The steelworks announced last week that it's cutting a quarter of the local workforce and the future of steel production, not only in Port Talbot but throughout the country, looks to be in a deadly downward spiral. The town itself is the butt of every joke, seen as dirty and sickly, marginalised, ravaged, riddled with alcohol and drug problems, suicides, depression, domestic abuse, young offenders, and quite literally passed over with huge motorway overpasses constructed in the '60s cutting through and over its streets. As travellers pass it by, speeding their way to the cities beyond, they are spared being confronted with the dirt and poverty beneath. It seemed to me that if the town was personified it would be just the sort of person Jesus would have been drawn to.

And whilst sitting one day in the chapel of St. Joseph on a visit to St. Peter's Basilica and surrounded by images of Christ's ministry, I was suddenly and overwhelmingly struck by a realisation. At that very moment, there were people in Port Talbot doing exactly the same work for those who needed it as Christ was depicted doing in the iconography of that corner chapel where I sat—ministering to the sick, the elderly, the dying, those who were lost, at their most vulnerable, most in need of help. It was at that moment that the underlying vision for the piece seemed to come together for me. From then on it was a case of trying to keep a balance between the project and its various strands having, on the one hand, an autonomous growth and, on the other, always being clear that everything had to fit within the context of the vision and connection that I found in that chapel. The interplay, between the very local and specific world of the town and the much deeper and universal world of Mark's version of the Passion, seemed to generate an experience for the performers and audience alike that was deeply meaningful and very emotional. Not just for people who understood the local meaning, but also for those who had no connection whatsoever to the town. The concept of midrash, which I was unaware of until reading your book, really resonated with me and encouraged me to follow where the overlap between the two worlds seemed to point. This proved hugely rewarding for the project.

I became more of a catalyst than anything else during the whole process. Keeping a strong sense of what was the guiding vision underlying and motivating the whole project for me, I tried to let the town itself guide how that vision would manifest itself in the performance. I would try and incorporate as many different and sometimes seemingly incongruous elements of the community as possible into the story and look for how they might suggest possibilities for how to depict them. So, for instance, I discovered that there was a children's circus skills group in a particularly disadvantaged area. I went to watch them doing a session and it became clear as I watched a few of them riding around on BMX bikes with their wheels on fire that there was a possibility of them creating a demonic nightmarish vision for my character when I was alone in the Gethsemane section of the story. That in turn suggested all kinds of other possibilities and that section became particularly powerful as a result.

Or, again, I discovered a local roofer who made small-scale versions of local buildings out of the slate he used on the roofs he mended in his work. He said that from his vantage point high up, atop the buildings, he had gained a different perspective on the town and a new appreciation of it and its people. It led me to having a scene, again in the garden of Gethsemane section, where my character speaks with his father who is working on the roof of one of the surrounding houses. A piece of slate from the roof has fallen and he asks me if I can see it anywhere. I find it and he asks me if I will pick it up. Their interaction suggests that in picking up the piece of slate my character is accepting his fate. The whole house will be saved by the sacrifice of one piece of it. The significance of the moment was increased by the sound of approaching police sirens.

The role I took on in the process of developing the piece was also reflected in the nature of the central character that I played. He had been a teacher in a local school who had disappeared, possibly as a result of some kind of breakdown—fear around losing his job, a broken marriage with a daughter involved—and who may or may not, according to local reports and sightings, have been living rough on the mountain overlooking the town. Forty days after his disappearance he emerges onto the beach at dawn on Good Friday and the three-day performance begins. He had lost his memory. No idea of his identity, his past or his family. He spends the next few days asking the town and its people to tell their stories. Finally, on the cross, he shouts, "I remember!", and he becomes a vessel for the collective memory of the town. So, as a character, he was more of a listener than a teacher—a catalyst, also.

> The war will come to your streets, and you will feel it in your own lives and on your own skin.
>
> (Chechen rebel leader)

Extract from email to Manic Street Preachers dated February 28, 2011: 53 days before the performance

It's now titled "The Passion of Port Talbot" and will be a non-stop three-day performance, beginning Good Friday and ending Easter Sunday night. It grew out of a conversation about the Passion play that used to be done in Margam Park. I saw it a few times growing up and it was very powerful for me. I'm not a Christian or religious in any specific way, but seeing theatre outside, and local people taking part, telling a simple but very emotional story about death and sacrifice, political oppression, violence and redemption and ultimately, compassion and love, really affected me. I had no interest in telling a story about events in Jerusalem 2000 years ago, but the story of the Passion provides a rich template for what we're doing.

It's a story about this town, now.

Occupied by a near omnipotent, multi-national, corporate entity, known as The Company, the town becomes the subject of a secret plan for demolition in order to exploit the unspecified "riches" that lie beneath it. The Company Man arrives by sea, surrounded by his private security force. Under the guise of construction for a new bypass road for the area—known as the "Passover"—they begin their relocation of the local population—at gunpoint. The local authorities, working on behalf of the town but officially sanctioned by The Company, prepare a grand welcome on the beach. A display of local culture, talent and above all, loyalty, all overseen by the local militia. The Resistance movement within the town is preparing a very different kind of welcome for The Company Man. They see his visit as a chance to strike a lethal blow to the corporate/military entity that keeps their town under oppressive occupation.

A Port Talbot school teacher, having disappeared 40 days previously, and rumoured to have had a breakdown and been living wild in the mountains above the town, appears on the beach at the same time. He emerges, having lost his memory, filthy and disorientated, no identity, no possessions, homeless and alone. Over the next three days we see how he asks the town to tell him their stories—what they hope for and what they've lost—and how he comes to complicate the Company plans for the area. Eventually, his galvanising and empowering presence is deemed too dangerous and he is made an example of. Taken to a local roundabout and publicly executed, his crucifixion inadvertently releases the power that has been lying dormant beneath the town all along. As his memory is restored to him he becomes a vessel for the history of the town and its people and all their stories come bursting forth.

Through the 72 hours of our performance we see: the ghost of a street come back with a warning, the dead walk among the gravestones and underpasses once more, hooded angels dance through the shopping centre evading police, demons on BMXs terrorise the labyrinthine back-lanes, the last night send-off for the last remaining Working Men's Club, a televised beachfront roundabout crucifixion, a makeshift refugee camp for the displaced families on Station Road, a moonlit meeting with a roofer who might be God, a Danse Macabre of sleep-walking pensioners, a three-hour procession where a whole town walks to a hundred drummers, and much more besides. The stories of the town and its people interweave with "the greatest story ever told", in a ritual of birth, death and renewal.

The performance will be taking place at various locations around the town over the three days and will involve as much of the local community as possible—at the moment, we have over a thousand local people involved. There'll be a series of scheduled, official episodes, and interspersed between them there will be continuous, unofficial action that people might happen across, and can follow if they wish.

I'm joined by the Cornish company Wildworks, who have a lot of experience in developing site-specific performances with communities. There'll be a core company of professional performers, all originally from the Port Talbot area, working alongside community performers, local performing groups and volunteers from the area.

We have marching bands, bell ringers, folk groups, male voice choirs, brass bands, rock groups, circus performers, graffiti artists, DJs, writers' groups, poets, opera singers, a harpist, fishermen, Lifeboat men, surfers, youth theatres, youth choirs, the WI, the Townswomen's Guild, slate workers, carpenters, builders, rugby teams, dance companies, gymnasts, horse riders, classic car enthusiasts, a landscape gardener and a donkey—the list is endless and growing every day.

That's not to mention the voluntary organisations and community groups that are at the heart of the piece. I want this story to be a celebration of community in general and the community of Port Talbot in particular. It is a town that has, quite literally, been overlooked.

One of the most defining features of the town is how it has been sliced through and swept over with bypass roads. Huge, monolithic structures, held up by elephantine grey concrete columns. Church spires, and terraced housing fighting for breath, as cars and lorries race overhead, on their way to neighbouring cities. Graveyards encircled by deafening motorway roar. This enforced isolation has led to both a subliminal acceptance on the part of its inhabitants that it does, indeed, have nothing worth stopping for or looking at, and, also, a strange preservation, some might say petrification, of certain things that many other towns seem to have lost. The bland and characterless homogeneity that has crept across the face of our towns has been slowed in its deathly drift here in Port Talbot, it seems. At least for now.

There is a visual aesthetic to the town that is unique, a combination of urban and rural, the steelworks and the sea, the sacred and the profane, the poetic and the brutish, all huddled together in amongst the pillars and between the mountains and the shore. As I meet more and more organisations and community service providers, a picture emerges of a town on the frontline: desperate needs met by heroic compassion with precious few resources. Generation after generation both dependent upon and poisoned by local industry. A population of 36,000 and out of that, 4000 children in the town are living in poverty. The highest percentage of young carers in the country. Highest suicide rate in the area. It's overwhelming.

Just over a year ago, sitting in the chapel of St. Joseph in St. Peter's basilica, the project suddenly became clear to me. Surrounded by images of the ministry of Jesus—attending to the sick, the dying, the young and the aged—I was suddenly overcome with the realisation that, at that very moment, back in my home town, there were people doing the very same work, for little or no money, with no support or resources. Constantly overlooked and ignored, until such time as people have need of them. Hidden behind doors and acronyms, they do the work that makes us uncomfortable, that we'd rather not acknowledge is going on or accept is happening, until we find ourselves in need of them. It's hard to face the fact that there's a 12-year-old girl caring for her mother who has both physical and mental disabilities, as well as her younger siblings who both suffer from fits—her father having disappeared—with little or no financial support, unable to qualify for home help. And on top of it all, she's being bullied at school. Her name is—and I went bowling with her and 17 other young carers the other night. She gets one night a week to be a regular 12-year-old. A carers' support group called Crossroads provides youth club facilities for young carers just to hang out together, play pool, get someone to talk to if they need it. Some as young as eight. They're just one of the groups we're working with on The Passion. And—will be one of our performers.

We're telling a story based upon the Passion narrative of the Gospels, but in a modern context, and firmly set within the town of Port Talbot. Woven throughout the piece will be the stories of the people we are meeting. The words of a woman who put her son into care because she knew the heroin addiction that was killing her was stopping her from being a mother. Her feelings of powerlessness and despair will inform the scene of a mother watching her son executed on a wooden cross on Aberafan beach roundabout.

Port Talbot is unique, but it's also every town. Under attack from a faceless enemy, turning us upon ourselves. Depleted and unsupported, but passionate and determined. By turns resigned and angry, violent and bored, proud and wasted. We don't need to be told anything, taught lessons, spoken to in parables. We just need to be listened to, our story told, our struggles witnessed. The character I play is just a vessel, emptied of memory, ready to be filled with the stories of the town. Reborn from the sea to listen and witness, and, finally, to take a journey into the unknown carrying their most precious and hard-won moments in his heart.

As I mentioned earlier, in this alternative Port Talbot there is an underground Resistance movement. Something along the lines of the activism I saw at the G8 and G20 summits when I was in Toronto last year. The so-called "Black Block" tactics. Small, semi-organised insurgent happenings. On the Saturday of our performance, I like the idea of balaclava-clad, "Black Block" bands mounting spontaneous performances around the town—on tops of buildings, in underpasses, on the top of cars or trucks. We need an anthem for the town and the Resistance movement, something the bands could play before the local militia shuts them down. Then in the evening at the Seaside Social Club Last Supper event, our Resistance band take the stage at the climax of a night of celebration, and play for all they're worth in front of the crowd. Giving voice to the voiceless, the unrepresented, the overlooked and the spat on. Into this come the security forces, checking papers, rounding up insurgents, and they either get taken away or they make their escape helped by the crowd. I would love you to be our band, and, if possible, create our anthem.

I'm not interested in telling a story about God or religion or faith. My faith is in people. I believe we have to make our stand and fight for the things that others would take from us. The things of real value. That which binds us. There is one basic truth for me—life is hard and we have to help each other. And the people who devote their lives to that truth must be celebrated. Stood up for. Listened to. And those who suffer, suffer for us all. That is why we have to hear their story, because it is our own. And if we do not recognise it as such then we are far gone indeed. Far gone.

They say you die twice. Once when you stop breathing, and again, later on, the last time someone says your name.

(Banksy)

Extract from email to Lily Bevan dated May 19, 2011: 26 days after the performance

It's been almost a month now since it finished and I went on a huge down afterwards. Really hard to let go and move on. It was the most extraordinary experience. The process of getting there, working with the community, getting involved with all the charities and service organisations, workshops, rehearsals with the core company, youth theatres, choirs, brass bands, rock bands, folk bands, dance companies, graffiti campaigns, films, online alternative reality games, websites. It was the biggest, most ridiculously ambitious project possible relative to the budget and timeframe. I've never felt more stress or anxiety in the lead-up to the performance. Such huge pressure and responsibility. No dress rehearsals or full techs of anything. Thousands of people, all except 15 of them non-professional; the majority never having done any kind of performing before. No idea how many people would show up, performers or audience. All outdoors, so no idea how the weather would affect things. No idea how the town itself might react, angry church leaders, unpredictable and very possibly quite drunk people everywhere, various local industry sponsoring the show slowly realising the story was attacking them, the possibility I might actually die or be seriously injured in any number of ways over the three days, and no-one really understanding what the fuck they were in or how it would work or really what it was even actually about—not the town, not the crew, not the company, not really the people I was working most closely with, writer, co-director, producers. A massive act of faith and trust, with me trying to keep it all in my head and heart, on the edge of hysteria and wild panic continually, working from the moment my eyes opened each day until the early hours of the next, not one day off for the final three months, writing, filming, workshopping, interviewing, devising, listening and so much talking, trying to explain, trying to motivate, connect, to get people to share what really mattered to them, to be brave, to stand up, to have a voice. I saw and heard things over those last three months that even now immediately bring me to tears, things that moved me so much with their beauty or their horror or their courage. I saw miracles happen, I saw lives change, I saw unbelievable struggle and difficulty, and people devoting their lives, in a very quiet and unassuming way, to helping with those struggles.

And then the three days of our story.

It shouldn't have worked, it should have been a mess. My greatest fear, and a very real possibility, was that it would just all grind to a halt, no-one knowing what was supposed to happen next, in front of a crowd that was full of disappointment and feeling angry and let down and blaming me. In the rain.

It started with an unannounced event at dawn on Friday morning at the sea. Three hundred people gathered under the most beautiful sunrise I've ever seen to witness a return. An old dying man stood on the grounds of his old-age home and sang a Welsh hymn to mark the beginning. A sort of call to prayer out across the sea. Figures emerged atop the dunes, as a group of sleep-dancing pensioners led the way to the sand and a dark, lost figure emerged onto the beach and made his way to the sea to be reborn. Sixty-four hours later, 12,000 people stood at a roundabout and watched him die on a cross and be mysteriously reborn again before them.

In between a miracle happened.

It's impossible to describe the events of those three days. I truly believe something else took over. It was like watching a miracle occur whilst being at its epicentre and knowing you have nothing to do with it. I understood faith and what it can do. The physics of belief. I watched a town that thought it was going to see one thing but realised it was watching itself and telling its own story. Life and art totally blurred. It was very frightening at times. The power that was unleashed and was coursing through that place. I could feel it, as could everyone that was there, and we were all changed by it. I understood how and why drama emerged and came to be. I understood the nature of sacrifice and ritual and shared experience and catharsis. But, ultimately, something mysterious and bigger than all of us that were there walked the streets that weekend, and we all knew it. It answered every question I've ever had. It banished every doubt. It proved every hope. About art. And life. And people.

And they came in their thousands upon thousands.

And the sun shone down every second on all of us.

And when it finished no-one left. Everything was transformed and none of us wanted to let go of what that feels like. I've dreamt about it every night for weeks. Can't think about anything else. And that's what's been hard since. Moving on and letting go.

7 A Neo-Calvinist sociology
John Carroll's metaphysical modernity

Peter Murphy

Guilt culture

Human beings behave badly, regularly. It begins young. The parent says 'no': the toddler shouts and stamps in a temper tantrum. The rage is palpable. Aggression swells up in the little monster. In many human societies that kind of violent rage is barely contained even among adults. Volatile, unpredictable, and dangerous savagery is commonplace. Sadism, carnage, and cruelty abound in them. They are populated by touchy unstable personalities prone to the same kind of explosive aggression that we see in tyrants from Stalin to Saddam Hussein. The endemic violence of contemporary Middle Eastern societies reminds us just how difficult it is to create civil societies. Pursuing conflicts and disputes by vehement, vicious, callous, and terrible means has been the rule, not the exception, in human history.

If Western Europeans were transported back to their own medieval past, they would discover a world of systemic violence, tumult, and disorder. Their premodern forebears had few ways of dealing with the brutishness and nastiness of life. They knew what they *ought* to do. Basic norms of behaviour are more or less universal. Everyone, even marauders and killers, know the essential *thou shalts* (Carroll, 2001: 154). These don't vary that much across societies, cultures, and civilisations. Yet managing to follow the basic norms in a self-controlled and disciplined manner is another matter altogether. What societies frequently lack are not norms but order. That insight permeates John Carroll's remarkable sociology. Constructive, productive order is principally the fruit of the modern age that begins in the 1500s. So too are many malign movements. Carroll's sociology is a masterful explanation of why this is so. His insight into the sources of the civilised foundations of successful societies is profound.

If we look at medieval Europe, what do we find? Societies that have limited means of constraining everyday violence and chaos. Medieval characters had two basic means of regulating violence and disorder. One was the eye of the community: shame. In shame or honour societies people avoid bad acts when someone else, a figure of authority, incites in them feelings of torment. This is achieved by eyeing the misbehaving person in a disapproving, shaming way. This is a form of face-to-face social regulation. It is not very effective in large socially anonymous towns. In addition to shame, the medieval world had a second way of instituting order. This was for persons to opt out of the brutish City of Man altogether and seek expatriation in the City of God. The medieval monasteries were exilic. Their rules imposed a discipline absent in the larger society. This approach, limited at best, was erased by the Protestant Reformation. In England, Henry VIII demolished the monasteries. Then in the Elizabethan age began the arduous process of building a conscience culture to replace the old inadequate shame culture.

Conscience culture provided the basic building-block for the handful of successful modern societies. This began with the expansive development of internal mechanisms of behaviour control, principally tormented feelings of guilt. But it did not stop there. Conscience-regulated action was just a cornerstone of an elaborate civilisational architecture that produced a small but impressive number of great modern societies. As Carroll observes, creating these societies was not easy. It was full of false starts, blind alleys, dead-ends, back tracking, missed opportunities, illusions, and delusions. Such is the human condition.

The voice of conscience is an inner authority. Most, though not all, human beings have a conscience. It allows them to regulate and channel aggression. The conscience's principal mechanism of control is feelings of guilt. These are the tormenting feelings that one has 'done wrong' or is about to 'do wrong'. Guilt feelings are not triggered by the external authority of the community but rather by normative authorities internalised in the individual conscience. The figure of the father who punishes the child for bad behaviour or the mother who withdraws her love are internalised by the child. The child who becomes an adult does not have to wait for an external authority figure to say 'this is wrong'. Internalised authority instead accompanies the individual everywhere. The voice of conscience says to itself: 'no, stop, don't do it, you should not have done that, you ought to do this'. Guilt torments wrongdoers to make amends. In some personalities guilt becomes dispositional (Carroll, 1985: 3, 10). Even if they have caused no harm, they still feel guilty.

Guilt feelings prompt a distinct range of behaviours. Some of these behaviours are prone to excess or episodes of fake virtue. Guilt is difficult to shake off. It can be channelled in all sorts of directions. Some are productive. Some are not. Guilt drives attempts to make amends by giving gifts, praising, and making efforts to be nice to people that the guilt-ridden have harmed or would like to harm. Often these gestures end in over-the-top and obsessive actions (Carroll, 1985: 17). Persons also assuage guilt by purification rituals (Carroll, 1985: 18–20). They obsessively wash and cleanse to make restitution. They also zealously guard against pollution (Carroll, 1985: 177–178). Self-sacrifice is yet another way of abating guilt. Ascetics live frugally; religious persons mortify the flesh (Carroll, 1985: 21–22). Guilt can give rise to self-punishment. Individuals flagellate, belittle, and denigrate themselves. They do so because their conscience tells them they have failed in some way.

Guilt manifests on a collective as well as individual scale. Contemporary green politics and late nineteenth-century American Progressive-era 'clean-up' of 'dirty' energy or 'dirty' politics are examples. It's more than plausible that

Germany's uncontrolled mass admission of a million refugees in 2015 had its roots in unresolved national guilt for the Second World War. Europe sacrificed millions in World War One in the name of a 'war to end all wars'. Group guilt can take very vindictive forms. Anxious classes in decline abate guilt with malicious racism, envious egalitarianism, and fulminating populism against their social rivals (Carroll, 1985: 26). If guilt is not carefully sublimated in productive ways, it can turn very nasty. If guilt cannot vent itself in constructive ways, its torments will find destructive outlets.

Modern societies did not invent internal authority. Yet in pre-modern societies it proved largely ineffective. The same is true in many failed modern societies. In medieval Europe, as Carroll points out, the difficulty was remission (1985: 99–105). Serious infractions of social norms were routinely forgiven. The Catholic Church sold indulgences. For a price, the Church would forgive all kinds of bad behaviour. This was the trigger of the Reformation; Martin Luther put his foot down in 1517. No more selling of forgiveness, he insisted. No more remitting sins. Carroll describes conscience and guilt as the foundation of successful modern societies yet also paradoxically as the underminer of them. In *Guilt* (1985) Carroll drew a distinction between two kinds of guilt (1985: 33–94). He maps the historical evolution of Western societies from the 1500s to today in terms of an epic tussle between persecutory and depressive guilt. Persecution guilt tends to drive persons to act. Depressive guilt functions as the modern substitute for medieval remission. It smuggles in through modernity's back-door the abatement of self-control and self-discipline that afflicts pre-modern societies.

Persecution guilt turns aggression outward. It projects and idealises punitive authority figures whose anger or displeasure can only be placated by virtuous behaviour. It induces individuals to control themselves so as to do right or avoid doing wrong. It also encourages them to become an authority figure in their own right. Such authority is not forgiving. It does not remit. It corrects, penalises, judges, castigates, and disciplines. It is not a nice authority. It is not lenient, sympathetic, pardoning, excusing, exonerating, or absolving. Nor does it wash away sins as in baptism. Depressive cultures, by contrast, rebuke persecution guilt. Depressive souls look on punitive authority as being harassing, bullying, intimidating, or hounding.

Depressive guilt turns aggression inward against the self. In doing so it paralyses, pacifies, belittles, and demoralises the self. The child that does wrong responds not by channelling aggression in the direction of doing right but rather by directing it to self-punishment. Depressive guilt is self-lacerating and masochistic (Carroll, 1985: 27–28). Rather than inciting the self to act in the right way, depressive guilt induces the self not to act at all (Carroll, 1985: 11–12, 69–71). It leads to procrastination, indecisiveness, fatigue, apathy, restlessness, sleeplessness, sadness, and melancholy. It dispirits. Young children experience authority in the form of a sanction or else the withdrawal of love and approval. The internal authority that deploys depressive guilt is disapproving rather than penalising. It elicits a sense in the culpable self that it is unlovable. Individuals spiral down into feelings of worthlessness or else into self-pity, complaint, and excuse. In the latter case, blame for the moral failures of the self is projected onto others (Carroll, 2001: 11).

The Calvinism of everyday life

Guilt sometimes makes people do unpleasant or even horrible things. But well managed, it can be very constructive. It becomes the energy of transcendental attachments (Carroll, 1985: 15). To be so, guilt first has to be channelled in the right way. Otherwise it goes off the deep end. The English Calvinists, the Puritans, were the great pioneers of modern constructive guilt culture. It is well known that they had plenty of over-the-top moments as well. Hostility to entertainment, theatre, and dance was an ascetic assuaging of guilt that gave Calvinism a bad name. In the 1640s the Puritans tried to outlaw Christmas. That gave rise to a spirited national debate on the merits of mince pies, plum-pottage, and holly decorations (Durston, 1985). Christmas celebrations of course were carried on regardless. That said, too much can be made of this. The Puritan model of authority was austere, abstemious, and severe. But the mechanics of guilt is not the same as the pattern of authority. The 1640s was part of the greater modern experiment of creating a guilt culture—and as Carroll observes, the results of this were often rampant (1985: 105–112). Lots of ways of mollifying guilt were tried, and often they were not very pretty. But at the same time the Puritans also began to make some remarkable breakthroughs. In many ways these were the genesis of successful modernity.

Carroll provides a thumbnail sketch of the stages of development of modern guilt culture (1985: 105–122). The first phase, 1600–1660, is the age of the English Calvinists. This was followed by the Augustan era of civilised guilt, 1660–1800. The first period mixed a harsh ascetic kind of authority with something of much greater lasting value. Alongside the image of an abstemious, self-denying authority, the Puritans developed productive sublimations of guilt. They systematically devised ways of channelling guilt into constructive activities, specifically work, saving, and companionate marriage. One made amends by endless work and industry. This was expressly different from Catholic good works (Carroll, 1985: 107, 148). Calvinism posed the question: what do I have to do to be saved? The answer was work, be frugal, save, be economical and industrious. Work in a systematic and sustained way. Do it with concentration and consistency. Work requires self-discipline and self-control. Don't act on impulse. Don't expect things to happen magically. Don't rely on charity or gift giving. These are momentary acts in time. What matters, industrious work, is unrelenting and unremitting (Carroll, 1985: 36, 97–98). It is permanent. It has no end-point.

This was a foundation stone of modern economies. With the Puritans came a surge in small employers and the self-employed. They relied on self-discipline and self-help to succeed (Carroll, 1985: 107). Calvinism drove the remarkable increase in literacy in Elizabethan England (Carroll, 1985: 106). It encouraged the do-it-yourself desire to read religious books and tracts for oneself. Do-it-yourself, though, did not mean by-yourself. Calvinism emphasised dualism as much as individualism. The pairing of husband and wife was central. Like work, the act of pairing canalised guilt productively. The aspired-to lifelong union of marriage was based on mutual attraction and free consent. It was anchored in love, companionship, and fellowship. Calvinism was instrumental in creating the view of husband and wife as helpmates (Carroll, 2008: 84).

Carroll draws the parallel between the Puritan notion of companionate marriage and the Platonic idea of a soul-mate (2001: 89–109). The self in a long-lasting loving union with another (their fated 'chosen one') experiences in everyday life a hint of a divine or mystical oneness or an enhypostatic-like union of two natures. As with a vocational calling, companionate marriage has sacred qualities. It binds together two selves that are contradictory but belong together (Carroll, 2001: 61). The self and the other cohabitate with an uncanny third party called 'we' (Carroll, 2001: 102–104). Companionate love is not the romantic swooning, intoxicated, capricious kind. It is calm, steady, and constant (Carroll, 2001: 108–109). It arises when two independent centres of gravity are bonded by grace into a union that is solid yet enlivening, stable but energising.

The theology of Calvinism was unusual even by Protestant standards (Carroll, 2004: 51–68). It held that God had already chosen those who are going to be saved and those who were not. Neither good works nor faith could alter this. The elect had been chosen before the world was created. The matter was predestined. Divine fate ruled. But as with much in Calvinism, this was paradoxical. For necessity freed individuals. It liberated them to undertake persistent, durable, unshakable activity in the world. Salvation was by the grace of God alone, *sola gratia*. There was only one intermediary between the believer and God, Jesus, *solus christus*. In this view, the Bible was not the voice of an external authority. Rather it was to be read and interpreted by each believer in light of their own conscience and understanding, *sola scriptura*.

Despite this or even perhaps because of it, typical Calvinists possessed an uncanny self-confidence that they had been elected by God before the birth of the world. In large part this was because Calvinist predestination theology precluded an anxious crippling search for signs of election. It said that the matter was already decided. No meritorious acts of free will, good choices, kind offices, sincere atonement, good works, or moral praise offered the slightest indication of a person's election. Calvinism said in effect: channel your guilt into intensive everyday work and activity. The rhythms, repetitions, progressions, and sequences of such work are calming for the nerves. It obviates even dispositional guilt. Work was not meant to be garlanded with praise or awards any more than churches were to be ornamented with icons or embellished with ritual and ceremony. Grave anxieties could be sublimated in vocations and soul-mate marriages. They could be absorbed in serious worldly activity that demanded time, sacrifice, concentration, and dedication. The effect of this was to redirect natural aggressive human drives into unremitting, burdensome, and often painful activity that nonetheless was constructive and satisfying. This is the core of successful modernity. Understandably it appeared in a rough-and-ready way in the first instance. Individuals from

Puritan backgrounds like Francis Drake led the way in Elizabethan-age adventures on the high seas. Freed from the incubus of doing outwardly virtuous good works or being conspicuously pious, the world of rational risk-taking opened up. Entrepreneurial activity flourished; so did science. Crossing the oceans and settlement in the New World followed.

Guilt is the tormenting feeling that one has disobeyed an internal authority. That authority, anchored in the conscience, embodies norms, rules, and expectations. Over time the type of internal authority changes. So then do the expectations of human behaviour. From the sixteenth century onwards, modern guilt culture evolved. In the beginning, its manner was often rough, harsh, and unbridled. By the eighteenth century it had found more civilised, polished, and restrained outlets for its torments. Carroll distinguishes between the rampant guilt culture of the early Protestant era and the more civilised guilt culture of the Augustan age. This is reflected in different kinds of authority in these different historical eras. In the early period the severe authority figure dominated; in the latter period affectionate authority, firm but relaxed, came to the fore. In families, the locus of stern authority tends to be male; affectionate authority, female. But in either case, whoever is the family authority figure has to deal with the in-born aggression of the young.

A prime function of any family is take little kicking-and-screaming monsters and socialise them. Parental authority has to bridle, subdue, and channel the innate aggression of the young. It has to transform it into useful or constructive drives. Aggression responds in kind to authority. It seeks symbolically to destroy it. Through most of the modern age, up until the twentieth century, aggressive feelings of the young were either parricidal or matricidal in nature depending on the historical context. Youthful resistance to authority was primarily directed outwards, not inwards. It is natural for authority to be challenged. Authority of all kinds is subject to mocking, sarcasm, rebellion, anger, violence, transgression, and more. In a guilt or conscience culture, the operation of authority is primarily internal rather than external. It manifests itself as the voice within. It responds to the aggressive foot-stamping of the child or the child-like adult by triggering in those personalities the inner torments of guilt. The consequence of this is that aggressive shrieking and table-pounding behaviours induce their own internal punishments. Guilt flagellates, tortures, abandons, interrogates, holds to account, distresses, persecutes, and afflicts the rebellious even as they defy authority.

The great innovation of Calvinism, psychologically speaking, was to create constructive ways of abating such torments by sublimating aggressive energies into long-lasting productive disciplines (Carroll, 1985: 154). As it matured, the natural belligerence of the child was channelled into the systemic disciplines of vocational work and companionate marriage. This was the great achievement of the early rough-hewn Calvinist culture. It provided the seeds that eventually grew into the most enduringly successful modern societies. To the basics of vocational work and companionate marriage were added the sublimations of affirmative high culture. What resulted was an affectionate Neo-Calvinism that Carroll most identifies with (1985: 118–122, 161). Its influence runs from the late seventeenth century till the beginning of the nineteenth century, overlapping with England's

Augustan age and the wider world of cultivated bourgeois Protestantism (Carroll, 2004: 115–134). This is the period when the major commercial institutions of modern capitalism were created as well as a lot of early industrial technology. The successes of this era rested on a tacit relaxed kind of Calvinism that was shorn of its outward severity but not its stoical disciplines. This was a Calvinism without the harshness and austerity of the forbidding, cold, distant authority figure. Authority (to which the child growing up directs its rebellions) became closer and warmer. It still said 'no'; but it was more patient, understanding, and tolerant in doing so. It responded to rebellion with wit, irony, and humour. Civilised guilt culture combined authority with liberty (Carroll, 1985: 163). This was what the Americans later on called ordered liberty.

Guilt may be a permanent feature of modernity but the internal authority that guilt responds to changes over time. The nineteenth century, for example, resurrected the stern authority figure. This was an effect of evangelical religion. Subsequently the forbidding evangelical authority figure mutated into the figure of the prohibitionist, a reforming and moralising authority. The prohibitionists tried to outlaw various kinds of consumption. Food, alcohol, and tobacco were common targets. Aggression was sublimated into a drive to purify society. This also extended to eugenic and racial cleansing and to campaigns against pollution, one of the most archaic forms of human taboo. Alongside prohibitionist authority, the twentieth century saw the rise of paternalistic authority. The old patrimonial king who fed the people was transformed into the legal-rational state that fed the people. Paternalism (the nanny state) indulged and rewarded poor behaviour (Carroll, 1985: 174–175). It overprotected and smothered citizens. At the same time it was eager to persecute them in the cause of purifying society. Many citizens internalised these au pair-like public authorities, modelling their conscience on them.

There were three important counter-movements to the rise of prohibitionist and paternalistic authority. The first were the death-of-God movements. Nietzsche's 1882 epigram predicted a nihilistic weakening of the internalised authority of modern guilt culture. As the twentieth century progressed, the voice of conscience that said 'no' or 'enough' would be heard less often. It was increasingly replaced by voices of permission. These refused to judge. In liberal democracies debauched internal authorities incessantly praised mediocre good works. They encouraged individuals to engage in virtue-signalling. The crisis of conscience, though, was much worse in totalitarian societies. There internalised authority made a virtue of murder, rape, torture, lying, and theft. This turned upside down the fundamental norms that authority generally takes for granted, however it interprets those norms. Everything, the inner voice said, is permitted. The worst behaviour became the best behaviour.

In the second counter-movement, the innate aggression of the psyche against authority was turned inwards. This counter-movement often allied itself with prohibitionist and paternalistic authorities. In conjunction with them it became the dominant social psychological mode of the twentieth century. Aggression turned inwards depresses. It channels aggression into dissatisfaction with the self. The result is terrible restlessness, hypochondria, serial relationships, promiscuity,

A Neo-Calvinist sociology 73

Faustian striving, devitalisation, impotence, self-flagellation, melancholy, lassitude, and insomnia (Carroll, 1985: 177–190). It tries to distract and sooth itself by fidgeting, over-eating, over-dosing, over-buying, and consuming every kind of novelty that appears (Carroll, 2001: 146; 1985: 179). The depressed self is impatient, twitchy, and easily agitated.

We can look back at the last century and see it as a function of prohibitionist, paternalistic, and nihilistic authority. Challenges to authority, far from finding productive outlets, were channelled into ascetic-masochistic, depressive, and anarchic channels. That is what a cultural pessimist might conclude. But in fact there was a third affirmative counter-movement. It came from an unlikely source: Neo-Calvinism.[1] Far from being a relic of the past, Calvinism, albeit much transformed and often barely recognisable, managed to insert itself slyly into the culture and everyday life of the West in ways that continued informally to counter the nihilisms, meliorisms, paternalisms, and psychological self-negations of the twentieth century.

In many ways twentieth-century Western culture was a mess. Yet latent within it was a durable, hard-to-eliminate, productive current. John Carroll, arguably, has been the most significant, certainly the most insightful, intellectual exponent of this current. One of its chief achievements was to preserve and extend the process of constructive sublimation of authority-resisting human energy. The classic Calvinism of the Christian era created a culture based on work as a vocation, companionate marriage, and an anxiety-abating soteriology of predestination. Neo-Calvinism continued this and creatively extended it in the post-Christian, God-is-dead, faith-is-abandoned age (Carroll, 2001: 25–26). A key, Carroll argues, is not to be too preoccupied with the moral law. Kierkegaard was right. Ethical religion killed religion (2001: 30–31; 2007: 55–56). All societies more or less have analogous prohibitions on murder, theft, fraud, and greed. They encourage fidelity and veracity. They reject idols and false gods. From these ethical laws cascade the specific norms and rules that define specific societies at specific times. Yet neither ethics nor rules are the pivotal point of religion. As St. Paul said with respect to salvation, 'you are not under law but under grace' (Romans 6:14). Neo-Calvinism pursues this notion with alacrity.

Churches played an historical role in propagating respect for the moral law. There are societies where that remains an important function. But in key Western societies that is no longer the case. Instead, the thousands of life-time hours that their denizens spend watching detective mysteries on television alone guarantees that everyone is relentlessly exposed to fundamental moral laws. That has left churches to harp on about superannuated secondary moral rules like celibacy or virginity before marriage. Almost no one takes these seriously. The problem, as Carroll frames it, is not simply that these rules are obsolete but that ethical religions are obsolete. He calls them water religions. They lack a sense of the spirit, the sacred fire or *pneuma* (Carroll, 2001: 27–28, 32; 2007: 25, 33–34, 73–74, 77–78). The spirit is not baptismal. It does not wash away sin or guilt. Rather, it is pneumatic. It is like the hot air that we breathe out (Carroll, 2007: 35). Air that is heated expands in volume or pressure. So analogously does the soul. There is a sacred fire in the soul (Carroll, 2001: 5). Some human beings placed under great pressure respond with astonishing actions that attest to the remarkable power of the spirit roused by the soul on fire. Thunderous, earth-shaking acts become possible in response to the crushing weight of necessity.

Think of it this way: rules are invoked by authority. Parents say 'no'. The energy generated in resisting authority (by way of anger, sarcasm, spite, protest, argument, ninety-five theses nailed to a door, or whatever) has to go somewhere. Some rebellious individuals become rule-makers. The new boss replaces the old boss. Carroll's Neo-Calvinism implies that the best outlet for rule-defying energies are sublimations classic and new. These allow persons in everyday life to periodically make contact with the sacred. We do this when we find an inspiring vocation or a durable love (Carroll, 2001: 89–111, 129–149). Not everyone succeeds in doing this. Some fall into narcissistic, violent, conquering, persecutory, jealous, possessive, and demonic kinds of love. Others opt for empty, instrumental, opportunistic careers or else they take jobs that generate income but no inherent authority or satisfying purpose (Carroll, 1985: 199–200).

One of the things that makes Carroll's sociology of everyday life especially interesting is the way he extends the idea of the great sublimation of energies beyond love and work. There are other ways in modern everyday life, Carroll observes, of making a connection with the sacred. Sport is one of these (Carroll, 2008: 42–68). So also is competition in business (Carroll, 1985: 39). Increasingly important today are DIY activities like house renovation (Carroll, 2008: 229–239). The self-help, companionate aspects of these projects echo the Calvinist past (Carroll, 1985: 172–173). So does the focus, commitment, and attention to detail and beauty they require. The DIY sector is becoming increasingly important in contemporary economies (Murphy, 2017). It underscores behaviour that is active and productive rather than passive and depressive. The leisure-time analogue is pursuits like walking or exploring the landscape. Such activities connect human beings to something larger. They elicit feelings of calm and stability.

Everyday activities that connect us to the sacred are marked by inwardness, intense concentration, balance, grace, and form. The head bowed in work is meditative and contemplative (Carroll, 2001: 139). Such work is guided not by inert rules but abstract patterns. It creates things that fit, that are in their right place. It is sacred work (Carroll, 1985: 153). It harmonises. It achieves equilibrium and calm. It uses timeless proportions (Carroll, 2001: 147–149). The high-point of Western culture is not the search for consistency (the promise of justice or the golden rule) but rather the hunt for a kind of beautiful order that negates the wilful violence, anarchy, and mayhem typical of most societies. Ultimately it is not legal justice or ethical codes that achieve this, but simple abstractions. Limits not excess, verticality and uprightness ('here I stand'), not slouching and crouching, are a couple of these (Carroll, 2001: 170).

In the eyes of the Neo-Calvinist, knowledge is blind. It misleads (Carroll, 2001: 154). Intuition is more reliable. The knowledgeable person knows the rules. Extended households, tribes, states, and nations, like all institutions, often suffer from being bound by rules and codes rather than grace and balance. The Neo-Calvinist view is that the government that governs least governs the best. Politics as opposed to government grapples with fateful necessity: with the often awful sacrifices required in the moments of crisis (Carroll, 2001: 143). In crises, great leaders like Lincoln and Churchill answer the call of destiny. But politics as a vocation is rare. The stoical deism it demands is incomprehensible to most would-be leaders. Politicians naturally have big egos. But rarely do they have the soul of a statesman. They chase power but fail to understand authority, which connects with a higher order of things. Few could ever find themselves saying as Churchill did when he returned to high office in 1940 after his wilderness years that he was walking with destiny (Churchill, 2013).[2]

To move in step with a higher order requires a kind of self-abandonment. Individuals lose their self in work or companionate life. They relinquish some of their ego so they can connect with the sacred order of things. The soul has a tiny spark of the divine. It is in touch with the epic time of Kairos instead of the ordinary time of Chronos (Carroll, 2007: 38). It is the part of us that is able to sweep away distraction. It allows us to concentrate. The ego has profane goals that it wants to attain. The soul's goals are hallowed. The soul elicits from individuals exceptional achievements. It pushes to one side the income, power, benefit, or status-seeking of the ego. It makes room for devotional goals. These are the objectives of achieving something beautiful, well designed, elegantly executed, precisely operated, poised, orchestrated, composed, or choreographed (Carroll, 2008: 25–27, 38–42, 60–62). The soul unifies mind, body, and environment. It provides the transcendental grace that syncs what normally is set apart. People in sports or the professions, those who do service work or housework, artists and writers: all can experience moments of uncanny integration. Every faculty, motion, condition, and person involved harmonises. The great sublimations are governed not by rules and laws but by a sense of grace and balance (Carroll, 2001: 31).

On its own the ego cannot answer the old question, 'how am I going to be saved?' (Carroll, 1985: 213). The post-Christian West no longer believes in an after-life, so it has stopped using the language of salvation. But the same underlying issue remains. Now the question is phrased, 'how can I find meaning in life?' The touchy, vulnerable, fragile ego of the normal, anxious, puny human being draws comfort from approval-seeking and virtue-signalling. Under the influence of the soul, reticence replaces egoism. Intellectual modesty abandons the fatal conceit that human beings control things. They do not. Rather than control, the soul adapts to the larger epic scheme of things. It bows gracefully to the providential workings of nature and society. It halts fruitless efforts to control outcomes by procedural rules or expert knowledge. The soul achieves a graceful adjustment to providence by using its in-built intuitive sense of balance, proportion, and fit. This allows it to revise, amend, adjust, and vary as the social summer turns to autumn, then winter, then spring, and back again to summer.

Metaphysical modernity

Neo-Calvinism is Calvinism after the death of God. It is Calvinism de-churched, de-institutionalised. Yet Neo-Calvinism stems directly from the premises of

Calvinism. If the Bible is to be read for oneself, *sola scriptura*, rather than being interpreted by others, then there is no ultimate point in the existence of churches (Carroll, 2008: 10). If the only intermediary between God and the believer is Jesus, *solus christus*, then you do what Carroll did—you re-tell the story of Jesus. This is the Jesus who is abandoned by God, who experiences God as absent, dead-to-him, and who replaces God with his own incandescent, rock-like *I am*, personifying the sacred potential within each human being (Carroll, 2001: 29–30; 2007: 24, 54, 62). Jesus is not the messiah who will save us but rather the human-like personification of courage and stoicism able to stand up to abandonment and betrayal (Carroll, 2007: 70–71). The spirit of *I am* is not clannish, communal, tribal, statist, or national. It is existential and individual. Carroll's work can be described in two ways. He is a sociologist of culture and a sociologist of everyday life. Both these bear directly on Neo-Calvinism. Religion in general after the death of God becomes a cultural rather than institutional phenomenon. Church-going shrinks but religious themes continue to permeate societies through archetypal stories. Novels and films replace the catechism. Recorded music supplants the hymn-book.

Successful modernity is metaphysical. It is outwardly a world of choice, free will, selection, options, picks, and variety. These are elements of what makes it what it is. Yet behind its freedoms lie metaphysical phenomena. These manifest in John Calvin's Neo-Stoicism and the Calvinist Deism of Abraham Lincoln, among many other interpretations of inexorableness. Liberty is complemented and underwritten by a sense of destiny, fate, or necessity (Carroll, 1985: 227–231; 2001: 150–172). Without these, selves wander aimlessly. They waste time on pointless activities (Carroll, 1985: 164). Their freedom is fickle and wilful. As Carroll describes, in response to boastful anxiety and feckless behaviour Calvinism defined a persona grounded in quiet anonymity. This was the person of shy reserve (Carroll, 1985: 149, 166; 2004: 129; 2007: 34). Having replaced praiseworthy good works with unremitting hard work, modesty followed. Carroll cites Australia's most important Prime Minister, Robert Menzies. Like many key modern political leaders, Menzies was a Presbyterian. He observed that what matters in a nation is not the gossip of fashionable suburbs or the self-promoting chatter of officials but what happens in the homes of 'people who are nameless and unadvertised' (Carroll, 2008: 86).

Those who are reserved avoid being the centre of attention. They balk at blowhard celebrity and tell-all, show-all behaviour. The reticent lower their eyes. Head down, they look away from the things that should not be seen or heard (Carroll, 1985: 216, 221). Anxiety-driven attempts to appear grand or be seen with important people are shunned (Carroll, 1985: 186–187; 2008: 12). Instead the shy, withdrawn person bows down to something larger. In the first instance this envelope is provided by the rhythms of a calling and the cycles of durable companionship. Like everything long-lived, these bear marks of the everyday suffering called experience. Such experience prepares us to deal with the modern phenomena of markets, industries, cities, and publics. These operate in fate-like ways. They cycle up and down. They swing like a pendulum back and forth.

Human choice, planning, and intervention have limited effects on modern social sub-systems. The maxim 'let it be', *laissez-faire*, is often good advice in the face of their clockwork-like mechanisms. Modern individuals who think that free will determines what is important are usually in for a rude shock. Despite appearances, most modern large-scale social processes are not progressive but rather providential in the sense of being recurring, repeating, seasonal, and deterministic (Carroll, 1985: 156–158). Patient souls harness themselves to and harmonise with the larger implacable, cyclical, forces of modern life (Carroll, 2001: 163). They steady things that threaten to capsize. They are constant when others waver and vacillate. They calm frenzies. As fragile egos panic, they assert a simple, firm, unshakable *I am* (Carroll, 1985: 233). This is the rock of 'being' in contrast to the non-entities, the craven, effete 'non-beings' who flee, cower, tremble, and dissemble in fear (Carroll, 2008: 13).

Calvinism produced a parallax personality: elect and confident yet reserved and humble in the face of a larger, weighty, sometimes crushing order of things. Such high-achieving but diffident, worldly yet introverted, personalities are subsumed by feelings of awe before the cosmos and the forces of fate. This, Carroll suggests, is the highest sublimation of all. It exists with or without God. It is sacred but not necessarily theistic or even deistic. The early Calvinists had already moved far in this direction: *solo gratia*, salvation alone by the grace of God set aside faith and piety for the fateful decisions that God had already made before the creation of the world. Where there is no faith, Carroll muses, human beings are still able to live with great questions in mind. They engage in puzzlement and curiosity, directed with fear and hope towards the forces of fate. This is metaphysical modernity. God is dead, faith is no more. But musing about fate, destiny, and necessity remains (Carroll, 2001: 13–14). Moderns still ask reverential questions about and praise the sacred order of things (Carroll, 1985: 39). Western societies do this through archetypal stories. They always have. This begins with Homer. It is followed by the classical Greek tragedies of Aeschylus and Sophocles, the Biblical story of Jesus, the paintings of Vermeer and Poussin, the novels of Austen, James, and Melville, through to the masterful Westerns of John Ford (Carroll, 1985: 154–161; 2001: 21–43, 66–88, 158–164; 2004: 69–92, 115–134, 221–254).

Freedom, Carroll notes, is the modern faith (2001: 165–166). Moderns are fascinated by freedom of choice. Yet the more trivial the matter, the more plausible this freedom is (Carroll, 2001: 156). The things that really matter to us—life and death; war and peace; the rise and fall of nations—are governed by fate and destiny. We don't determine them. Despite what they often tell themselves, moderns are not free to make themselves into whatever they want to be (Carroll, 2001: 155). For all the proclaiming of our free will, what is really important is the way that we bow down before the higher hidden order that frames each individual's fate. We can do this in awe or as victims, complaining and whining. Carroll repeatedly draws parallels between Calvinist necessity and ancient Greek tragedy. He makes less of comic fatalism than he might. He recognises the role of comedy as a structural form in companionate marriage. Shakespeare's Beatrice and Benedick in *Much Ado about Nothing* is a cultural model for the drollness of the happy marriage (Carroll, 2001: 105–106). Yet Carroll is mainly drawn to the model of classical tragedy and its modern analogues. The transcendental role of irony, humour, wit, satire, and sardonicism was pointed out by Kierkegaard and practised by the Augustans. It is underplayed in Carroll's cultural sociology. Like tragedy but with happier results, the comic outlook captures those absurd paradoxical truths that constitute the metaphysical inlay of modernity. These enigmatic truths fuse contraries into complementarities. They bind fate and freedom into one.

While Calvinism is a decidedly modern world-view, its sense of destiny challenges the modern anti-metaphysical understanding of freedom. Calvinist actors are yoked by necessity yet are responsible for what they do. Potent Kierkegaard-type paradoxes arise from this (Carroll, 1985: 150; 2004: 59, 186–190; 2007: 28, 30, 32–33, 48). The strange deterministic-liberty of Luther's 'here I stand, I cannot do otherwise' bridges between the story of the enigmatic man-divinity Jesus forsaken by God and the lone stranger in twentieth-century movies who saves the besieged community (Carroll, 2001: 69–70; 2007: 23–34). All partake in Kierkegaard's absurd truth. This truth meshes together profound contradictions. In so doing it generates meaning. *The detached save the involved. Free acts are driven by necessity. Steel is nailed into flesh. The paralysed man walks. Light emerges from the dark. Grace animates gravity. The elect are humble.* Such truths are a kind of *aletheia* (Carroll, 2007: 66). They speak to the soul rather than the mind (Carroll, 2007: 30). They overcome the deathliness of the dispirited (Carroll, 2001: 4). Such uncanny metaphysical truths undo the lassitude, weariness, fatigue, and exhaustion of depressive moderns who are hounded by masochism and spiritual paralysis, their energy drained from them.

Metaphysical modernity with its deep and fruitful paradoxes stands in tension with anti-metaphysical modernity. The latter's stories contain no sacred truths. Anti-metaphysical modernity averts its eyes from classical tragedy and divine comedy. It is characterised by a repeated loss of nerve, depressiveness, and hysteria. It turns freedom into nihilism or despotism. It abandons disciplined sublimations for indulgent remissions. It wrecks affirmative high culture and bureaucratises the universities (Carroll, 2008: 143–158). It lacks the power of paradox. It is bereft of metaphysical modernity's weighty, potent, energising enigmas. These invest life with meaning. They are the sources of sacred order. Without such order, life is miserable. With it, Carroll concludes, life glows.

Notes

1 Neo-Calvinism is used in a secular sense. I do not mean by Neo-Calvinism the Dutch Calvinist theology associated with Abraham Kuijper (1837–1920) or the recent American spike of New Calvinism, but rather the tacit post-Christian Calvinism that is embedded in everyday life and culture.
2 'I felt as if I were walking with destiny, and that all my past life had been but a preparation for this hour and for this trial' (Churchill, 2013: 220).

References

Carroll J (1985) *Guilt.* London: Routledge and Kegan Paul.
Carroll J (2001) *The Western Dreaming.* Sydney: HarperCollins.
Carroll J (2004) *The Wreck of Western Culture.* Melbourne: Scribe.
Carroll J (2007) *The Existential Jesus.* Melbourne: Scribe.
Carroll J (2008) *Ego and Soul: The Modern West in Search of Meaning.* Melbourne: Scribe.
Churchill W (2013) *The Second World War.* London: Bloomsbury.
Durston C (1985) Lords of Misrule: The Puritan War on Christmas, 1642–60. *History Today* 35(12): 8–14.
Murphy P (2017) *Auto-Industrialism: DIY Capitalism and the Rise of the Auto-Industrial Society.* London: Sage.

8 The eclipse of metaphysics[1]

Keith Tester

> Fear not therefore: ye are of more value than many sparrows.
>
> (Luke 12:7)

Like the humanism it dissects, John Carroll's work is haunted by the skull Holbein's *Ambassadors* will have to tread upon as soon as they move (Carroll, 2004). Their only way out of the gilded prison is over the skull and through the shadow of death. The project of a metaphysical sociology, treating 'the meaning questions that confront all humans—Where do I come from, What should I do with my life, and What happens to me when I die' (Carroll, 2014), explores the fear and hubris keeping the two Ambassadors, and after them all of us who are the subjects of the legacy of Western humanism, struck and stuck rigidly to the spot, and it also points towards the source of the courage the Ambassadors lacked despite— or maybe because of—their extravagantly displayed worldly prowess and power. Metaphysical sociology suggests we ought to draw on the deep truth humanism sought to deny, walk over the skull and *Be*. The *fear* of death can be overcome, even though the *fact* of death never can, through the existential assertion *I am* (Carroll, 2007; Tester, 2010).

Humanism too was built on the assertion of the *I am*. But it stressed the *I* a little too much. Humanism made the *I* the centre, measure and motivator of all things. Perhaps its strongest and starkest announcement is in Shakespeare's *Coriolanus*. Coriolanus took humanism and the humanist *I* to something like its zero point when he sought to 'stand As if a man were author of himself And knew no other kin' (*Coriolanus* V.iii: 35–37[2]). The play's tragedy swung on the 'as if'. Coriolanus discovered how we are *not* entirely the authors of ourselves and *do* have other kin. He discovered how we are inextricably situated in restraining and constraining empirical circumstances. Coriolanus also discovered the deadness of a life without meaning other than its empirical self. Despite the confidence of humanism, *Coriolanus* shows how the *I* is *not* the self-sufficient maker of itself.

The version of *I am* embraced in Carroll's work is different to the humanist hubris of Coriolanus. Now it is an *I am*, within an order of absolute laws which we transgress at our peril . . . they bequeath to each individual human at birth some sort of personal spirit, leaving us to hope . . . that we may do our best with the way it directs us and the way it conditions our responses.

(Carroll, 2008: 254)

It is, then, an *I am* seeking to know the spirit given to it *at*, or maybe even *before*, birth. It is an *I am* seeking to know what it was in the beginning and shall be at the end. In short, the *I am* of Carroll's *metaphysical* sociology is to a significant degree nonempirical and in the first instance unconditioned by the empirical circumstances in which it is fated to seek to become what it is to *Be*.[3] Empirical and conditioned circumstances are the *context* of the assertion *I am*. Consequently metaphysical *sociology* explores how these circumstances have an impact upon the sense of what Carroll calls 'some sort of personal spirit'.[4] This spirit is to be discovered through adherence to the Delphic principles running through Carroll's work. The first of these is *know thyself*. The extent to which empirical and conditioned circumstances can help or hinder this knowing is reflected in the second principle: *nothing too much* (Carroll, 2002, 2010[5]). Acceptance of the guidance offered by these principles overcomes the fear of death because it is in conformity to and with a Being *knowing itself* without distraction by the allure of the empirical *too much*. The continuity of *I am* with death is taken as given, and the deeper the knowing of thyself the more death is invested with meaning. The three metaphysical questions become almost sequential: knowing where I come from (*know thyself*) guides what I ought to do, and by doing what I ought to do (*nothing too much*) I can *Be* in the moment and aftermath of my material death. I shall *Be* even in the shadow of death because *I am*. Consequently, unlike Holbein's *Ambassadors*, I can move. Unlike them I am *never* dead behind the eyes.

This is where the situation gets complicated. The point is this: We are the subjects of unchosen historical circumstances in which death could well have no necessary link whatsoever with *any* 'sort of personal spirit'. We might well adhere to the Delphic principles and *Be* but in these, *our*, unchosen circumstances the chance of the meaningful death can be taken away from us through no virtue or fault of our own. We are the subjects of circumstances in which the presumptions of metaphysical sociology are challenged irrespective of what we may or may not have done ourselves. Is it possible to know thyself when there is no reason to assume we shall die naturally or in circumstances making any sense, and when the moment of our death is possibly also the *terminally too much* moment of the death of everyone and everything? This is the question shadowing us, put in its starkest form.

This chapter resolves upon the question and seeks to explore its implications for metaphysics, the meaning of our death and, by extension therefore, the meaning of our life.

The chapter identifies and explores a *historical contradiction* between the sociological (as empirical and conditioned reality, as unchosen circumstances) and metaphysics (as nonempirical and unconditioned reality, as a 'sacred order', to use Carroll's term).[6] The exploration has two main sections. In its first part the chapter settles on the question of the status of metaphysics in these unchosen circumstances and seeks to establish the *historical specificity* of these circumstances. They are called the *Last Age*. Indeed, being able to identify the specificity of these unchosen circumstances justifies the use of words like 'we', 'us' and 'our'. They are neither rhetorical nor lazy but, instead, references to a historical collective identity. The second part of the chapter develops the preceding discussion by looking at Michelangelo Antonioni's film *L'eclisse* (1962). It is amongst the most significant works of cultural production of the late twentieth century, and even though it has been consigned to the safe sanctuaries of 'film history', it continues to resonate if it is taken seriously as a living engagement with the world we still share with it. Of course there has been change since the early 1960s, but there has been continuity too, certainly in terms of the contradiction between the empirical and the metaphysical.

The Last Age

Adorno gave the title 'Dying Today' to one of the concluding sections of his *Negative Dialectics* (Adorno, 1973: 368). The very title raises the question. To talk about dying *today* is to imply something special and specific about these particular historical circumstances, something making death and dying *now* different to *yesterday*. Of course for Adorno what made the difference was Auschwitz. As he famously said, the historical event signified by the name 'Auschwitz' has 'paralyzed' metaphysics. 'There is no chance any more for death to come into the individuals' empirical life as somehow conformable with the course of that life', he wrote (1973: 362). 'Conformability' is precisely the presumption of metaphysics, and Auschwitz has torn the presumption apart. *Being* according to the Delphic precepts—a life and death conformable to them—made absolutely no difference when it came to deportation to Auschwitz and murder when there. Every victim was treated the same. The individual invested with 'some sort of personal spirit' by metaphysics was demeaned into just one more victim passing through, one more item to be dealt with as efficiently as possible, and so, 'in the concentration camps it was no longer an individual who died but a specimen' (Adorno, 1973: 362). Death was detached from life, and knowing thyself in terms of *Being* was replaced with knowing thyself purely through excessive suffering.[7] This shadow now hangs over all. It is not necessarily something experientially likely, but it hangs as a historical possibility and as a wound in our world. It is now known—and indeed *ought* to be known[8]—how a certain set of circumstances and intentions might drastically subordinate 'some sort of personal spirit' to the death of the specimen.

Can culture remedy the paralysis and rescue metaphysics from the historical circumstances of the camps? According to Adorno, the answer is a firm *no*. After all: 'All post-Auschwitz culture, including its radical critique, is garbage'. Adorno went on: 'Whoever pleads for the maintenance of this radically culpable and shabby culture becomes its accomplice, while the man who says no to culture is directly furthering the barbarism which our culture showed itself to be' (1973: 367). According to Adorno, culture offers no chance of meaning for those of us who come after Auschwitz. To accept this culture without question, or to make the case for a return to culture allegedly lost, is to be complicit in the conceits of the world which made the camps possible in the first place. But to reject culture because of its complicity in barbarism is simply a barbarism of its own, one reducing the human to the empirical alone and, therefore, universalizing one aspect of what the camps forced its victims to become. This is a further twist to the knife of paralysis and it indicts the Delphic principles along with everything else. By Adorno's understanding, then, Auschwitz puts a howling and blood-stained question mark against the metaphysical.[9]

Adorno's arguments about the fate of metaphysics are apposite and appropriate. But do they actually cut to the heart of the question of dying *today*? Unfortunately and terribly, the answer is *no*. Adorno sought to make sense of a massive historical shift. After Auschwitz and the camps, humans are no longer simply mortal and moving towards individual natural death (barring combat, morally neutral accidents and natural events). Auschwitz was a practical lesson in the possibility of the *exterminability of humans* as specimens and not individuals. After Auschwitz it is necessary to think about the deliberately prosecuted *unnatural death of humans, not just individuals*. But when Adorno wrote about the paralysis of metaphysics an event had already happened which forced a far more fundamental maxim. No longer is it just the case that specimens might be exterminated. Now there has to be a concession of the possibility of the *exterminability* of *humanity* itself. What can be exterminated is not just humanity in the moral sense, but humanity in the most material sense. Humanity as a species can now be the object of an unnatural death. This is the true and terminal extent of dying today. We are no longer *just* after Auschwitz. We are *also* after Hiroshima and Nagasaki.[10]

The identification of a shift from 'all humans are mortal' through the stage of 'all humans are exterminable' to the final 'humanity is exterminable' is drawn from Günther Anders (1956: 148). He spoke about how in the middle of the twentieth century total war and genocide had created a situation in which 'for Europeans natural death was an unnatural or at least an exceptional occurrence' (Anders, 1956: 148). The claim is over-inflated and obviously meant for polemical effect, but the central point is clear and compatible with Adorno's remarks. Natural death was completely eliminated in the camps, as was the associated presumption of the conformability of the individual's death with their life. But Anders went on to add the next historical event: Auschwitz certainly, but also Hiroshima and Nagasaki. Now the *natural death* has potentially become *unnatural* at a *global* level. The bombing of Hiroshima and Nagasaki showed how we 'are mortal not only as individuals, but also as a group, and . . . are granted survival only until further orders' (Anders, 1956: 148). Natural death applies only in the absence of administrative orders to the contrary.

Adorno took for granted the continuation of something or other after Auschwitz. After all, had he not, he would have been unable to call all post-Auschwitz culture *garbage*. Culture has to continue after the event in order for it to be garbage. But Anders identified the next stage and pulled out its implications. Before the advent of the bombs death was imagined as an individual or group occurrence within a human world which would nevertheless continue. But we cannot make such an *assumption* any longer. We need to confront the full implications of the possibility of the end of absolutely everything: 'today our fear of death is extended to all of mankind; and if mankind were to perish leaving no memory in any being . . . everything will have been in vain' (Anders, 1956: 149). This is the circumstance of a drastic challenge to conventional metaphysics. Metaphysics seeks to establish and provide meaning but these unchosen historical circumstances raise the possibility of everything being completely in vain and, therefore, utterly *bereft* of meaning.

Two claims follow from the possibilities signified for us by Hiroshima and Nagasaki. First of all, it becomes legitimate to use collective nouns such as 'we', 'us' and 'our'. This collective identity is created by the shared lived experience of the shadow of the unnatural death. *We are* because we might all die together, leaving absolutely nothing human. Consequently this collective identity is *specific in time*. It is stuck in a perpetual present. The past, when individual humans could die a natural death and in the usual course of things need only worry about accident, illness or disaster, has become a nostalgic reverie. Neither can there be a guarantee of a future in which any or all of us shall be remembered. Indeed: 'the distinction between the generations of today and of tomorrow has become meaningless' (Anders, 1962: 495). The second claim therefore concerns what makes these historical circumstances, our time, different to any other. On this point Anders was quite clear. These are unchosen—yet human-made—historical circumstances which can only end in a negative sense, with the end of everything. As such: 'however long this age may last, even if it should last forever, it is "The Last Age": for there is no possibility that its "differentia specifica", the possibility of our self-extinction, can ever end—but by the end itself' (Anders, 1962: 493).[11]

Anders confronted the metaphysical implications of the advent of the Last Age. The old metaphysical question of how *ought* we to live, the question which is of course implicit to and guided by the Delphic principles, has been contradicted, and pressed out, by something considerably more basic. The Last Age is a circumstance in which the balance is tilted very far away from matters of nonempirical and unconditioned meaning and firmly towards the empirical and conditioned alone. Now the question is not how *ought* we to live but, simply, *will* we live (Anders, 1962: 493)?

Of course there is a cynical rejoinder to the question raised by Anders in 1962. *Will we live? Well evidently, yes we shall*. But still we live all the time overshadowed by the Last Age's possibility of the exterminability of humanity. This is the circumstance in which we search for meaning. As soon as this point is made, another question emerges, one which is in the first instance more *sociological* than *metaphysical* but one which is nevertheless of fundamental consequence to metaphysics. Shall we live? Self-evidently, yes. But *how do we live in the Last Age?* This matter is explored in the next section.

The eclipse

Carroll's *The Wreck of Western Culture* (2004) proceeds through concentration on a range of works of art, literature and film. They are held to be masterpieces because they 'have tapped the deepest truth of their time. They are illuminated by what they have touched'. There are two types of illumination. Carroll's work separates out those works which 'judge their contemporary world by the light of ... higher truths' on the one hand from, on the other, the 'unsettling' works not 'in touch with the eternal powers and their laws'. This second group, the works lacking contact with the eternal, 'rattle their times, imposing on them a commanding turmoil' (Carroll, 2004: 9).

One of the main traits of the Last Age is its relative *lack* of evident turmoil. Given what the Last Age might involve, peace seems to have been made with it rather easily. Orwell noted the paradox on one of the Age's first mornings. In October 1945 he wrote with wonderful and bitter understatement: 'Considering how likely we all are to be blown to pieces by it within the next five years, the atomic bomb has not roused so much discussion as might have been expected' (Orwell, 1945). The most obvious reason for the silence is because of immediate shock, but Orwell's point has not really become less valid with time.

So why the *continued* silence? There are two explanations. The first can be drawn from Herbert Marcuse. We say nothing about the possibilities unleashed at Hiroshima and Nagasaki because we are too scared to unsettle the apparatus claiming to protect us, even as it goes about the production of the means of creating *another* Hiroshima and Nagasaki (Marcuse, 1991: x). The second explanation goes rather deeper and comes from Anders. The threats of the Last Age are met with silence because they are completely beyond human imagination and understanding: 'It is difficult enough to visualize someone as not-being, a beloved friend as dead; but compared with the task our fantasy has to fulfil now, it is child's play' (Anders, 1962: 496). It is our task to imagine circumstances completely beyond our powers of imagination. Yet this cannot be done, and silence ensues. By Marcuse's argument it is safest to say nothing, and by Anders's argument it is impossible to say anything.

How then might it be possible to answer the question of how we live now, in the Last Age? Can the approach of *The Wreck of Western Culture* be used in these circumstances? After all, contemporary culture is itself complicit with the Last Age and yet, to recall Adorno, the rejection of culture is simple barbarism.[12] Carroll's first set of works, those judging the present by reference to higher truth, could too easily fall into the trap of seeming to be nothing more than 'sanctimonious', to recall Adorno (1973: 361), because they are too out of balance with the circumstances of the Last Age even to be able to speak to the times. If cultural works are going to be able to *speak to* the Last Age, they must logically then be of Carroll's second sort. The speaking cannot be a return to the past (sanctimony) or the promise of a future (fantastic futurism) because *the Last Age is a perpetual present*. Therefore the culture speaking *to* these circumstances will rattle by 'imposing on them a commanding turmoil'.

Works of this order *can* be found, although they are few and far between and, like everything worth finding, they are sometimes hidden away in the dusty recesses of cultural memory or neutered by celebration. They are explorations of how we live now, and they illuminate *precisely because* they impose turmoil on what is otherwise left in placid silence. Michelangelo Antonioni's exceptional film *L'eclisse* is one of the very best of these works.[13]

L'eclisse was released in 1962, and is the final instalment of an informal trilogy of films (also including *L'avventura* of 1960 and *La notte* of 1961) which, however, look forward to *Red Desert* which was made by Antonioni in 1964. All of these films have two things in common. The first might seem banal, but it is what makes them *sing*. They all feature Antonioni's muse Monica Vitti (as Bibi Andersson or Liv Ullmann was to Bergman, so Vitti to Antonioni). The second dimension of the similarity is more significant. They all explore how it is the historical fate of men and women nowadays to live in circumstances which do not need them as individuals and, furthermore, in which any resonance of meaning has been eclipsed. This final point is wonderfully intimated at the beginning of *L'avventura*, where the dome of St Peter's lurks in the distance but is about to be hidden from view by a rapidly developing housing estate. In all of these films the distinctly human dimension is challenged, and Antonioni intimates this by how he uses actors as if they were architectural props. Each of the films is profound and necessary, but of the four it is arguably *L'eclisse* which most unflinchingly confronts the *silence* of the Last Age, *accepts* it, *magnifies* it and, in so doing, *illuminates* it little by little. *L'eclisse* illuminates by rattling the curtains and the blinds keeping the light out of the Last Age.[14]

Curtains are opened in the very first scene of *L'eclisse*. Vittoria and Riccardo have spent the night at his house discussing the end of their affair. The scene is incredibly claustrophobic. The two characters are placed in a room that has become a prison, the only sound comes from an electric fan and Vittoria paces around, looking for an exit she seems to be reluctant to take. She walks over to the window and opens the curtains. Outside, a mushroom-shaped water tower looms in the early morning grey light. The film, then, begins *after the event*. Vittoria leaves and walks home through the empty streets of the EUR district of Rome, with its fascist-modernist architecture (although Antonioni is more interested in the deserted streets which are presented as roads to nowhere than with the buildings). Riccardo follows her, but this love affair is over. Vittoria goes to visit her mother, finding her in the maelstrom of Rome's Stock Exchange. She starts a languid affair with her mother's stockbroker, Piero. They arrange to meet one evening. Neither turns up: 'What does it mean that a couple fails so portentously to meet at a street corner despite protestations of eternal love?', asks Seymour Chatman (2008: 40). *L'eclisse* ends with one of the greatest scenes in film history. The camera goes to the places Vittoria and Piero have been in the past, would have been had they bothered to meet and shall never share in the future, if there is one. The camera moves to a newspaper headline implying an impending nuclear war, and the film ends with a close-up of an illuminated street lamp. As Cowie says, this burning light 'could refer to the title of the film or suggest the conflagration that will shortly engulf the arid, mineral world Antonioni has scrutinized. The predominant feeling engendered by these shots is . . . one of finality' (1963: 45).[15] The narrative of *L'eclisse* is as slight as this quick outline shows, but as with all of Antonioni's best work the 'story' is little more than a vehicle to explore mood, sensibility and the relationships of characters locked in circumstances not of their own choosing.

L'eclisse is set in the eternal present of the Last Age. The future is eclipsed by the doubt and finality of the final scene, and the past is no more than the debris of what now seems like ancient history. Neither future nor past is a horizon *of*, or *for*, action. Everything happens in the present and there is no obvious sense of the perception of meaning beyond the empirically present. Such is the fate of love, the desire for which is one of the main themes of the film, precisely because love offers some hope of meaning. Love is now or it is not, and the lover is now or they are not. Riccardo simply disappears at the end of his relationship with Vittoria, and her subsequent affair with Piero is always and only in the present. For them, to love is to engage in the empirical practices of love, and as soon as these practices can no longer carry the meaning sought in them, they become little more than charades to be regarded indifferently. It thus becomes possible to answer Chatman's question about the meaning of the lovers' failure to attend the date they had arranged. It means absolutely nothing other than their failure to be there, and it means nothing because despite the desire of Vittoria and Piero to find meaning in a love relationship, their affair means nothing beyond the times of its presence. Where everything is empirical, we love today but not necessarily tomorrow. Or, to put it in the way of an old adage: out of sight, out of mind.

Something similar happens to death. It too becomes the affair of an empirical present and evidently without any meaning otherwise sought and invested in it. There are two deaths in *L'eclisse*. The first is announced at the Stock Exchange. A broker has died and trading is suspended for one minute after a formal and conventionally platitudinous announcement is read out over a microphone. Everyone stands in bored silence obviously planning their next investments, and they all immediately spring back into action as soon as the minute ends. The dead broker is never mentioned again. The second death is visited upon a drunken joyrider who steals Piero's car and drives it straight into a lake. The car is lifted out of the water, with the arm of the driver hanging limply over the side. But as the lifting happens one of the watching crowd falls into the water, to the amusement of everyone else. The driver is forgotten and no one seems at all moved by what has happened, except for Vittoria herself, at least for a little while.[16] As Luca Pasquale points out, 'death is not associated with the disappearance of feelings—since feelings are non-existent. Death is a simple fact' (in Martini, 2007: 310). Death is not conquered and neither is it a source of fear. The metaphysical need remains unanswered because it has been replaced with an indifferent *what does it really matter?*[17]

The question of 'what does it really matter?' is deeply cynical but quite apposite to the Last Age, for two reasons. First, the question is valid because the exterminability of humanity itself *could* be construed as signifying the indifference and unimportance of the death of any individual. Second, the question is fitting because it reveals the sociological consequences for metaphysics of what *L'eclisse* identifies as the place to which turn is made when the empirical seems to be the only discernible source of meaning, and when love and death are all too likely to have been felt to fail. The turn is to *money*.

Money is not abstract in *L'eclisse*. Rather, it is signified and a lived experience in the Stock Exchange. This is pretty much the only place in the film where there is something approaching what appears to be a passionate and meaningful life. It is almost as if Coriolanus has reappeared as a bourgeois stockbroker. The Stock Exchange is a theatre of conflict and of a kind of war in which each is the author of themselves and admits of no other kin than money. The minute's silence for the dead broker is no more than a hindrance to financial profit and loss. Furthermore, although Vittoria meets her mother at the Exchange, the latter is far too busy giving instructions to the brokers, and then far too busy haggling with market traders, to pay attention to her daughter. Vittoria is of her mother's past, not her present. The thinning of social bonds is also seen in Piero's reaction to the theft of his car. He talks about how much it will cost to repair, or whether it might be better now to sell it. He is quite unconcerned about the drunk driver. For Piero the death does not really matter much at all, at least not when it is compared to questions of money or trying to create an opportunity to kiss Vittoria on their subsequent walk. Money eclipses everything else. It has the ability 'to reduce the highest as well as the lowest values equally to one value form and thereby to place them on the same level, regardless of their diverse kinds and amounts' (Simmel, 1990: 255).

Money then does two things. First, the ability of money to fill the present, and its ability to excite some kind of passion, offers an empirical compensation for, and distraction from, the finality of the Last Age. There is no need to think about metaphysical problems when there is money to be made and spent, and indeed no real space to think about them when all is noise. Yet in what does such passion and excitement consist? It is difficult not to recall Macbeth's bitter description of life as a 'walking shadow, a poor player / That struts and frets his hour upon the stage / And then is heard no more. It is a tale / Told by an idiot, full of sound and fury, / Signifying nothing' (*Macbeth* V.vi: 24–28). Second, even if questions were to turn to metaphysical matters, to the problem of meaning, answers are all too easy to find in the circumstances of the domination of money. As Simmel put it, everything is made to count the same and becomes interchangeable: 'higher values . . . are for sale for the same kind of value as groceries, and . . . also command a "market price"' (1990: 256). The answer to metaphysical investigations therefore consists in what can be bought and sold. All imaginable values are conditioned by empirical circumstances and are exchangeable, one for the other.

These circumstances challenge the Delphic principles. There is nothing stable and certain through and in terms of which to know thyself and, more obviously, the focus on money—the practical dominance of money as the only arbiter of value and meaning—runs directly contrary to the maxim of nothing too much.

Most everyone in *L'eclisse* wants too much and none of them can really be said to know thyself. The only exception is Vittoria, who at least glimpses the walls of the prison in which she is trapped and is the most enigmatic character in the film. Unlike every other character in *L'eclisse*, she is aware of her lack of a sense of a 'personal spirit', but she has no idea where or how to find it.

L'eclisse rattles because it reveals the absence of a commanding truth, at the levels of both circumstance (the Last Age) and empirical being (the lives of men and women). It establishes a sensibility through which it becomes possible to glimpse how the Last Age is silent about what makes it the Last Age, but also how the Age offers remarkably loud and noisy distractions from confrontation with this *sociological* challenge to *metaphysical* matters.

Conclusion

Walter Benjamin spoke about how these are the circumstances of 'a perception whose sense of the sameness of things has grown to the point where even the singular, the unique, is divested of its uniqueness' (1985: 250).[18] He anticipated one of the truths of the Last Age. The comment was made in his discussion of photography and the fate of *aura*, and it also offers a useful way of pulling together the themes of this chapter.

Metaphysics, and specifically the concern to make death meaningful, can be construed as an exercise in the investment of the individual with an *aura* in as much as it implies the unique presence of the *I am*. After all, the very statement *I am* is also an implicit *I am not* something else, and therefore it is an expression of the sense of singularity. The Last Age is a historical circumstance in which the uniqueness of the *I am* in the face of death has tended to become *completely imperceptible*. This is the resonance of Adorno's use of the word 'specimen' to describe *dying today*. Uniqueness and singularity are also undermined by how money makes everything comparable in the same quantitative terms. The ensuing question, then, is *how do we live in the circumstances of the possibility of our being or becoming mere specimens?* How do we live in circumstances divesting the unique and instead raising the profoundly anti-metaphysical question: *what does it really matter?* This is the pressing issue which usually occasions only silence. Antonioni's film *rattles* because it pulls aside the curtain of silence, enabling us to go on in these circumstances, and it *provokes questions*.

Towards the very end of *L'eclisse* the camera focuses on the back of a woman's head. She is walking to a street corner and her hair is immediately recognizable as Vittoria's. The woman looks over her shoulder to check if it is safe to cross the road. Her face can be seen. She looks tense, anguished and unfamiliar. She is not Vittoria. This is a woman whose uniqueness and singularity has been challenged. Her *aura* has become largely imperceptible in two ways.

First, like all of the characters in *L'eclisse*, she is shown in the glaring light and *without shadow*. The light washes her out. In Antonioni's vision, shadow has passed over to architecture. The historical world is possessed of a brooding, mysterious atmosphere of light and shade, whereas its inhabitants have no defence from the blast of light flattening them out, leaving them defenceless on the blasted heaths of formerly utopian dreams. The woman looks back with precisely the gaze which Benjamin saw in an early photograph of Kafka. She looks at the world, and at us who see her, in an 'excluded and god-forsaken manner'. Her gaze and her self, like Kafka's, lack what portraits formerly intimated about their sitters: 'There was an aura about them, an atmospheric medium, that lent fullness and security to their gaze' (Benjamin, 1985: 247). The dead-eyes of Holbein's *Ambassadors* could be taken to suggest an inscrutable and singular interior life, but the fearful eyes of the woman on the corner suggest only the insecurity of the specimen. She is only *contingently* present, and she *knows* it. Second, the woman's *aura* has become imperceptible because she is *denied uniqueness*. Antonioni traps us into taking the woman to be Vittoria. Their hair styles are identical, and all the time she might be Vittoria there is a sense of relief. The mystery of the closing sequence of *L'eclisse* is redeemed because the main character of the film has reappeared, and now there shall be closure. But the woman turns around, and it is not Vittoria at all. Despite her hair, and despite the expectation of Vittoria's reappearance, the woman is someone who has never obviously been seen before, and indeed she is never obviously seen again.[19] She and Vittoria transform one another into specimens.

This moment pulls the rug out from under the silence of the Last Age, the silence shielding us from the full implications of the divestment of the presence of the unique and the singular. It *rattles* the silent acceptance of sameness or, more pointedly, the *specimen*. Even though we have just spent time with Vittoria, actually, it turns out, we have not really recognized her singularity at all. If we had, we would have noticed subtle differences between her and the woman at the corner. We have actually *failed* to acknowledge Vittoria's struggle to *Be*, and *failed* to acknowledge her attempt to assert her unique *I am*. Vittoria evidently does not really matter to us at all. Alternatively, if we are disappointed the other woman is *not* Vittoria, then *she* does not matter to us. Either way of perceiving the woman is barbaric. Had we not silently, easily and immediately reduced the woman to a specimen defined by a fashionable hair-style, we might not have fallen into the trap Antonioni set. But we did.

Benjamin wondered: 'is not every square inch of our cities the scene of a crime? Every passer-by a culprit?' He asked a question of the photographer which is also the question Antonioni makes all of us confront: 'Is it not the task of the photographer—descendent of the augurs and haruspices—to reveal guilt and to point out the guilty in his pictures?' (Benjamin, 1985: 256).[20] *We* are the guilty, and we are guilty of the crime of silently accepting the fate of the specimen which is the tendency of the Last Age. How can this guilt be absolved? Can it be absolved? Well, the first step towards answering those questions is to be found in the task of appreciating (in both senses of the word) the presence of the unique and the singular. It consists in the work and discipline of the perception of *aura* both *despite* and *in spite of* the Last Age. The second step is the determination to respect and support the secure *Being* of this presence. Thus can *begin*—but *only* begin—the refutation of the question, *what does it matter?*

Notes

1 I would like to thank Sara James for her excellent comments on an earlier version of this chapter.
2 Carroll's work settles its account with *Coriolanus* a little too quickly when it dismisses the play as no more than 'a partial and inferior reworking of the Brutus theme' (Carroll, 2004: 50). Despite the debts to the historical material from which it draws, and despite the historical context it emphasizes, the play can be read as the clearest statement of humanist arrogance and its comeuppance in the circumstances of the resistance of others, relationships and institutions. *Coriolanus* is a very deep and disturbing teaching of the now sentimentalized lesson of Donne's 'no man is an island'. Shakespeare shows how the I seeking to assert itself according exclusively to its own will is *inhuman*: 'He was a thing of blood, whose every motion / Was timed with dying cries' (*Coriolanus* II.ii: 110–111; see also Kermode, 2000: 249).
3 Here I am alluding to a claim of Leszek Kołakowski: 'Metaphysical questions and beliefs reveal an aspect of human existence not revealed by scientific questions and beliefs, namely, that aspect that refers intentionally to nonempirical unconditioned reality'. Kołakowski continues to add an important qualification: 'The presence of this intention does not guarantee the existence of the referents. It is only evidence of a need, alive in culture, that that to which the intention refers should be present' (Kołakowski, 1989: 1–2).
4 There is a very great deal of post-Weberian Calvinism in Carroll's version of metaphysical sociology. *Ego and Soul* (Carroll, 2008) and *The Existential Jesus* (Carroll, 2007) can be read as essays on *vocation*. Carroll's work might even be understood as starting where Weber finished in the last few paragraphs of *The Protestant Ethic and the Spirit of Capitalism*. It confronts how we became, and seeks to make us question whether we are prepared to remain, no more than the notorious: 'Specialists without spirit, sensualists without heart; this nullity imagines that it has attained a level of civilization never before achieved' (Weber, 1976: 182). The essay on *Terror* is an inquiry into how 'this nullity' was challenged on and by 11 September 2001 (Carroll, 2002).
5 Coriolanus learnt neither of these lessons until it was too late, and maybe not even then. He completely fails according to the principle of *know thyself*, and because of this neither does he know what *nothing too much* might mean. Only at the end of the play is there any glimmer of his appreciation of these precepts and precisely then he must die. Coriolanus died twice: first of all as the self-made and independent man he asserted himself to be in his humanist hubris, and second as a material body. In his case the first death was the worst and made the second desirable.
6 I am identifying an inescapable *contradiction* in which there will be and can be no 'winner' between the metaphysical and the sociological. The metaphysical and the sociological can neither prove nor disprove one another because they refer to different—incommensurable—criteria of proof (Kołakowski, 1989). However, their relationship can be extremely firmly tilted in one direction, and *as if* to the exclusion of the other. Consequently the job is to lever open *both* the metaphysical and the sociological, and to reveal the *as if* to be historically contingent, not inevitable.
7 It is important to *try* to think *with*—because it is impossible to think *through*—the fate of a group of Dutch Jews who attacked a German Police detachment. They were tortured in Buchenwald and Mauthausen. Of them Arendt wrote: 'For months on end they died a thousand deaths, and every single one of them would have envied his brethren in Auschwitz and even in Riga and Minsk. There exist many things considerably worse than death, and the S.S. saw to it that none of them was ever very far from their victims' minds and imagination' (Arendt, 1994: 12). It is impossible to know what this might mean, and yet *it happened*.
8 Why *ought* we to know? 'A new categorical imperative has been imposed by Hitler upon unfree mankind: to arrange their thoughts and actions so that Auschwitz will not

    repeat itself, so that nothing similar will happen' (Adorno, 1973: 365). See also the essay 'Education after Auschwitz' in Adorno (2005).
9. These paragraphs are a massive gloss and simplification of Adorno's position, and admittedly and explicitly so. There has been no exegetical concern here. This is for two reasons. One: there is already too much exegesis on Adorno and, instead of simply doubling his thought, it is almost certainly better to try to encounter it for oneself—read Adorno, not the commentaries on Adorno. Two: as will become clear, for the purposes of this chapter Adorno's comments on Auschwitz are a stepping-stone to the next stage of the discussion. It would be unwise to get side-tracked here. But one side-track is worth highlighting. Adorno's argument is at the level of metaphysics, and it is worth comparing it with the argument of survivors like Victor Frankl who stressed the search for meaning in the camps. See Frankl (2004).
10. Adorno's work never confronts Hiroshima and Nagasaki directly. But for some this does not mean he ignored it. For instance, according to Gene Ray: 'Hiroshima is a latent topos that erupts repeatedly in Adorno's postwar oeuvre' (2005: 183). Yet to justify this claim Ray can point to only three texts, and by my reading at least Hiroshima is such a 'latent topos' in at least two of them as to be virtually invisible. But let Ray's contention be conceded. The question *still* remains: why was Hiroshima only a *latent* topos?
11. This is the essence of the presently fashionable debate about the anthropocene age. It is a second-nature which shall shortly become treated as if it were a first-nature Last Age. And of course the argument also applies to climate change. For a connection of these arguments to climate change, see Tester (2016). One of the best discussions of climate change opening to metaphysical questions is provided in Vetlesen (2015).
12. There is complicity where a post-apocalyptic future is presented as intelligible in pre-apocalyptic terms and as a more or less horrid (usually Hobbesian) version of the present. Witness Hollywood's dystopias.
13. The handful includes the work of the British pop artist Colin Self. For an introduction to Self's work see Martin (2008). A case can also be made for Nevil Shute's novel *On the Beach*.
14. There is another reason for discussing an Antonioni film. Carroll's work is influenced by, although by no means imitative of, the work of Philip Rieff. Rieff did not like Antonioni at all. He thought the film-maker a less-than-first-rate fighter against any conception of a sacred order (Rieff, 2006: 8). This is to attribute to Antonioni a polemicism the great films of 1960–4 lack. *L'avventura, La Notte, L'eclisse* and *Red Desert* are considerably more nuanced than Rieff allows. Jonathan Rosenbaum gets it *exactly* right in his essay accompanying the Criterion release of *L'eclisse*: 'It's almost as if Antonioni has extracted the essence of the everyday street life that serves as a background throughout the picture, and once we're presented with this essence in its undiluted form, it suddenly threatens and oppresses us. The implication is that, behind every story, there's a place and an absence, a mystery and a profound uncertainty, waiting like a vampire at every moment to emerge and take over, to stop the story dead in its tracks. And if we combine this place and absence, this mystery and uncertainty into a single, irreducible entity, what we have is the modern world itself—the place where all of us live, and which most stories are designed to protect us from' (Rosenbaum (2014). I owe this reference to Sara James).
15. The burning light anticipates the burning film in Bergman's *Persona*. The shadows produced by the light emitted in nuclear explosions are of the same physical order as the shadows making up photographic images. On this last point see Deutsche (2010).
16. Vittoria and Piero see the lifting of the car when they are happily walking together: 'Vittoria's gaiety shrivels immediately: she is disturbed not only by the macabre element in the scene [the dead driver's hand dangling over the side of the car] but also by Piero's obliviousness to its victim' (Cowie, 1963: 44). This is what makes Vittoria a compelling figure and an anticipation of Giuliana, Vitti's next role with

Antonioni, in *Red Desert* (1964). Like Giuliana, Vittoria feels the need for a meaning and meaningfulness the empirical and conditioned world is either unable to provide or decidedly refutes. The tragedy of both is their inability to find what they know they need. Specifically, the tragedy is how Giuliana is the only future Vittoria could likely imagine.

17 '"What does it really matter?" is a line we like to associate with bourgeois callousness, but it is the line most likely to make the individual aware, without dread, of the insignificance of his existence' (Adorno, 1973: 363).

18 Notice the nuance of Benjamin's argument. He is not making a claim about the *disappearance* or *destruction* of aura. The claim is about the *perception* of aura. The difference is cause for hope, not despair.

19 It is impossible to be *certain* whether she has been seen before or whether she is seen again. It is only possible to be certain of the failure to perceive her either before or after she turns her head. This is exactly the point.

20 Remember, Delphi was not just a place of the two principles stressed by Carroll. Delphi was also the site of an oracle, as Carroll himself makes clear in his *Greek Pilgrimage* (2010). Meanwhile, the haruspices to whom Benjamin refers were Rome's readers of auguries from the entrails of animals.

References

Adorno TW (1973) *Negative Dialectics*, trans. E.B. Ashton. London: Routledge & Kegan Paul.
Adorno TW (2005) *Critical Models: Interventions and Catchwords*, trans. Henry W. Pickford. New York: Columbia University Press.
Anders G (1956) Reflections on the H Bomb. *Dissent* 3(2): 146–155.
Anders G (1962) Theses for the Atomic Age. *The Massachusetts Review* 3(3): 493–505.
Arendt H (1994) *Eichmann in Jerusalem: A Report on the Banality of Evil*. London: Penguin.
Benjamin W (1985) *One Way Street, and Other Writings*, trans. Edmund Jephcott and Kingsley Shorter. London: Verso.
Carroll J (2002) *Terror: A Meditation on the Meaning of September 11*. Melbourne: Scribe.
Carroll J (2004) *The Wreck of Western Culture: Humanism Revisited*. Melbourne: Scribe.
Carroll J (2007) *The Existential Jesus*. Melbourne: Scribe.
Carroll J (2008) *Ego and Soul: The Modern West in Search of Meaning*. Melbourne: Scribe.
Carroll J (2010) *Greek Pilgrimage: In Search of the Foundations of the West*. Melbourne: Scribe.
Carroll J (2014) Death and the Modern Imagination. *Society* 51(5): 562–566.
Chatman S (2008) *Michelangelo Antonioni: The Complete Films*. Cologne: Taschen.
Cowie P (1963) *Antonioni, Bergman, Resnais*. London: The Tantivy Press.
Deutsche R (2010) *Hiroshima after Iraq: Three Studies in Art and War*. New York: Columbia University Press.
Frankl VE (2004) *Man's Search for Meaning*. London: Rider.
Kermode F (2000) *Shakespeare's Language*. London: Penguin.
Kołakowski L (1989) *The Presence of Myth*, trans. Adam Czerniawski. Chicago, IL: University of Chicago Press.
Marcuse H (1991) *One-Dimensional Man: Studies in the Ideology of Advanced Industrial Societies*, second edition. London: Routledge.
Martin S (2008) *Colin Self: Art in the Nuclear Age*. Lausanne, Switzerland: AVA Publishing.

Martini G (2007) *Michelangelo Antonioni*. Bologna, Italy: Edizioni Falsopiano.
Orwell G (1945) You and the Atomic Bomb. *Tribune*, 19 October.
Ray G (2005) *Terror and the Sublime in Art and Critical Theory: From Auschwitz to Hiroshima to September 11 and Beyond*. New York: Palgrave.
Rieff P (2006) *My Life among the Deathworks: Illustrations of the Aesthetics of Authority*. Charlottesville, VA: University of Virginia Press.
Rosenbaum J (2014) *L'eclisse*: A Vigilance of Desire. Available at: www.criterion.com/current/posts/359-l-eclisse-a-vigilance-of-desire.
Simmel G (1990) *The Philosophy of Money*, second edition, trans. Tom Bottomore and David Frisby. London: Routledge.
Tester K (2010) Telling Stories about Jesus: A Conversation with John Carroll. *Cultural Sociology* 4(3): 379–394.
Tester K (2016) Per un Futuro Temibile. In Bordoni C (ed.), *Immaginare il Futuro*. Milan, Italy: Mimesis, pp. 149–152.
Vetlesen AJ (2015) *The Denial of Nature: Environmental Philosophy in the Era of Global Capitalism*. London: Routledge.
Weber M (1976) *The Protestant Ethic and the Spirit of Capitalism*, trans. Talcott Parsons, second edition. London: George Allen & Unwin.

9 Digital Western dreaming

Marcus Maloney

Introduction

In John Ford's Western epic, *The Searchers* (1956), Ethan Edwards leads a band of frontiersmen on a quest to find Debbie, his young niece kidnapped by Comanche Indians. Over many years, and stretched across the film's arresting Monument Valley backdrop, the search party gradually dwindles to just Ethan, himself and Martin Pawley, a part-Native American man who had been adopted as a boy by Debbie's murdered parents. *The Searchers* is a central modern text in the work of sociologist, John Carroll, and the scenes in which Ethan and company journey through Monument Valley echo key aspects of Carroll's thinking. First, there is the quest itself. A small party of men, and eventually just two, wander the frontier, deeply unsure about what they hope to achieve. Indeed, this is no simple, rational quest to rescue the proverbial damsel in distress. Ethan makes clear on a number of occasions that, having been torn from the cultural milieu into which she was born, and presumably re-socialised into Comanche life, Debbie would be better off dead. This, then, is instinctively about culture, and about how life loses its meaning when cultural ties are undone. The Monument Valley backdrop tells us something else important about Carroll's sociology. As Ethan makes his way across its desolate vastness, his dogged pursuit is witnessed by the many sand-stone monoliths that inhabit the landscape like somnolent gods. A higher order frames this human story, though we can never quite be sure about the extent to which it pays heed to our goings-on.

This chapter explores certain key dimensions of Carroll's metaphysical sociology through an exploration of four noted video game narratives: *Bioshock, The Last of Us, Red Dead Redemption* and *That Dragon, Cancer*. To the reader uninitiated into this digital space and emergent cultural sphere, video games might seem an unlikely, perhaps even heretical, place to study Carroll's grand sociological themes. Indeed, since the early days of the medium, video games have, at best, been largely dismissed in public discourse as a time-wasting escapism, and the exclusive domain of boys and young men with little better else to do. At worst, video games have been viewed as a dangerously antisocial pursuit that rewards violent inclinations (e.g., Anderson & Dill, 2000; Irwin & Gross, 1995) and, more recently, as a medium that encourages unhealthy attitudes towards women (Ratan et al., 2015). As with any caricature, there are grains of truth to these negative assessments, but such indictments fail to take into account both the numerous 'positive potentialities' (Bertozzi, 2014) of video games and the medium's intriguing evolution as a unique narrative medium. The purpose of this chapter is thus two-fold: to demonstrate the relevance of Carroll's sociology to a particular aspect of the 21st-century digital culture; and to highlight, by way of noted examples, the increasing capacities of video games to tell stories of cultural significance.

A different kind of sociology

Carroll's work represents a different kind of sociology to that with which readers might be familiar. Both within and outside its borders, sociology has become increasingly synonymous with inequalities and social justice, and Carroll is less at odds with this focus than simply a world apart. By his own estimation, Carroll's (e.g. 2008a: 3) sociology follows Weber, a self-classification that rests on two pieces in Weber's diverse body of work: the conclusion to *The Protestant Work Ethic and The Spirit of Capitalism* (1905), and the later lecture, *Science as a Vocation* (first published in 1946). In both, Weber questions the capacity of secular humanist culture to sustain itself without a guiding spiritual framework, and this apprehension over the 'disenchantment of the world' (Weber, 1946: 155) is at the heart of Carroll's work. In truth, however, he is better understood as a *Nietzschean* sociologist. Indeed, the Weberian disenchantment explored by Carroll is, even by Weber's (e.g. 2002: 191) own admission, merely an extension of Nietzsche's earlier critique of modernity.

It is beyond the scope of this chapter to attempt a full survey of Carroll's sociology (see chapters from Dickson, Murphy and Tester for broader and illuminating surveys). In the reading of video game narratives offered here, I focus on two core dimensions. This first is Carroll's Nietzschean inquiry into the modern crisis of meaning. Famously encapsulated in the German philosopher's 'Death of God' (Nietzsche, 1882) proclamation, it is essentially a concern over the shaky metaphysical foundations of secular culture—that hubristic modern effort to place the individual human, rather than God, at the centre of all things. In *The Wreck of Western Culture*, Carroll's (2004: 1) assessment adopts the form of searing indictment akin to Alan Bloom or Philip Rieff:

> We live amidst the ruins of the great, five-hundred-year epoch of humanism. Our culture is a flat expanse of rubble. It hardly offers shelter from a mild cosmic breeze, never mind one of those icy gales that regularly return to rip us out of the cosy intimacy of our daily lives and confront us with oblivion . . . We are homeless in our own homes.

In later works—most notably *The Western Dreaming* (Carroll, 2001) and *Ego and Soul* (Carroll, 2008a)—the indictment is significantly tempered by Carroll's examination of the cultural forces that continue to offer metaphysical solace to ordinary people. In *Ego and Soul*, cultural vitality is principally found in the common sense of the lower-middle-classes, and in the narratives of popular film and television that still grapple with the 'big questions' (Carroll, 2008a). In *The Western Dreaming*, hope lies in the enduring relevance of archetypal stories wrought from our Ancient Greek and Christian foundations: 'The Western world is in the process of being thrown back onto its deepest resources' (Carroll, 2001: 6). Importantly, however, hope here remains tentative. While 'the stories are close by [and] some have unwittingly found them' (Carroll, 2001: 6), the sparks of vitality struggle against the broader cultural malaise that informs *The Wreck of Western Culture*'s more damning critique.

The second aspect of Carroll's sociology to which this chapter is indebted is his broader reading of culture itself. Increasingly central to Carroll's evolving view of what 'culture is, and does' (Carroll, 2008b: 5) is the role of narrative as metaphysical anchor and binding social force: 'Without the deep structure of archetypal story, a life has no meaning ... Without Story, the temptation has been to withdraw into self' (Carroll, 2001: 9, 11). Here, Carroll echoes Nietzsche's (2003: 40) view of culture as a redemptive 'veil of illusion', only without the latter's more cynical inference of wilful human misapprehension. Perhaps more importantly, narrative has also increasingly become Carroll's principal methodology. This is true in two senses: in his use of narratives as a means of reading cultural trends; and in the way he has increasingly presented his own theses as narratives in and of themselves. From an empirical perspective, such an approach to cultural inquiry will always remain open to critique, though Carroll appears to view himself as a somewhat unique mixture of storyteller and sociologist. Indeed, when engaging with Carroll's sociology, one must first take a Kierkegaardian leap of faith and embrace the idea that truth and fiction might be one and the same.

Carroll's methodology appears to place as much, if not more, stock in the insights of art and narrative as it does in any form of scholarship. Here, the act of telling resonant stories represents the 'collective consciousness' (Durkheim, 2006) of culture working through the storyteller and his/her individual sorrows and passions. In other words, the great storytellers are vehicles through which a society 'tells itself what it is' (Orgad, 2014: 137). In *The Wreck of Western Culture*, Carroll's choices of significant texts convey two dimensions of his thinking to which he has largely held in subsequent writings. First, and as outlined, the key works are those with wide and enduring appeal that seek to illuminate our shared metaphysical dilemmas. Moreover, Carroll sees venerable lineages operating here in which seminal earlier texts find themselves reborn in later ones—to give one of the more idiosyncratic examples (Carroll: 2002), he sees David Fincher's *Fight Club* (1999) as the late-modern heir to Joseph Conrad's (1899) *Heart of Darkness*. Echoing literary critic Frank Kermode (1979: 81–83), Carroll (2007: 7) appropriates[1] the Jewish term 'midrash' to denote this process: 'the art of reworking stories so as to bring them up to date'. With respect to the second dimension of his thinking, Carroll adheres to a broader definition of narrative 'texts' in which painting and sculpture sit naturally alongside the more conventionally understood narrative mediums of literature, theatre, film and television. Here, Rembrandt and Poussin are as much *storytellers* as William Shakespeare, Joseph Conrad or John Ford. In later works, Carroll (2008a) argues that popular film and television have all but replaced their high-culture counterparts as the most vital spheres. Most recently, he has suggested that television has now overtaken cinema in cultural pre-eminence. For Carroll (2015a), this most recent shift begins with *The Sopranos* (1999–2007), HBO's existential take on the mobster genre in which mob boss, Tony Soprano, laments the meaninglessness of his life on his therapist's couch.

A different kind of narrative[2]

In this chapter, I argue that the metaphysical themes highlighted by Carroll have also begun to emerge in the increasingly mainstream digital space of video games. There are two starting points for understanding what sets video games apart from the similarly visual mediums of film and television as a vehicle for narrative: the notion of video games as a 'ludic' phenomenon—or video games *as games*—and the accompanying notion of interactivity. In the emergent field of games studies, much debate has focused on the extent to which video games should, first and foremost, be seen as a ludic, rather than narrative, phenomenon (Simons, 2007). Indeed, while the heated tensions that once marked this debate have abated (Wesp, 2014), consensus on how to define the field's central concept remains (fascinatingly) elusive. To briefly summarise my own open position, while Juul (2005: 224) is right to argue that 'narratives are basically interpretative, whereas games are formal', the distinction works more in the abstract than it does across the increasingly diverse contemporary landscape of what we, perhaps now loosely, call 'video games'. Moreover, to quote Swalwell and Wilson (2008: 3), any understanding of contemporary video games that fails to recognise the increasing inseparability of narrative and gameplay 'is suggesting a definition and a range of enjoyment in gameplay far narrower than that used by players, journalists, and industry professionals'. The emphasis here is thus broadly on video games as a 'fictional form' (Atkins, 2003), and the case studies I examine can each be seen as noteworthy examples of games 'that borrow heavily from literary and cinematic conventions in the construction of something that resembles a game/fiction hybrid' (Atkins, 2003: 22).

Conversely, the notion of interactivity—of the 'passive' spectator becoming the 'active' player—is equally crucial to understanding even the most story-driven video game. Darley's (2000) formulation, in which he highlights the paradox inherent in the passive spectator/active player distinction, provides a useful basis from which to proceed. According to Darley (2000: 151), however much a game might aspire to narrative sophistication, narrative itself is always, to some degree or another, 'decentered' against the medium's instrumental ludic precepts. In turn, any notion that the player possesses a more active relationship with video games than does the spectator with cinema rests on a narrow, kinaesthetic understanding of 'activity':

> Players are often perceived as being more active than viewers are, yet, this is only true—or at least with respect to the computer game—in a vicariously 'physical' sense . . . interactivity in the computer game involves a kind of relative or regulated agency: the constraints of the game allow players to choose between a limited number of options. However, such 'active participation' should not be confused with increased semantic engagement. On the contrary, the kinds of mental processes that games solicit are largely instrumental and/or reactive in character . . . passive spectators of conventional cinema might be said to be far more active than their counterparts in newer forms.
>
> (Darley, 2000: 163–164)

Again, Darley's characterisation of video games as being principally kinaesthetic and 'goal oriented' is more or less accurate depending on the game in question. Indeed, traditional lines of prioritisation between the medium's ludic and narrative dimensions are very much blurred in contemporary games such as *Journey* (2012) or the similarly existential *Dear Esther* (2012), both of which possess a relative scarcity of challenging puzzles and so forth, and even less in the way of the frenetic gameplay often associated with the medium.

In viewing gameplay as a discrete aspect of video games, Bogost's (2007) notion of procedural rhetoric is helpful. Evaluations of the medium's capacity for meaning-making and 'semantic engagement' are often informed by an implicit view of gameplay as a sort of ideologically neutral, or empty, backdrop against which narratives, meanings and other interpretable aspects of a more traditional text might (or might not) emerge. For Bogost (2007: 340), gameplay itself is a form of rhetoric in which, whether consciously or unconsciously, a given game's ludic systems inevitably convey a worldview: 'We must recognize the persuasive and expressive power of procedurality. Processes influence us . . . the logics that drive our games make claims about who we are, how our world functions'. Here, Bogost offers a view of formal gameplay systems comparable to film studies' understandings of 'realism' in cinema in which 'the mechanical imitation of nature' (Arnheim, 2006: 158) is always underpinned by an 'implicit ideology supporting and structuring a given work' (Wood, 2006: 46). With respect to this study, it is thus important to engage in a 'different kind of literacy' (Atkins, 2003: 61) in which gameplay can be no less suffused with meaning than the more explicitly rhetorical dimensions of narrative and representation.

Bioshock

Irrational Games' *Bioshock* is widely cited as an example of what video games have begun to achieve as a narrative medium. It is also a game that very much operates in Carroll's thematic territory. Set in 'Rapture'—a dystopian underwater city founded on a sort of hyper-allegiance to the objectivist philosophy of Ayn Rand—*Bioshock* is a first-person shooter (FPS) in which the player engages in bloody combat as the narrative teases out the mysteries of the city's downfall and the hero/avatar's true purpose. Praised for both the immersion of its dystopian world-building and the weight of the themes with which it grapples, the game is essentially an interactive reimagining of Conrad's *Heart of Darkness*.[3] Echoing Conrad's meandering departure-journey-arrival structure (Carroll, 2002)—a structure that proves ideally suited to this player-driven mode of storytelling—*Bioshock* functions as a Nietzschean critique of modernity's secular attempts 'to find in individual being some quality that might give enduring dignity to the human condition' (Carroll, 2015b: 611).

In *Bioshock*, the 'quality' in question, the 'saving truth' (Carroll, 2002: 33) that is ultimately exposed as fraudulent, is Ayn Rand's (1957: 735) belief that, through unrestrained individualism, humankind might find a heaven 'here and now and on this earth'. The mouthpiece for Rand in *Bioshock* is Rapture's founder, Andrew Ryan: a shadowy, Kurtz-like figure modelled off the sort of mid-20th-century American entrepreneurs who found themselves taken with Rand's (1957) seminal *Atlas Shrugged*. Much like Marlow's search for Kurtz, *Bioshock* takes the player on a journey through the 'horror and absurdity' (Nietzsche, 2003: 40) of Rapture and towards a confrontation with the reclusive Ryan. The city itself is in ruins and, echoing the Atlantis of Plato's (380 BCE) *Republic*, its submergence conveys the notion of a civilisation drowned by its own hubris. Scattered across *Bioshock*'s various environments are the remnants of Rapture's citizenry: a deranged collection of subhumans who serve as the FPS's requisite enemy combatants. Hostile and altogether pitiful, they exist solely to gratify their own individual consumptive desires which, in this case, centre on a power-giving drug referred to as 'ADAM'. To meet the game's increasing challenges, the player is also compelled to consume ADAM—the pessimistic allusions to our own consumer society are clear.

Again, like Carroll's reading of Kurtz, the objectivist Ryan is *Bioshock*'s failed 'new Christ, the one for our time who might point the way, teach how to live, explain the meaning of it all' (Carroll, 2002: 34). The supreme individualism on which Ryan founds Rapture is summed up in one of the many 'audio logs' the player is encouraged to discover across the game: 'A man chooses, a slave obeys'. The moment the player sets foot in the underwater city, the consequences of this ideology are exposed as Kurtz's 'The horror! The horror!' (Conrad, 2007: 98). In isolation, *Bioshock* could be viewed as a narrower critique of Randian individualism, rather than the broader, Carroll-esque critique of humanist ambitions being argued here. However, in *Bioshock*'s two sequels, both essentially the same in core narrative structure and gameplay, the thematic backdrop is redirected towards an indictment of other redemptive modern philosophies. Set in Rapture once more, *Bioshock 2* shifts the focus onto the city's collectivist counter-movement. Here, it is the Orwellian tendencies inherent in secular notions of a shared 'humanity' that come under scrutiny. The third game in the series, *Bioshock Infinite*, takes the player to the new destination of 'Columbia': a city in the sky founded by the religious fundamentalist, Zachary Hale Comstock. In Columbia, Comstock's nostalgic desire to resurrect Christian-American society has become an oppressively autocratic state governed by notions of racial purity, and by blind devotion to its human founder, rather than to God. Indeed, Columbia's 'artificial firmament' (Maloney, 2015: 158) is built on the self-negation that underpins all fanaticism: the ostensible force with which Comstock has constructed his new Christian society is an inversion of his unconscious profanity. Viewed together, then, the three *Bioshock* instalments can be seen as a bleak tripartite assessment of the supra-ideological revolutionary impulses that modernity's crisis of meaning habitually engenders.

The Last of Us

Lowering its sights onto the struggles of ordinary people, and one of the most awarded video games in the history of the medium, Naughty Dog's *The Last of Us* (2013) offers an interactive retelling of both Cormack McCarthy's (2006) *The Road* and Robert Kirkman and Tony Moore's (2013) similarly themed comic book series, *The Walking Dead*. In much the same fashion as these close literary descendants, *The Last of Us*' post-apocalyptic setting essentially functions as a backdrop for exploring questions of ethics and morality, and the challenge of doing what is right when the cultural 'veil of illusion' is lifted. To summarise the plot, the player adopts the role of single father, Joel, whose daughter is killed by police when they try to flee Austin, Texas during a nation-wide pandemic. The game opens with this as prologue, a device aimed at establishing the repressed grief underpinning Joel's motivations as the player's avatar. Twenty years later, Joel is a smuggler living in the wake of a society that has ripped itself apart. Now, there are only tenuous pockets of community, along with the oppressive state troops who police quarantine boundaries and the roving gangs who prey on the weak. Outside the city's boundaries also reside hostile swarms of mindless, zombie-like victims of the pandemic who serve as the game's principal moment-to-moment gameplay antagonists. Still broken by the death of his daughter, Joel is offered a large sum of money to smuggle a young girl named Ellie out of Austin and into the hands of 'the Fireflies': a seemingly virtuous revolutionary enclave seeking to restore democracy to America. Ellie's significance lies in her unique immunity to the disease, and the Fireflies believe they can develop a vaccine by examining her biological makeup.

As stated, *The Last of Us* explores the challenges of maintaining a sense of morality amidst devastation and chaos. In the 'Five Theses' that frame *Ego and Soul*, Carroll (2008a: 4–5) draws a decisive and contentious line between the singularity and function of a given culture, on the one hand, and the universality of morality, on the other:

> Unconsciously, all humans know the true and the good, and are inwardly compelled to find what they know, through their lives and what they see. They sense that there is some higher order framing their existence . . . Culture is those myths, stories, images, rhythms, and conversations that voice the eternal and difficult truths . . . Cultures are singular. Fundamental moral laws and human rights are universal.

Post-apocalyptic narratives test Carroll's thesis by exploring what happens to people when the sociocultural restraints that seem to elicit principled behaviour—Rieff's (1990: 37) civilising 'thou-shalt-nots'—are severely undermined. On the face of it, the verdict in stories like *The Last of Us* is mixed: while central characters usually confirm the thesis through their dogged moral fortitude and self-sacrifice, they operate against a social milieu very much governed by the 'everything is permitted' logic of Dostoyevsky's *The Brothers Karamazov* (first published as a serial in 1879–80). However, on closer inspection of *The Last of Us*, the message is quite clear: morality is always a matter of 'individual conscience' (Carroll, 2008a: 101) regardless of whether a given culture gives collective 'voice' to its 'fundamental laws'. When these laws are broken—as in the cases of the exploitative gangs and the oppressive, similarly cruel border troops—the wrongdoers have merely acted in what Sartre (2003) would call 'bad faith'. The immorality of such characters simply makes them *less human*, and arguably no better than the shuffling zombies that skulk the city's outskirts.

Furthermore, during their treacherous cross-country journey to meet the Fireflies, it is the young Ellie, rather than Joel, who emerges as the story's moral centre. She teaches the broken man how to be whole again, and how to live compassionately. This is important: born into a post-pandemic world of anomie, Ellie should by all rights be as feral as the worst of the gang members. In *The Road*, McCarthy (2006: 5) portrays a similar father–son dynamic: the former sees the latter as his 'warrant' and postulates that 'If he is not the word of God God never spoke'. When Joel and Ellie finally reach the Fireflies, the core message of individual conscience is brought to the fore. Joel discovers that the group intends to remove a portion of Ellie's brain in order to examine, and hopefully extract, whatever it is that makes her immune to the disease. This will kill Ellie and, reluctant as they ostensibly seem, the group's scientists are adamant that this represents humanity's only hope. Choosing the sanctity of individual life over the utilitarian needs of the 'theoretical masses' (Carroll, 2008a: 99), Joel kidnaps an anaesthetised Ellie, fighting his way out of the Fireflies' compound. A humanity that would intentionally kill innocents is not worth saving—the means never justify the ends.

During the final stages of *The Last of Us*' second act, there is a scene that demonstrates the unique power of video games as a narrative medium. A key element distinguishing this from most other post-apocalyptic stories is that it is set in an America gradually being reclaimed by nature, rather than in the sort of wasteland George Miller established in his Australian desert-inspired *Mad Max* franchise (1979–2015). Joel and Ellie arrive in Salt Lake City and, while traversing the ruins of a large bus station, the young girl glimpses something remarkable outside and presses Joel to join her on a balcony to take a closer look. Presumably originating from some now-disused zoo, it is a family of giraffes foraging across the station's grounds. One of the adult giraffes lifts its head towards the balcony to greet the pair and Ellie pats the out-of-place creature. Importantly, Joel only follows suit in this gesture of affection if/when the player responds to an onscreen prompt. Joel and Ellie then take a moment to watch as the family drifts away across the disused grounds, an environment that now appears more liberated than rundown.

Like Tony Soprano's captivating suburban encounter with ducks in *The Sopranos* (Carroll, 2015a; Maloney, 2015: 116–117), the existential respite of this event speaks to a 'higher order'—indeed, everything else in *The Last of Us* feels as though it orbits around this one brief moment. In cinema, the significance of such moments is commonly conveyed by a 'lingering shot': the audience is required to bear witness for as long as the director sees fit, and whether they like it or not. By placing control of Joel in the hands of the player during this sequence, *The Last of Us*' designers ostensibly relinquish their narrative authority, and can only *hope* that their audience will linger with Ellie on the balcony long enough to absorb the full poignancy of what is being offered. Indeed, any player who purchased *The Last of Us* wishing only to fight zombies and gang members is free to pull Joel immediately away from the balcony in order to trigger a return to the video game action. As in real life, such moments of abiding significance are only accessible to those with the requisite tools of contemplation, those with 'ears to hear'.

Red Dead Redemption

The Western cinematic oeuvre of John Ford looms large in Carroll's sociology. Indeed, in arguably his most recognised book, *The Wreck of Western Culture*, Carroll devotes far more space to its exegesis than to Conrad's *Heart of Darkness* or any other similarly important work. Central though it remains to both film criticism and American cultural history, the Western as a cinematic genre has seen a steady decline in relevance over recent decades. As Agresta (2013) laments, 'Other, newer genres like superhero movies . . . have cowboy movies outgunned with younger generations and international audiences'. True as this may be in cinema, 2010 saw a marked video game revival of the Western in Rockstar Games' *Red Dead Redemption*. Among the highest-selling games of that year, and with a highly anticipated sequel scheduled for release in 2018, *Red Dead Redemption* is a genuine Western in every sense, rather than the sort of digital shooting galleries with 'cowboys and Indians' aesthetics that preceded it. The plot sees the player adopt the role of John Marsden, a retired outlaw who is offered amnesty by government authorities in return for bringing members of his former gang to justice. Having also taken his wife and son hostage, Marsden is left with no choice but to acquiesce to the government's Mafioso-style offer. In gameplay terms, *Red Dead Redemption* follows the 'open-world' format of Rockstar Games' wildly successful *Grand Theft Auto* franchise (1997–2013) in which players are given free rein to inhabit the virtual world as they see fit, moving the story forward at their own pace and engaging in free-form (and often violent) activities in the interim.

While its aesthetic and soundtrack evoke Sergio Leone's spaghetti Westerns, and Marsden himself is arguably more Eastwood than Wayne, *Red Dead Redemption* is an interactive narrative steeped in Ford. The story itself, with its themes of revenge, tragedy and the birth of modernity, combines elements from *The Searchers* and *The Man Who Shot Liberty Valance* (1962). The core narrative structure—again, a meandering one that naturally lends itself to the video game format—follows the former. Marsden's cross-country mission to capture or kill 'Dutch's Gang' echoes the journey of Ford's Ethan: 'Nothing will stop him. For seven years he rides through the snows of northern winter to the scorching desert summer' (Carroll, 2004: 240). Also like Ethan, Marsden is 'a very violent man, at any point as likely to add to the moral havoc as restore order' (Carroll, 2004: 240). Here, however, the player is encouraged to enact these destructive character dimensions as an integral part of the gameplay experience, especially during the free-form moments in between the narrative's progression. More importantly, the metaphysical purpose of Marsden's violent mission to rid society of its last vestiges of savagery represents a Ford-like 'clearing of the field' (Campbell, 1993: 338) in the founding of modernity: 'The desolate and dangerous frontier is being tamed for the future, so that decent communities can settle and build. This is the making of America' (Carroll, 2004: 237–238).

According to Carroll, Ford would ultimately come to see the quixotic nature of his foundation myth through the process of building his cinematic oeuvre. As Kathleen Yorke puts it in *Rio Grande*, 'All this danger to serve people as yet unborn—and probably not worth saving'. In this sense, *Red Dead Redemption* is very much post-Ford: a reverent contemporary evocation of the director's myth in which a cynical critique is also embedded. Unlike Ford's modern representatives who seem more effete than nefarious, *Red Dead Redemption*'s bureaucrats and bean counters are explicitly presented as self-serving creatures who disingenuously hide behind the values of 'democracy and the Constitution, of education and development' (Carroll, 2004: 249). When authorities arrest the local snake oil salesman, the knowing Marsden demands they let him loose: 'He's a harmless old fraud, the kind of man who built this country'. The sense of what has been lost in modernity's civilising of the 'untamed frontier' is also conveyed in the various virtual environments that the player can inhabit across the game. The smaller settlements and open plains are hives of gameplay activity and danger. The fictional industrialising centre of 'Blackwater', like Shinbone at the end of *The Man Who Shot Liberty Valance*, is lifeless: 'All is clear and distinct, but the streets are dead' (Carroll, 2004: 250).

For modernity to fully establish itself, the savage hero who cleared the field must himself also finally depart the scene. In *The Searchers*—Ford's earlier, more hopeful work—Ethan simply rides into the sunset. In *The Man Who Shot Liberty Valance*, the entire narrative orbits around the death of the similarly violent hero, Tom Doniphon. *Red Dead Redemption*'s Marsden must also take 'the pollution of all the blood-guilt with him' (Carroll, 2004: 246) as the final establishing stage, and in this more cynical reading of Ford's myth, it is the corrupt authorities who make it so. Unbeknownst to Marsden, he is the final outlaw on their list of men to kill and the ensuing tragedy is again conveyed with a force unique to the video game form. Having made sure his wife and son are safely away from his ranch, Marsden readies himself for the inevitable confrontation with the posse sent out to end his life. The sequence begins with a non-interactive cinematic 'cut scene' in which Marsden edges open a barn door to see sixteen men with guns at the ready. After taking a deep breath in resignation, he fully opens the doors to face his antagonists. The scene then shifts into gameplay mode, with control of

Marsden placed back into the hands of the player. At this late stage of the long interactive experience—length of play can be anywhere from 18 to 40 hours or more, depending on how long one wishes to inhabit the virtual West—the player will ideally have come to feel as accomplished in gunplay as Marsden himself is meant to be in the narrative. However, while ostensible control is placed in the player's hands at the onset of the shootout, there is no way of 'winning' the gameplay sequence. However skilled the player might have become during the game, and however many antagonists he/she is able to dispense with during this sequence, the shootout can only end in Marsden's death. This, quite literally, is gameplay as an expression of heroic tragedy.

That Dragon, Cancer

The final video game under examination is very different to those discussed thus far. Winner of the 'Games for Impact' award at the Game Awards 2016, *That Dragon, Cancer* (2016) is a low-budget 'indie' title from Numinous Games, a small team headed by husband and wife designers, Amy and Ryan Green. While *That Dragon, Cancer* has not enjoyed the wide appeal of the other games studied here, and therefore fails to meet a key criterion in Carroll's view of what constitutes texts of cultural significance, the game warrants inclusion for what it says about the possibilities of high art in the digital era. The main function of all art, according to Carroll (2008a: 2–3), is to grapple with the 'three age-old, fundamental questions . . . "Where do I come from?", "What should I do with my life?", and "What happens to me at death?"' For Carroll, as suggested, one of the important cultural trends of the previous century is high art's abdication of this responsibility in favour of an abstraction 'emptied of all spiritual and moral content' (Carroll, 2008a: 124). In its patent aspirations to high art rather than entertainment, *That Dragon, Cancer* suggests there may yet be life in this allegedly enervated and nihilistic cultural arena.

That Dragon, Cancer is a video game only in the most fundamental sense of giving its audience a sense of interactive control in how things play out within a digital space. Through a series of dream-like abstracted sequences, the game invites the player to inhabit the Green family's deeply personal journey in dealing with the all but inevitable death of their young son from a rare form of brain cancer. Both of them devout Christians, Amy and Ryan Green wanted to convey to others the 'grace' (Green, n.d.) inherent in such irrevocably heart-breaking experiences. For this game designer couple, the interactivity of their chosen medium made it an ideal forum for their message:

> We made a film about a couple that loses their only son to cancer. We also wrote a children's book . . . However, none of those could do what I believe an immersive videogame can do . . . The truth is that any game that has been created or will be created contains only the illusion of choice. Dialog trees, branching narrative, and puzzle mechanics all drive the player towards a predetermined end . . . I believe that the creator of any universe

has the power to limit choice. But a good creator gives choice because they empathize with the player. This creator recognizes that the player has been hurt, and treated viciously. This creator wants the player to love his son, like he loves his son. This creator ultimately wants good for the created world, and for its inhabitants.

(Green, n.d.)

In other words, video games provide self-contained universes in which designers lend only a cursory sense of freewill to players. The narrative itself is predetermined and, in this case, tragic. The allusions here to the Green's religious outlook on life are clear. However, *That Dragon, Cancer* ultimately represents the couple's struggle to maintain their beliefs amidst the senselessness of their son's passing.

With its 20th-century abstract-modernist aesthetic, integration of audio recorded by the family during the tragic period and postmodern self-referencing of video game tropes, *That Dragon, Cancer* is undoubtedly a game with contemporary high art aspirations. However, it is most noteworthy in its use of these techniques to return high art to the function that Carroll argues has long been abandoned by its other traditional forms. Indeed, the interactivity of the piece—the invitation from designers to inhabit the pain of their experiences—complements the artist's ideal aim of lending to his/her particular anguish a more universal sense of the 'eternal, primal suffering' (Nietzsche, 2003: 25). Importantly, and as suggested, while Amy and Ryan Green are both practising Christians, the overarching message of *That Dragon, Cancer* is not one of blind faith. On the contrary, and in a narrative tradition that stretches back to the works of both Dostoyevsky and Leo Tolstoy, the unfolding tragedy rests on the tension between Amy's withdrawal into notions of an afterlife and Ryan's ever-increasing descent into Nietzsche's 'horror and absurdity'. Ultimately, a peace is found not unlike Weber's (1946: 155) appeal to stoicism in the face of modern ambivalence: 'It is an invitation to walk in the garden with those that suffer, and struggle; who make mistakes; who doubt; and are trying their hardest to love in a world that seems undone' (Green, n.d.).

Everything old is new again

The four case studies examined here suggest that, as an emergent narrative medium, video games are providing a new forum for retelling key stories in the modern cultural tradition—a phenomenon that Carroll himself might see as a form of digital 'midrash'. It would be an overstatement to suggest that these retellings—the doomed search for charismatic secular guidance; the struggle to maintain morality in the face of cultural disintegration; the tragic nature of modernity's foundations; and the modern fragility of religious faith—attain the level of pre-eminence that marks their literary and cinematic forebears. However, the existence of such themes in this digital space is nonetheless significant. Indeed, while there may not yet be a 'masterpiece' of video games akin to, say, Conrad's *Heart of Darkness* or Ford's *The Searchers*, the medium is demonstrating in these case studies an unmistakable inclination to place itself within the cultural traditions that Carroll's sociology helps illuminate. There is a paradox here that echoes Wolcott's (2013: 121) thoughts about the 'conservative impulse' in 1970s punk rock, and Wood's (2006: 353–354) assertion of what truly amounts to 'innovation' in art: that is, rather than being best understood as birthplaces of the never-before-seen, new and resonant creative phenomena can often represent a return to the 'deepest resources' of what has come before.

In terms of understanding the digital innovation through which these video games have sought to renew stories of modern cultural significance, what we are seeing is the integration of interactive elements that invite the audience to become 'players' rather than 'spectators'. While the narratives themselves may be largely predetermined, the journeys from beginning to end are marked by a sense of audience participation in precisely how things play out. It is a form of storytelling that aligns itself to the broader characteristic of digital cultural 'prosumption' (Beer & Burrows, 2010) in which consumers of a given cultural artefact become agents in the production process. While this dynamic is more explicit in the user-generation of amateur videos on YouTube, or in similar content across other social media platforms, video games can be seen as an arena for more traditional author-driven storytelling in which prosumption tendencies nonetheless assert themselves. All of this, in turn, echoes the late-modern 'individualising' shifts traced by Giddens (e.g. 1991) and Beck and Beck-Gernsheim (e.g. 2002) whereby culture has increasingly become a 'do-it-yourself' (Beck & Beck-Gernsheim, 2002: 47) arena in which ordinary people are compelled to 'produce, stage and cobble together their biographies themselves' (Beck et al., 1994: 13). Indeed, a game like *Bioshock* can very much be seen as Conrad's *Heart of Darkness* re-imagined for audiences who now expect higher degrees of agency in their engagements with narrative.

If you were to ask the average player what the interactivity of inhabiting video game narratives elicits, he/she would be likely to respond in terms of 'immersion'—to quote Stuart (2010), 'We lose ourselves in games'. In the earlier days of cinema, this sense of losing oneself in the presence of alternate worlds—that spatially and temporally destabilising sense of 'really being there'—was similarly crucial to the appeal of the moving image. However, while we may still be compelled by any number of onscreen film or television narratives, the moving image itself has gradually lost much of its novel power as an immersive technology.[4] To understand what is occurring in audiences' captivation with these immersive narrative innovations is to once more enter into a paradox. Here, I turn to Carroll's own deepest resources: the work of Nietzsche and, specifically, *The Birth of Tragedy* (Nietzsche, 1872). In this, Nietzsche's first and arguably most influential book, the philosopher outlines his theory of the nature and origins of Ancient Greek tragedy. While Nietzsche's theory of Greek tragedy is 'complex . . . and fraught with apparent contradictions' (Maloney, 2015: 5), his core insight into the medium's origins helps shed light on any immersive narrative innovation.

According to Nietzsche, the earliest forms of Greek tragedy saw the actors, chorus and audience, along with any rational distinctions between fiction and reality, all folded into each other within the greater 'Oneness' (Nietzsche, 2003: 17) of storytelling as a transcendent ritual event. Indeed, what *we* would categorise as an 'audience'—in terms of passive spectators distinct from what is occurring on stage or screen—had no equivalent at the birth of tragedy: 'there was no fundamental opposition between the audience and the chorus: for everything was simply a great, sublime chorus of dancing, singing satyrs' (Nietzsche, 2003: 41). The increasing rationality that, over time, would ultimately come to define Ancient Greek thought and culture would see a corresponding shift in the conception of theatrical representation towards something comparable to how we conceive of theatre, film or television today: that is, as fictional forms from which we, as audience members, remain spatially and temporally at a distance. In this sense, the immersive interactivity of video games can be seen as an attempt to return to the oneness of storytelling; a oneness in which 'reality' dissolves and, like the earliest ancient Greeks, we become fully invested members of that 'great, sublime chorus'.

In conclusion, these four video games demonstrate a marked impetus towards Carroll's metaphysical 'big questions'—those questions of individual and collective meaning that cut across the social and economic divisions with which conventional sociology has become increasingly associated. As a digital medium historically dismissed as little more than base entertainment, this maturation of video games speaks to the human-social inclination to infuse even our most ostensibly ignoble pursuits with deeper cultural functions; with what anthropologist Clifford Geertz (1973: 449), in his influential study of Balinese cockfighting, refers to as 'a kind of sentimental education'. As stated in this chapter's introduction, video games might seem an unlikely site for metaphysical inquiry, and I remain unsure of how Carroll himself—a scholar of archetypal stories who has argued 'that with any story, it is the major telling that counts' (Carroll, 2001: 16)—might view the work undertaken here. However, as Carroll (2015a) implies in his more recent assertion that television has transformed itself into Western culture's principal 'generative source', we need to stay open to the possibility that the 'timeless challenge of culture' (Carroll, 2015a) might again be taken up in newer cultural forms that begin life inauspiciously, as mere 'entertainment'.

Notes

1 In Jewish theology, midrash is a complex concept that resists simple definition. It is perhaps most easily equated to biblical exegesis and Kermode's and Carroll's use of the concept as more or less a stand-in for terms such as retelling, reinterpretation or re-imagining is, by Jewish theological standards, very loose.
2 This section represents a revision of my earlier games studies outline in Maloney (2016).
3 Another similarly lauded video game, *Spec Ops: The Line*, offers a second interactive retelling of *Heart of Darkness*, further confirming Carroll's argument about the significance of this core narrative across the modern cultural landscape. Taking its thematic cues more from Francis Ford Coppola's *Apocalypse Now* than from Conrad's original work—and thereby curtailing certain key elements in Carroll's reading of the blueprint—the game is peripheral to this discussion.
4 The recent and all but failed effort by Hollywood to promote 3D imagery as the new standard in commercial cinema can be seen as an attempt to revitalise the medium's immersive powers.

References

Agresta M (2013) How the Western was lost (and why it matters). *The Atlantic.* Available at: www.theatlantic.com/entertainment/archive/2013/07/how-the-western-was-lost-and-why-it-matters/278057.

Anderson CA and Dill KE (2000) Video games and aggressive thoughts, feelings, and behavior in the laboratory and in life. *Journal of Personality and Social Psychology* 78(4): 772–790.

Arnheim R (2006) *Film as Art.* Berkeley, CA: University of California Press.

Atkins B (2003) *More than a Game: The Computer Game as Fictional Form.* Manchester: Manchester University Press.

Beck U and Beck-Gernsheim (2002) *Individualization: Institutionalized Individualism and its Social and Political Consequences.* Thousand Oaks, CA: SAGE Publications.

Beck U, Giddens A and Lash S (1994) *Reflexive Modernization.* Stanford, CA: Stanford University Press.

Beer D and Burrows R (2010) Consumption, prosumption and participatory web cultures: An introduction. *Journal of Consumer Culture* 10(1): 3–12.

Bertozzi E (2014) The feeling of being hunted: Pleasures and potentialities of predation play. *Games and Culture* 9(6): 429–441.

Bogost I (2007) *Persuasive Games: The Expressive Power of Video Games.* Cambridge, MA: MIT Press.

Campbell J (1993) *The Hero with a Thousand Faces.* London: Fontana Press.

Carroll J (2001) *The Western Dreaming: The Western World is Dying for Want of a Story.* Pymble, NSW: HarperCollins.

Carroll J (2002) *Terror: A Meditation on the Meaning of September 11.* Melbourne: Scribe.

Carroll J (2004) *The Wreck of Western Culture: Humanism Revisited.* Melbourne: Scribe.

Carroll J (2007) *The Existential Jesus.* Melbourne: Scribe.

Carroll J (2008a) *Ego and Soul: The Modern West in Search of Meaning.* Melbourne: Scribe.

Carroll J (2008b) The Greek Foundations of the West. *Thesis Eleven* 93(1): 5–21.

Carroll J (2015a) These days, we face our most difficult truths through HBO. *The Australian.* Available at: www.theaustralian.com.au/news/inquirer/popular-cultures-renaissance-led-by-hbo/news-story/0eedf641f56da1f3e1f01244e6c1f7db.

Carroll J (2015b) Authenticity in question. *Culture and Society* 52(6): 611–615.

Conrad J (2007) *Heart of Darkness.* London: Vintage Books.

Darley A (2000) *Visual Digital Culture: Surface Play and Spectacle in New Media Genres.* London: Routledge.

Dostoyevsky F (1958) *The Brothers Karamazov.* London: Penguin Books.

Durkheim E (2006) *On Suicide.* London: Penguin Books.

Geertz C (1973) *The Interpretation of Cultures.* New York: Basic Books.

Giddens A (1991) *Modernity and Self-Identity: Self and Society in the Late Modern Age.* Stanford, CA: Stanford University Press.

Green R (n.d.) Why games need grace. *Gamechurch.* Available at: http://gamechurch.com/why-games-need-grace.

Irwin AR and Gross AM (1995) Cognitive tempo, violent video games, and aggressive behavior in young boys. *Journal of Family Violence* 10(3): 337–350.

Juul J (2005) Games telling stories? In: Raessens J and Goldstein J (eds.) *Handbook of Computer Game Studies.* Cambridge, MA: The MIT Press, pp. 219–226.

Kermode F (1979) *The Genesis of Secrecy: On the Interpretation of Narrative.* Cambridge, MA: Harvard University Press.

Kirkman R and Moore T (2013) *The Walking Dead, Vol. 1: Days Gone Bye*. Berkeley, CA: Image Comics.

Maloney M (2015) *The Search for Meaning in Film and Television: Disenchantment at the Turn of the Millennium*. Basingstoke: Palgrave Macmillan.

Maloney M (2016) Ambivalent violence in contemporary game design. *Games and Culture* (Online First). Available at: http://journals.sagepub.com/doi/full/10.1177/1555412016647848.

McCarthy C (2006) *The Road*. London: Picador.

Nietzsche F (1974) *The Gay Science*. New York: Vintage Books.

Nietzsche F (2003) *The Birth of Tragedy*. London: Penguin Classics.

Orgad S (2014) When media representation met sociology. In: Waisbord S (ed.) *Media Sociology: A Reappraisal*. Cambridge: Polity Press, pp. 133–150.

Plato (1968) *Republic*, trans. Bloom A. New York: Basic Books.

Rand A (1957) *Atlas Shrugged*. New York: Dutton.

Ratan RA, Taylor N, Hogan J, Kennedy T and Williams D (2015) Stand by your man: An examination of gender disparity in *League of Legends*. *Games and Culture* 10(5): 438–462.

Rieff P (1990) *The Feeling Intellect: Selected Writings*. Chicago, IL: The University of Chicago Press.

Sartre JP (2003) *Being and Nothingness*. London: Routledge.

Simons J (2007) Narrative, games, and theory. *Games Studies* 7(1). Available at: http://gamestudies.org/0701/articles/simons.

Stuart K (2010) What do we mean when we call a game 'immersive'? *The Guardian*. Available at: www.theguardian.com/technology/gamesblog/2010/aug/10/games-science-of-immersion.

Swalwell M and Wilson J (2008) Introduction. In: Swalwell M and Wilson J (eds.) *The Pleasures of Computer Gaming*. Jefferson, NC: McFarland, pp. 1–12.

Weber M (1946) Science as a vocation. In: Gerth HH and Mills CW (eds.) *From Max Weber: Essays in Sociology*. New York: Oxford University Press, pp. 129–156.

Weber M (2002) *The Protestant Ethic and the 'Spirit' of Capitalism*, trans. Baehr P and Wells GC. London: Penguin Books.

Wesp E (2014) A too-coherent world: Game studies and the myth of 'narrative' media. *Game Studies* 14(2). Available at: http://gamestudies.org/1402/articles/wesp.

Wolcott J (2013) *Critical Mass: Four Decades of Essays, Reviews, Hand Grenades, and Hurrahs*. New York: Doubleday.

Wood R (2006) *Personal Views: Explorations in Film*. Detroit, MI: Wayne State University Press.

10 Ego-terrorism

The benefit of an anarcho-psychological perspective of terrorism

Wayne Bradshaw

The threat of terrorism is not new, but the question of what motivates terrorists remains unresolved. In *Break-Out from the Crystal Palace* (1974), John Carroll delineated an "anarcho-psychological tradition" of critique that emerged from the ideas of Max Stirner, Friedrich Nietzsche and Fyodor Dostoevsky. This strain of metaphysical critique enables an examination of terrorism that portrays it as an attempt to overcome doubts about the meaning and purpose of life by imposing structure on the flux of modernity. For the terrorist persona, fundamental questions about the possibility of meaningful action and the value of a single life can find their resolution in symbolic acts of violence. In *Terror: A Meditation on the Meaning of September 11* (2002), Carroll provided his own reading of the meaning of the September Eleven terrorist attacks to a West that has lapsed into decadence. In it, he suggested that the perception that terrorism is the product of global economic inequality and American imperialism "misreads a metaphysical crisis" as a crisis of morals (2002: 97). Though not explicitly indicated by Carroll, the critique provided by *Break-Out from the Crystal Palace* and the writings of generations of terrorist philosophers directly relate to his reading of the character of Usama bin Laden in *Terror*. By pulling together the thought of Stirner, Nietzsche and Dostoevsky, Carroll has provided the foundation of a strain of metaphysical critique capable of describing the terrorist persona and the rational and moral constructions that underpin it. Applied to the polemics, manifestos and manuals of terrorists of different ideological waves of terror, Carroll's critique reveals a persistent terrorist persona that is obsessed with achieving self-realisation through violent struggle against institutionalised morality.

As uncomfortable as it is for the modern West to accept, terrorism is eminently *rational*. To understand its rationality, however, it is necessary to first understand how terrorists generate meaning in the world they occupy. That is, to understand the terrorist act, one must first understand the terrorist persona. Identifying the terrorist persona in turn requires a metaphysical critique such as the anarcho-psychological critique that Carroll provides. Fifteen years after the World Trade Centre was destroyed, Western nations continue to ask what motivates terrorists to perform morally reprehensible acts. A metaphysical critique reframes this question by asking what violence means to terrorists instead of searching for its source in the founding ideologies of their movements. It reaches beyond the characteristics of ideology to interrogate terrorist ideas about the purpose of life and action in a manner which demonstrates the breadth of terrorist constructions of meaning and warns against reductionist conceptualisations of terrorists as mere ideologues. Despite the ideological and political diversity of terrorists past and present, metaphysical critique reveals the extent to which they share a consistent idea of what amounts to meaningful action. In the case of the anarcho-psychological critique emerging from Carroll's *Break-Out from the Crystal Palace* (1974), consideration falls upon the terrorist persona's relationship with ideology and morality. It involves identifying the intersections between the ideas of individual terrorist theorists and the ideas of Stirner, Nietzsche and Dostoevsky, and then determining the extent to which these intersections are shared between the different ideological waves of terrorism. Ideas common both to the anarcho-psychological and terrorist tradition can then be used to establish aspects of the terrorist persona. Finally, the full extent of the anarcho-psychological critique can then be brought to bear on the terrorist persona to identify the flawed logic that leads it to rationalise the use of indiscriminate violence.

The anarcho-psychological tradition that Carroll describes in *Break-Out from the Crystal Palace* (1974) draws together the shared ideas of Max Stirner, Friedrich Nietzsche and Fyodor Dostoevsky to produce a consistent metaphysical critique. It is a critique founded on the perspective that natural morality is an illusion, that all moral values are constructions of the ego, and that it is the responsibility of the individual to overcome such constructions when they serve as impediments to self-realisation. Along with liberal-rationalism and Marxism, Carroll argues that anarcho-psychology represents one of the three great intellectual traditions that "have supplied contemporary Western civilization with its key social images of man" (1974: 1). It is distinct from the other two in that it represents a repudiation of the "progressive secularization of the religious quest for truth" that "governs the flow of all intellectual currents in Europe over the last three centuries" (Carroll, 1974: 5), and from its first complete representation in Max Stirner's *The Ego and Its Own* (1995, originally 1844), it has mounted an unremitting assault on the objectivity of morality and ideology. Its critique is anarchic in so far as it rejects the legitimacy of all external value structures, while its preoccupation with the ego as a foundation for the creation of new values provides it with its psychological and moral components.

Carroll suggests that the targets of the anarcho-psychological critique are "the ideological veneers which distort human communication, which inhibit individual fulfilment and enjoyment, and thereby preclude self-realisation" (1974: 17). It presents a threefold assault on the objectivity of morality, ideology and economics. The logic of the critique is encapsulated in Carroll's description of Stirner's

> insistence that not only is the God of religion a projection of man's alienated self, but so is every ideal, every cause, every "fixed idea", for they all entice men into following a *spook* which is neither of their creation nor within their power.
>
> (1974: 21)

Stirner's preferred response to the tyranny of "fixed ideas" is neatly expressed when he suggests that:

> *I* am my species, am without norm, without law, without model, and the like. It is possible that I can make very little out of myself; but this little is everything, and is better than what I allow to be made out of me by the might of others, by the training of custom, religion, the laws, the State.
>
> (1995: 163)

The anarcho-psychological critique suggests that ideology, like morality and economics, is a tool of control that finds its origin in the mind. Stirner suggests that it must either serve the individual as property or will inevitably come to control the individual as a "spook" haunting the mind. For the proponent of the anarcho-psychological critique, the struggle for self-realisation is a struggle for ownership of ideas. This effort to take ownership over ideology is repeatedly demonstrated in the writings of successive terrorist theorists. Carroll observed the capacity of this critique to account for the values of artists, bohemians and students (1974: 1), but its application can also be turned upon the terrorist, anarchist or otherwise.

An anarcho-psychological approach to the terrorist persona suggests that the process by which dominant moral frameworks become destabilised by insurrectionary egoism may be as important as the prevalence of revolutionary ideology in forming waves of terrorism. Anarcho-psychology as a form of metaphysical critique is relevant to conceiving the terrorist persona because terrorist descriptions of society, like those of Stirner and Nietzsche, "develop as a critique of existing patterns of human thought and behaviour," while "their driving ambition is to provide the key to a revalued world" (Carroll, 1974: 17). Like Stirner and Nietzsche, terrorists confront the monolith of institutionalised morality by identifying it as an alien construction while simultaneously attempting to circumvent absolute relativism by imposing a new system of values that instead find their origin in the self. The terrorist persona is then led to suggest the importance of the criminal act to the process of overcoming the "fixed ideas" of institutionalised morality. In *The Ego and Its Own* (1844), Stirner proposed that the state calls its own violence "law" while branding the individual's violence "crime" [*Verbrechen*], and that "only by crime does [an individual] overcome [*bricht*] the state's violence when he thinks that the state is not above him, but he is above the state" (1995: 176). Nietzsche too suggested in *Beyond Good and Evil* (1886) that "[a] criminal's lawyers are seldom artists enough to turn the beautiful terribleness of the deed to the advantage of him who did it" (2003a: 97). For political revolutionaries grounded in an egoistic world-view, this logic can seem a strident call to violent action.

Adapting Carroll's anarcho-psychological critique to the study of terrorism suggests that the terrorist persona is characterised by its attempts to render ideology subject to *will*, rather than be governed by it. One side of the process of self-realisation that flows from this persona demands the creation of a personal ideology; another requires the destruction of the rational foundations of external ideologies. Whether it be anarchism's critique of the state's exclusive right to use violence, the New Left's "smash monogamy" initiative, or anti-colonial and jihadist assaults on the rights of multinational superpowers, the anarcho-psychology of the terrorist persona demands the destabilisation of existing ideological institutions by arguing that they are built to serve a decadent hegemony. The irony that the terrorist's own ideological standpoint is built on equally subjective foundations is inconsequential because it is imposed by the ego rather than from without. The terrorist persona's commitment to ideology and the terrorist act itself is an outwardly directed performance of their strength of will and accordingly contains its own signification.

A weakness of the existing discussion of terrorism is that it has become dominated by a preoccupation with the role of radical ideology in inspiring political violence. While crucial to understanding terrorism, the pervasiveness of ideological analysis has come at the expense of the equally important endeavour of subjecting terrorism to metaphysical critique. In 2008, Michael Chertoff, the then secretary of the US Department of Homeland Security, observed that "Al-Qaeda and like-minded organizations are inspired by a malignant ideology, one that is characterized by contempt for human dignity and freedom and a depraved disregard for human life" (2008: 11). His perspective captures a popular sentiment that terrorists are slaves to a dogma that pits itself against the rights and freedoms of the individual. This view leaves crucial aspects of Islamic fundamentalist terrorism unaccounted for, such as the preoccupation of terrorists throughout history with achieving rights and freedoms for individuals they claim to represent. For instance, the Islamist Sayyid Qutb's essay "Jihad in the Cause of God" from his book *Milestones* (1964) is from the outset foremost concerned with *jihad* as a means of defending the "freedom" of Muslims (2004: 394). Focusing on the control Islamist ideology seems to exert over its adherents rather than the apparent incongruity between Islamist and liberal ideas of freedom, Chertoff proposed that the ideological roots of contemporary fundamentalist Islamic terror largely draw from the reservoir of twentieth-century Western totalitarian thought (2008: 12). Certainly, terrorism contains within it the effort to thwart the ambiguity of the modern condition, but it approaches this task egoistically, by imposing the terrorist self on the flux of modernity. By failing to recognise the complex dialogue between freedom and control that lies at the heart of the terrorist persona, Chertoff cuts off Islamism from a history of terrorism that also includes nineteenth-century anarchist and twentieth-century anti-imperialist movements. Without the complementary insight of Carroll's metaphysical critique, ideological critique seems to suggest there is little continuity between the various waves of terrorism, and little to be gleaned from the terrorists of the past when trying to understand the terrorism of the present.

Carroll's metaphysical critique, when applied to the history of terrorist thought, dispels the illusion that waves of ideology have produced entirely discrete kinds of terrorism. It also suggests that terrorists are not necessarily merely the victims of malicious ideologies. On the contrary, they are at times the manufacturers and owners of ideology, using it as a means of achieving self-realisation. The process of using ideology in this way does, however, seem to push terrorists inexorably towards pure dogmatism. Instead of asking what terrorism is, or what terrorists want, a metaphysical critique asks what terrorism means to terrorists and their sense of self. Within the context of Carroll's anarcho-psychological critique, terrorism is an attempt at self-realisation by overcoming imposed moral boundaries. The terrorist persona longs to rise above morality and create new moral structures of their own choosing. The terrorist attack itself is an example of violent insurrection against moral institutions imposed on the individual by society. The terrorist persona engages in acts of criminal violence not only to foment widespread revolution, but to demonstrate the persona's own liberation from moral strictures. This second goal is achieved at the very moment the terrorist attack takes place. The material overthrow of the state, capitalism or the West becomes concomitant to the symbolic performance of its overthrow. Like Raskolnikov in *Crime and Punishment* (1866), terrorists tend to seek a moment of self-realisation at the very instant a grievous crime against morality is committed, because the criminal act itself amounts to a rejection of morality's capacity to govern the individual. Considering Dostoevsky's *Notes from Underground* (1864), Carroll suggests that "[s]cientific laws, or what Dostoevsky calls with some irony the laws of nature, enclose whoever accepts them like stone walls" (1974: 113). Like the underground man of Dostoevsky's novel, the terrorist persona "calls for the anarchist demolition of the new authority" (Carroll, 1974: 113), beginning with the rejection of the capacity of law to govern the self. The suicide attack takes this logic to its most extreme point, where even self-destruction becomes a reasonable cost of a grand symbolic crime against institutionalised morality.[1]

Applied to the study of the terrorist persona, Carroll's anarcho-psychological metaphysical critique reveals new details in the historical landscape of terrorism. A dominance of ideological critique in the study of terrorism has encouraged its conceptualisation as a series of ideological "waves" of violence occurring since the late nineteenth century. It has seemed otherwise impossible to reconcile the values of nineteenth-century anarchists, early twentieth-century nationalists, mid-twentieth-century Marxists and twenty-first-century religious fundamentalists. In this regard, the work of David Rapoport in establishing the existence of four discrete waves of terror has been paramount. Breaking the history of terrorism into waves of anarchist, anti-colonial, New Left and religious ideology (Rapoport, 2004: 47), Rapoport seeks to understand the forces that operate *within* each wave, but also isolates each one from the others, even when multiple waves are simultaneously active. Where the ideological critique of terrorism focuses on the internal consistencies of a given wave of terrorism, and what marks it as distinct from the others, a metaphysical critique, such as one adapted from Carroll's anarcho-psychology, integrates the waves by depicting a persistent terrorist persona. The terrorist persona is a shared egoistic metaphysical perspective that emerges in the mid-nineteenth century and is re-enacted in both the practice and theory of each ideological wave of modern terrorism.

The project of establishing a metaphysical critique of terrorism that can complement and sometimes contest the dominant ideological critique has already begun in earnest. As part of the project of developing a sociology of modern culture, John Carroll, Max Weber and Theodore Adorno have all contributed to describing the character of the terrorist persona, as indeed have others including Émile Durkheim in *Suicide* (2002, originally 1897), Terry Eagleton in *On Evil* (2010) and Frank Furedi in "Youth Rebellion that Embraces Authority" (2014). Nietzsche himself considered the character of the anarchist revolutionary in both *Thus Spoke Zarathustra* (2003c, originally 1891) and *Beyond Good and Evil* (2003a, originally 1886), where he condemned it to varying extents. In his portrayal of Pyotr Stepanovich Verkhovensky[2] in *Demons* (2006, originally 1872), Dostoevsky provides his own depiction of the terrorist persona. There are surprising points of intersection between the personas they describe: intersections that are intensified when viewed in the context of the writings and seminal texts of subsequent waves of terrorism. It is important to note that establishing a consistent terrorist persona is not the same as establishing a consistent cause for terrorism, any more than establishing a shared ideology within a wave of terrorism amounts to discovering a cause for terrorism within that wave. Instead, it assists in understanding the variety of forces that drive individuals towards violent insurrection. It also strives at identifying the way individuals and groups rationalise terrorist acts and perceive the commission of these acts as a meaningful endeavour.

Existing metaphysical critiques of terrorism

The terrorist persona emerges as one response to the anxiety produced by the conditions of cultural modernity. Terrorism in its contemporary form is a phenomenon that finds its earliest fully fledged examples in the anarchist violence of the nineteenth century. Randall Law suggests that the "French Revolutionaries introduced the language and purpose of modern terrorism in the late eighteenth century," and over "the second half of the nineteenth century and the first few decades of the twentieth, the number of groups devoted to the use of terrorism grew rapidly, as did the number of guises in which terrorism appeared" (2009: 74). Terrorism as it is understood today developed in tandem with cultural modernity. The contemporaneousness of cultural modernity and modern terrorism suggests the importance of the sociology of modern culture to developing a metaphysical critique of terrorism. Faced with the threat of dehumanising scientific rationality on the one hand and the chaotic flux of total relativism on the other, the terrorist persona instead elects to thwart ambiguity with a structure that finds its locus in the ego itself. For the terrorist persona, meaning is found in terrorism as a vocation dedicated to imposing the individual ego on both scientific rationality and the flux of relativism.

In *Science as a Vocation* (1970, originally 1917), Weber describes the societal conditions that produce the metaphysical crisis of modernity. Applying Carroll's anarcho-psychological critique to the way the terrorists confront this crisis suggests that the terrorist persona finds meaning in imposing its will on reality. Lawrence Scaff suggests that Weber "realized that challenges to the 'organic' cycle of life and its sense of 'wholeness' can lead to a search for alternatives, for counter-cultural routes of escape from the iron cage of modern forms" (2000: 103). The terrorist persona presents one such attempt to escape. Weber observes that "civilized man, placed in the midst of the continuous enrichment of culture by ideas, knowledge, and problems, may become 'tired of life' but not 'satiated with life'" (1970: 140), leading to an eventual disillusionment with the broader project of Enlightenment. Scientific rationality, he suggested, itself shattered the dreams of the Enlightenment, and after "all these former illusions, the 'way to true being,' the 'way to true art,' the 'way to true nature,' the 'way to true God,' the 'way to true happiness,' have been dispelled" (1970: 143) by reason, the modern condition demanded that "the individual has to decide which is God for him and which is the devil" (Weber, 1970: 148). Just as Tolstoy's response to this dilemma was to reject a science that fails to address the meaning of life (Weber, 1970: 143), terrorists too respond by rejecting the foundation of scientific rationality that girds modernity. Rather than succumbing to the abyss of total relativism that remains after the abolition of scientific reason, the terrorist persona falls back on the crutch of the ego as a foundation for meaning in a meaningless world. Because "[w]hat is hard for modern man, and especially for the younger generation, is to measure up to *workaday* existence" (Weber, 1970: 149), the egoistic persona of the terrorist is appealing to those who look not for the rational analysis of the teacher, but the leadership of a preacher who imposes structure and meaning on modern existence.

While John Carroll's *Terror: A Meditation on the Meaning of September 11* (2002) is, at its heart, an exploration of the internal response of Western civilisation to the most significant terrorist attack to occur on American soil, it is at the same time a metaphysical characterisation of Usama bin Laden. Carroll identifies in the character and bearing of Usama bin Laden an analogue of John Ford's Liberty Valance, with both being an inversion of the idealised hero of the Wild West transformed into a self-possessed nemesis of decadent Western civilisation (2002: 6). In Ford's *The Man Who Shot Liberty Valance* (1962), Lee Marvin's Valance is the archetype of the "bad man" of the American western. Carroll observes that he stands "in his monumental badness" (2002: 7) as a test of will for the two leading men of the film, James Stewart's lawyer Ranse Stoddard and John Wayne's rancher Tom Doniphon. Valance is defeated not through valour but deception, and although Stoddard becomes lauded as "the man who shot Liberty Valance," his legend is founded on a lie. Carroll describes both Valance and Usama as Satanic figures who, confident and assured, match the gaze of American might and ask "What kind of man are you, Dude?" (Carroll, 2002: 7). Carroll suggests that Usama bin Laden's goal is not the establishment of a utopian state modelled on an Islamic ideal, but to assert *himself* as an existential adversary of Western civilisation (Carroll, 2002: 8). Islamism is an ideology he uses to provide a foundation for action. This view suggests that terrorism arises from a combination of a credible but immense *will*, an ideological program, and the capacity to view the dominant institutional framework itself as an *other* to be overcome.

Ultimately, terrorism is a kind of praxis that amounts to "pseudo-activity" as it is described by Theodore Adorno. In response to criticism that "his refusal to translate Critical Theory into a program for political action" amounted to a "resignation" from political life (Bell, 2014), Adorno offered an important critique of revolutionary self-realisation through praxis in the form of a radio address in 1968, itself entitled "Resignation." Included in his intended audience of "the radical student movement and Soviet intellectuals like György Lukács" (Bell, 2014) were certainly the likes of Ulrike Meinhof, the militant journalist who went on to co-found the Red Army Faction two years later. Adorno's critique of theory-informed praxis is also applicable to a broader terrorist program of self-realisation through action. "Resignation" provides a blueprint for the relationship between terrorist ontology and ideology. His description of pseudo-activity suggests a model that helps us understand the theatrics of terrorist violence:

> Pseudo-reality is conjoined with . . . pseudo-activity: action that overdoes and aggravates itself for the sake of its own publicity, without admitting to itself to what extent it serves as a substitute satisfaction, elevating itself into an end in itself.
>
> (Adorno, 2005: 291)

The spectacle of terrorist attacks and concern with the publicity of demonstrations of "propaganda of the deed" are reinforced by a conceptualisation of the terrorist act as self-fulfilling. Egoism leans upon ideology as an avenue to self-realisation through action, and ideology runs unchecked by being continually reinforced by the confidence of the ego in being the source of all value. Adorno warns of the co-dependency of ego and ideology that takes root at the point of praxis when he suggests that "[i]deology lies in wait for the mind which delights in itself like Nietzsche's Zarathustra, for the mind which all but irresistibly becomes an absolute to itself" (1973: 30). It is into this very trap that multiple waves of terrorists fall; overconfident in their will and capacity for action, they are pushed towards a programme of self-assured annihilation.

Where the metaphysical critique of cultural modernity touches upon the phenomenon of terrorism, it hints at the importance of anarchic nihilism and unrestrained egoism to the character of the terrorist persona. Approached from this angle, the relationship of the terrorist with ideology recasts ideology as both a construction of the ego and an object of personal property. The dominant ideologies of society are neither produced nor owned by the terrorist ego, and instead become obstructions that must be overcome. Through praxis, the terrorist loses control over ideology and the relationship becomes reversed, with the formerly "owned" idea becoming a new imposed morality. Destructive violence becomes the only kind of act that retains any meaning, as a negation of all potentially obstructive thought. Locating the origin of all values within an individual ego that seeks self-realisation through the destabilisation and destruction of value systems imposed on the ego from without, this attitude finds its origins in the "anarcho-psychological tradition" that Carroll describes in *Break-Out from the Crystal Palace* (1974). Carroll suggests that the shared perspective of this tradition emerged independently in the work of Max Stirner, Nietzsche and Dostoevsky in the mid-to-late nineteenth century.

The history of ego-terrorism

The egoistic terrorist persona and application of an anarcho-psychological critique of society are employed by terrorist writers as diverse as the revolutionary Karl Heinzen (1809–80), the Russian collectivist anarchist Sergey Nechaev (1847–82), the individualist anarchist Emma Goldman (1869–1940), the anti-colonial theorist Frantz Fanon (1925–61), the Red Army Faction leader Ulrike Meinhof (1934–76) and the poet-philosopher of political Islam, Muhammad Iqbal (1877–1938). In "Murder" (2004, originally 1849), Heinzen proposed that while all killing is undesirable, the state's claim of "special privilege" to the use of murder means it is the responsibility of revolutionaries to undermine the exclusivity of this right (2004: 58). He called murder "the principal agent of historical progress" (Heinzen, 2004: 57), and posited the need for weapons capable of giving "a few lone individuals the terrifying power to threaten whole masses of barbarians" (Heinzen, 2004: 65). Viewing terrorism as a pragmatic consequence of an already established egoism, he suggested that "egoists begin the murdering, and the men of ideas reply in kind," where "the 'ultima ratio' of both is quite simply the obliteration of their enemies" (Heinzen, 2004: 57). Moral outrage is, according to Heinzen, "closely linked to the self-interest of those reacting," and the "courageous bearing of the murderer seems to be of equal weight in the scales of judgement as the success of the attempt" (2004: 60). He suggested that murder is justified wherever it furthers self-interest and is committed with audacity, and in his own case this means the advancement of collectivist anarchism. It is not his ideology which he uses to justify killing, but an anarcho-psychological reading of the historical use of murder.

Another collectivist, Nechaev proposed in his *Catechism of the Revolutionist* (2004, originally 1869) that the revolutionary is required to break "every tie with the civil order and the entire cultured world, with all its laws, properties, social conventions, and its ethical rules" (2004: 71), and that all things are moral if they serve to foment revolution. By doing so he suggested even the ethics of socialism itself were no moral impediment to an act that brought the revolution closer to fruition, because the terrorist is not subject to ideology. The egoistic terrorist brings about ideological revolution by moving beyond notions of good and evil. Emma Goldman openly suggested in her preface to *Anarchism and Other Essays* (1917) her admiration for the work of both Stirner and Nietzsche. Nietzsche, she wrote "called for a state of society which will not give birth to a race of weaklings and slaves," while "Stirner's individualism contains the greatest social possibilities" and the necessary avenue to a liberated society (Goldman, 1917: 50). In her memoir, *Living My Life* (2006, originally 1934), Goldman recalled responding to the charge by her lover Edward Brady that Nietzsche's "ideal is the superman because he has no sympathy with or faith in the common herd," by arguing that Nietzsche's "aristocracy was neither of birth nor of purse; it was of the spirit" (2006: 126). She went on to suggest that "Nietzsche was an anarchist, and all true anarchists were aristocrats" (Goldman, 2006: 126), linking anarchist revolution to aristocratic egoism.

Fanon's first major work, *Black Skin, White Masks* (1986, originally 1952), is bookended by egoism. In the introduction, he recalled that "Man's tragedy, Nietzsche said, is that he was once a child," but that "we cannot afford to forget that, as Charles Odier has shown us, the neurotic's fate remains in his own hands" (1986: 12). The closing pages of the book first suggest his Stirnerian desire "[t]hat the tool never possess the man" (Fanon, 1986: 231), before evoking Nietzsche's aphorisms in a final prayer that implores, "O my body, make of me always a man who questions!" (Fanon, 1986: 232). More importantly, Fanon proposed a kind of violent action that, grounded in egoistic self-will, rises above *ressentiment*.[3] He suggested that consciousness desires to become absolute, and "wants to be recognized as a primal value without reference to life, as a transformation of subjective certainty (*Gewissheit*) into objective truth (*Wahrheit*)" (Fanon, 1986: 217–218). To this end, he proposes "actional" rather than "reactional" violence as a means of circumventing the resentment that exists in every instance of reaction, taking his cue from Nietzsche's *Will to Power* (1901) (Fanon, 1986: 222). Fanon came to ask, "Was my freedom not given to me then in order to build the world of the *You*?" (1986: 232), in an intonation of messianic egoism that proposes to remake the world in his own image and provide a model for others to remake it in their own. His objective was not dissimilar to that of the anarchism that preceded it, but involved substituting the institutionalised morality of whiteness for the institutionalised morality of the state.

Jeremy Varon's authoritative history of the Weather Underground Organisation and the Red Army Faction, *Bringing the War Home* (2004), suggests the importance of an egoistic ontology to the actions of the two groups. He proposes that both organisations attempted a path between ideological Marxism and ontological egoism, at once aspiring to transcend capitalist individualism and achieve self-realisation through the transgression of state-imposed morality (Varon, 2004: 9). Meinhof's observation that "[t]he progressive moment in the burning of a department store doesn't lie in the destruction of commodities but in the criminality of the act, its breaking of the law" was an expression of this kind of insurrectionary and egoist agenda (Meinhof quoted in Varon, 2004: 41). It can also be seen in the recollection of David Gilbert, a former member of the Weather Underground Organisation, that the purpose of a "push on sexuality was to defy society's norms and restrictions" (Gilbert, 2012: 140). Varon's argument that a "real" existence "for New Leftists meant 'being what one becomes upon rejection of the conventions' learned through one's mainstream socialization" (2004: 88) once again reiterates the importance of rejecting institutionalised morality to terrorist self-realisation.

Once the impetus to equate Islamist terrorism with religious dogmatism is set aside long enough to propose that it might share an egoistic vocation with its predecessors, the relationship can be traced to the inception of political Islam. The works of the poet-philosopher Muhammad Iqbal and the literary critic Sayyid Qutb are crucial to understanding the formation of this relationship. Iqbal was a central player both in the development of the independent state of Pakistan and of the evolution of political Islam. His major work in English, *The Reconstruction of Religious Thought in Islam* (2012, originally 1930), is a series of essays largely concerned with the renewal of Islamic thought in the context of modernity. In it he espoused a philosophy of Islam grounded in an existentialist reading of the Qur'an. The work blended together Nietzschean egoism and the prophetic archetype, and suggested that the self seeks "knowledge, self-multiplication, and power, or, in the words of the Qur'an, 'the kingdom that never faileth'" (Iqbal, 2012: 68). From this position, he went on to argue that "[t]here are no pleasure-giving and pain-giving acts; there are only ego-sustaining and ego-dissolving acts" (Iqbal, 2012: 95) and proposed a model of "the prophet" as an insurrectionary egoist who "returns to insert himself into the sweep of time with a view to control the forces of history, and thereby to create a fresh world of ideals" (Iqbal, 2012: 99). As one example of this prophetic mode of engagement with the world, he considered the importance of Muhammad Ibn 'Abd al-Wahhāb to asserting just this kind of insurrectionary private judgement (Iqbal, 2012: 121), and tied it by extension to the broader project of Islamic puritanism and fundamentalism of which jihadism now asserts itself as part.

Iqbal's metaphysical approach to Islam girds the theoretical work of the Islamic scholar Sayyid Qutb. The impact of Iqbal's thought was not to advocate political violence, but to imbue the Islamic perspective with a character that promoted active engagement with the world as a path to realisation. He politicised (or rather re-politicised) Islamic thought. Farzin Vahdat suggests that while Qutb viewed Iqbal as having over-glorified the human "self" in his work, he agreed that Islamic revival was inhibited by mysticism's passivity and rejection of the self (2015: 95). Participation in the modern world had to be grounded in an Islamic "personality" [*khudi*], which Iqbal's work sought to construct (Vahdat, 2015: 95). This influence is demonstrated by Qutb's construction of *jihad* in his essay "Jihad in the Cause of God" in *Milestones*. In it he suggested that in "calling Islamic jihad a defensive movement . . . we must change the meaning of the word 'defense' and mean by it 'the defense of man' against all those elements which limit his freedom," identifying that these "take the form of beliefs and concepts, as well as of political systems, based on economic, racial, or class distinctions" (Qutb, 2004: 349). He expounded a programme that shares its targets with those of Stirner and Nietzsche; the institutionalised morality of Western civilisation and the mythological thinking that underpins them.

The influence of Qutb's thought on Islamic terrorism was recognised in the United States government's *9/11 Commission Report*, which stated that

> Usama Bin Ladin and other Islamist terrorist leaders draw on a long tradition of extreme intolerance within one stream of Islam (a minority tradition), from at least Ibn Taimiyyah, through the founders of Wahhabism, through the Muslim Brotherhood, to Sayyid Qutb.
> (National Commission on Terrorist Attacks upon the United States, 2004: 362)

The Commission did not recognise the influence of a broader history of terrorism on the Islamic strain, or of Iqbal on Qutb's conception of the Islamic "personality" and its relationship to action. These shortcomings are typical of an attitude to the study of terrorism that regards it as a purely ideological phenomenon.

These connections emerge only when the question is raised of what ideology and action mean to terrorists on a personal level, and how they engage with the two to give their lives purpose.

Conclusion

The anarcho-psychological approach to existence need not be condemned out of hand. Reading Stirner and Nietzsche is not *ipso facto* a precursor of terrorism. Just as it is frequently displayed by terrorists, the egoistic character is common to a host of individualist archetypes including artists, writers and philosophers. Furthermore, there is an important distinction between the kind of praxis endorsed by Stirner, Nietzsche and Dostoevsky and that was endorsed by Heinzen, Goldman and Iqbal. The first group highlight the importance of inner struggle and of overcoming one's self, and for them, the spooks, mythologies and *idées fixes* of ideology can only be meaningfully challenged through acts of thought. On the other hand, terrorism is an outwardly directed manifestation of an anarcho-psychological critique of society. Rather than a programme of inwardly directed self-overcoming through reflection and criticism, it pursues self-exaltation through acts of other-overcoming. Terrorists demand that the public bear witness to assaults on the foundations of institutionalised morality as emblematic of the indomitability of their will. This difference is crucial to understanding the objectives of terrorism and trying to combat its spread.

It can seem compelling to dismiss the terrorist act as merely a demonstration of *ressentiment*, emerging from the inability of radical political activists to overcome existing political structures. The seductive lure of this analysis is nowhere more apparent than in Nietzsche's depiction of anarchists in *Thus Spoke Zarathustra*. Nietzsche, through his speaker Zarathustra's parable of the "fire-dog," criticised the superficiality of anarchist revolutionary violence (2003c: 153). Zarathustra portrays the anarchist fire-dogs as "inventors of new noises" rather than "new values" (Nietzsche, 2003c: 153). He suggests that he has "unlearned belief in 'great events' whenever there is much bellowing and smoke about them," and that greatness is instead to be found "not in our noisiest but our stillest hours" (Nietzsche, 2003c: 153). Nevertheless, Nietzsche suggests more is at play in the violence of anarchist revolutionaries of his time than outward manifestations of hatred emerging from a sense of inadequacy as demonstrated by the "spiders" of liberalism and socialism (2003c: 123–126). Rather than an idealised, inwardly directed attempt at *self*-overcoming, Nietzsche identifies in the anarchist struggle an outwardly directed (and in his view, degraded) form of *other*-overcoming. The terrorist has failed to heed Zarathustra's warning:

> The noble man wants to create new things and a new virtue. The good man wants the old things and that the old things be preserved.
>
> But that is not the danger for the noble man – that he may become a good man – but that he may become an impudent one, a derider, a destroyer.
>
> (Nietzsche, 2003c: 71)

Nietzsche's criticism of anarchist violence explains the capacity of egoistic terrorists to engage in seemingly irrational behaviour and transgress the moral tenets of even their own ideological frameworks. Carroll's reading of Nietzsche, along with Stirner and Dostoevsky, provides the means by which the terrorist persona can be examined as the product of a flawed attempt to confront the existential crisis produced by the conditions of modernity. Particularly when dealing with the leaders and demagogues of terrorist movements, the anarcho-psychological critique that Carroll provides in *Break-Out from the Crystal Palace* serves to curb the ubiquity of ideology in contemporary studies of terrorism. As a form of metaphysical critique, it serves as a gateway to a better understanding of the terrorist persona and the way it generates meaning by imposing its will on the flow of history.

Notes

1 The wave of suicide bombings beginning in the 1980s that were perpetrated by the Tamil Tigers in Sri Lanka are of note here, as they were not grounded in the notions of religious martyrdom and heavenly reward typically invoked when considering religious fundamentalists' willingness to sacrifice themselves. Instead, self-destruction represents the terrorist persona's symbolic victory over the moral law of the state. Death places the individual beyond the reach of the state and its laws, circumventing its capacity to respond. This view suggests that suicide attacks are not only used tactically, but are the natural outcome of the terrorist persona's distinct approach to the task of self-realisation.
2 In his foreword to the novel, Richard Pevear notes the influence of the murder of the young radical Ivan Ivanov "by a group consisting of two students, an older writer, and their leader, a hanger-on in university circles with credentials from the anarchist movement abroad, the twenty-two-year-old nihilist Sergei Nechaev" (2006: vii). The author of the terrorist manifesto *The Catechism of the Revolutionist* (1869), Nechaev became the basis for the character of Pyotr, who was indeed "called 'Nechaev' in the first sketches of the novel" (Dostoevsky, 2006: viii).
3 Nietzsche discusses his own conceptualisation of *ressentiment* most clearly in the first essay of *The Genealogy of Morals*, where he portrays it as "a resentment experienced by creatures who, deprived as they are of the proper outlet of action, are forced to find their compensation in an imaginary revenge" (Nietzsche, 2003b: 19).

References

Adorno TW (1973) *Negative Dialectics*. London: Routledge.
Adorno TW (2005) *Critical Models: Interventions and Catchwords*. New York: Columbia University Press.
Bell A (2014) Notes on Adorno's "Resignation." *TELOSscope*, 23 April. Available at www.telospress.com/notes-on-adornos-resignation.
Carroll J (1974) *Break-Out from the Crystal Palace: The Anarcho-Psychological Critique: Stirner, Nietzsche, Dostoevsky*. London: Routledge.
Carroll J (2002) *Terror: A Meditation on the Meaning of September 11*. Carlton: Scribe.
Chertoff M (2008) The Ideology of Terrorism: Radicalism Revisited. *Brown Journal of World Affairs* 15: 11–20.
Dostoevsky F (1864) *Notes from Underground*. London: Vintage.
Dostoevsky F (1866) *Crime and Punishment*. Oxford: Oxford University Press.

Dostoevsky F (2006) *Demons*. London: Vintage.
Durkheim É (2002) *Suicide*. London: Routledge.
Eagleton T (2010) *On Evil*. New Haven, CT: Yale University Press.
Fanon F (1986) *Black Skin, White Masks*. Leichhardt, NSW: Pluto.
Furedi F (2014) Youth Rebellion that Embraces Authority. *The Australian*. Surry Hills.
Gilbert D (2012) *Love and Struggle: My Life in SDS, the Weather Underground, and Beyond*. Oakland, CA: PM Press.
Goldman E (1917) *Anarchism and Other Essays*. New York: Mother Earth.
Goldman E (2006) *Living My Life*. New York: Penguin.
Heinzen K (2004) Murder. In: Laqueur W (ed) *Voices of Terror: Manifestos, Writings and Manuals of Al Qaeda, Hamas, and other Terrorists from Around the World and Throughout the Ages*. Naperville, IL: Sourcebooks, 57–70.
Iqbal M (2012) *The Reconstruction of Religious Thought in Islam*. Stanford, CA: Stanford University Press.
Law RD (2009) *Terrorism: A History*. Cambridge: Polity.
National Commission on Terrorist Attacks Upon the United States (2004) *The 9/11 Commission Report*. New York: Norton.
Nechaev S (2004) Catechism of the Revolutionist. In: Laqueur W (ed) *Voices of Terror: Manifestos, Writings and Manuals of Al Qaeda, Hamas, and Other Terrorists from Around the World and Throughout the Ages*. Naperville, IL: Sourcebooks, 71–75.
Nietzsche F (1901) *The Will to Power*. London: Weidenfeld and Nicolson.
Nietzsche F (2003a) *Beyond Good and Evil*. London: Penguin.
Nietzsche F (2003b) *The Genealogy of Morals*. New York: Dover.
Nietzsche F (2003c) *Thus Spoke Zarathustra*. London: Penguin.
Qutb S (2004) Jihad in the Cause of God. In: Laqueur W (ed) *Voices of Terror: Manifestos, Writings and Manuals of Al Qaeda, Hamas, and other Terrorists from Around the World and Throughout the Ages*. Naperville, IL: Sourcebooks, 394–397.
Rapoport DC (2004) The Four Waves of Modern Terrorism. In: Cronin AK (ed) *Attacking Terrorism: Elements of a Grand Strategy*. Washington D.C.: Georgetown University Press, 46–73.
Scaff LA (2000) Weber on the Cultural Situation of the Modern Age. In: Turner S (ed) *The Cambridge Companion to Weber*. Cambridge: Cambridge University Press.
Stirner M (1995) *The Ego and Its Own*. Cambridge: Cambridge University Press.
Vahdat F (2015) *Islamic Ethos and the Specter of Modernity*. London: Anthem.
Varon JP (2004) *Bringing the War Home: The Weather Underground, the Red Army Faction, and Revolutionary Violence in the Sixties and Seventies*. Berkeley, CA: University of California Press.
Weber M (1970) Science as a Vocation. In: Gerth HH and Mills CW (ed) *From Max Weber: Essays in Sociology*. London: Routledge.

11 Mortality, time and embodied finitude

Margaret Gibson

Introduction

Mortality is our reckoning with time as embodied finitude:

> the resource of life in the finitude of time, that is to say, in death itself – requires us to surrender ourselves unreservedly to the fear that it arouses, and reconcile ourselves to remaining constantly in its grip. But leaving the governing of life to this nothing that is death, implies neither nihilistic heroism nor nostalgic regret. In the tragicomedy of a life which, far from recoiling before death, takes death into account, it demands rather the conjoining of grief and joy, of laughter and tears.
>
> (Dastur, 1996: 3)

This quote from the French philosopher Françoise Dastur speaks to a style of thinking about mortality encountered in John Carroll's "metaphysical sociology". Indeed, the tragic-comedy of modern life is a theme in much of Carroll's work (2001, 2008). Carroll reminds us that death is at the heart of modern tragedy as the perennial search for meaning in myths, religion and art. These forms of storytelling and aesthetics both represent and expose our ongoing struggle with mortality. And while life expectancy particularly amongst globally economic advantaged classes has been extended due to advances in health care, nutrition, disease control and medicine, it can have the effect of psychologically distancing death's reality inevitability lurking beneath the "surface" of our everyday lives (Carroll, 2014: 562). Moreover, what is perhaps felt even more acutely in a first world where consumerist comforts and life-extending medicines buffer death's immediacy is the need to salvage meaning and beauty out of the fleeting and fragile (Carroll, 2008).

The question, "how should we live?" – which is the Janus face of "how should we die?" – is a metaphysical sociological question at the centre of Carroll's work (2014). It goes hand-in-hand with a sceptical sociology that rejects the fantasies of "youthful idealism" (Carroll, 1980: 3) and an arrogant moralism of prescriptive, pious or dogmatic sociologies:

We should not expect too much of our knowledge, remembering that our minds are feeble in the face of Goliath reality, and that doubt and wit lead one further away from falsehood than do dogma and piety. Which is not to mock all seriousness, but to ensure that the intellectual's traditional inclination towards righteous indignation in defence of his [sic] certitudes is put off-balance.

(Carroll, 1980: 3)

As a sociologist of late modernity, Carroll's work heeds the fall in the historical practice of the grand narratives of modern political philosophy – notably, but not only, Marxism with its revolutionary idealism and terrifying realities (1980: 4). It is not uncritical of the market-driven rationalities of capitalism and its destructive and dehumanising logics (Carroll, 2008). Metaphysical sociology respects the question, and specifically the foundational questions that continue to impact human beings. It is neither naïve nor cynical in its response to the legacies of enlightenment thought and specifically humanist philosophy. It is perhaps more than anything hopeful while circumspect in its explorations of the modern human condition, moving and weaving its narrative in non-linear directions from the present into the past and the past into the present. Carroll does not turn away from the legacies of Western thought or denigrate the continuing value of high art and philosophy: "It is art that works at the frontier of our understanding, taking account of changing times, helping us to understand the world we inhabit, and our place within it" (2011: 216). Focusing on the important questions of human existence in late modernity, Carroll's work asks questions such as: how should we live and find meaning in a secular, godless world? How and where do people in secular society find beauty, awe and moments of transcendence? Is death the end of our individual story and does this matter? These types of questions are important precisely because "religious answers have waned, and individuals are subject to the dispiriting possibility that the random and the absurd rule the human condition" (Carroll, 2014: 562).

In the spirit of homage to Carroll's embrace of aesthetics and narrative forms, this chapter takes as its key text the film *Amour* (2012) by the Austrian auteur Michael Haneke. Through undertaking a close reading of this film, the chapter considers the question "how should we die?" in an age where secular democracies and first-world economies are governed by the institutionalisation and medicalisation of ageing and death. For many in the secularised West, the historical time of God as the giver and taker of life has been surpassed by advanced medical technologies that both create and support life beyond the capacity of mortal bodies. God, imagined as a transcendental signifier, can operate as a boundary point or limit enabling human decision-making and agency. This does not mean that God exists or is a specifically religious principle; it simply means that she/he/it functions as a frontier through which we dare to traverse as well as comfortably work within.

The question, "how should we die?", also presupposes that the history of human science and medicine has transformed the human body and the natural world to the point that the notion of "a natural death" is a contested idea. Medicine's capacity to extend the limits of our lifespan in providing machines that support our bodies beyond their mortal capacity already creates moral crisis in hospitals and law courts around the world. In this context, the resilient question "how should we die?" is ever-more prescient as it brings to the fore a number of conflicting divisions between the secular state and religious institutions as well as underlining the differences between secular and scientific world-views that can jar against religious value systems. The urgency of protecting the vulnerable is foremost to the difficult task of addressing the question of dying since human law is as fallible as human religion. Perhaps one can only be vigilant in protecting the vulnerable – the dying, the very old, the disabled and other marginal groups whose agency is often circumvented by institutional frameworks.

This chapter does not seek to provide definitive or prescriptive answers to the question of "how should we die?". Rather it responds to this question in a manner that provokes thinking and questioning. Haneke is a perfect fit for a Carrollian style of sociology since his films never settle upon on any secure foundations or moral answers that would immediately impose a boundary or limit upon thinking and contemplation. Haneke's films, like Carroll's writings, shake us up because they trace the tragedy of the quotidian.

In "Death and the Modern Imagination", Carroll develops an important thesis which frames the argument and central concerns of this chapter. He writes:

> The modern era opens, metaphysically speaking, with Hamlet and Don Quixote. Hamlet's first significant encounter is with death, in the form of the ghost of his murdered father. His most powerful love scene takes place in the graveyard reminiscing tenderly to the skull of Yorick, the Court Jester who had played with him as a boy. His one "felicity", as he calls it, is to die. Hamlet confronts us with the big modern question: "To be or not to be?" . . . It is a long meditation on suicide, on whether Hamlet should kill himself . . . The encounter with death, which has paralysed him, has also emptied him of any capacity for saving illusions . . . Hamlet illustrates Tolstoy's later dictum that if death becomes meaningless then so does life.
>
> (2014: 562–563)

The modern condition is one of existential fragility in the capacity to sustain a meaningful existence in the face of death without salvation or redemption in some beyond or afterlife. Carroll suggests that the depressive mode, which is Hamlet's fate, is the default condition of modernity where meaning, purpose and saving illusions (religious or otherwise) so easily fall away to expose us to the nothingness beneath and beyond our life in the here and now. It is important to grasp that this "depressive condition" marked in the character of Hamlet cannot be saved by calling it a psychological or mental illness requiring treatment or cure. There is no cure or saving for this existential condition. Psychology and psychiatry may provide therapeutic remedies but when they conceal our true condition as time-bound mortal beings, they – like religion – become a comforting illusion. We are fragile when our lives and the lives of others go awry and we must look to what we have left of value or meaning in order to stave off utter despair.

Bonds of love strengthened and supported by the aesthetic and natural worlds of art and beauty are central in sustaining a meaningful life in late modernity. The ability of art to transport us beyond the here and now can be powerfully expressed in film, and Haneke's extraordinary aesthetic triumph *Amour* (2012) is exemplary. What also makes this film particularly efficacious is its representation of the quotidian. We are granted rare access into the lives of a bourgeoisie couple whose world is enriched by a shared love of beauty and art. They are a couple whose love for each other cannot be separated from their love of art, and especially music.

The subject matter of this film intersects with debates about assisted suicide or assisted dying (voluntary and involuntary, physician or non-physician assisted). The film also speaks to the vulnerabilities of old age, particularly when compounded by illness and disabling circumstances. Like death and dying, the ageing in first-world cultures and economies is subject to institutionalised and medicalised trajectories: the longer people live, the more institutionalised they are likely to become. Gillard and Higgs speak of this in terms of "ageing without agency" (2010) and identify this as a significant issue for those in the fourth age – those over eighty years of age whose disease profiles and frailties make them vulnerable to the decision-making of others. There is also a narrowing of what I call "spatial citizenship" in the reduced presence/visibility of elderly citizens occupying and moving through public spaces, shopping centres, parks, beaches and so on. The frail elderly can so easily become anomalous bodies, subjects-out-of-place, when they appear in the cut and thrust of busy city-spaces. In a "risk society" (Beck, 1992) the priority of safety, above freedom of movement, reduces the likelihood of a vulnerable sector of society maintaining visible citizenship across a range of social or public spaces. Those advanced in age rarely die outside death's regular and regulated institutions – private homes, aged care facilities, nursing homes and hospitals. The consequence is that the reality of death becomes a "shock"; perhaps even a "trauma" in cultural geographies that control the risk of affective exposure and witnessing of human vulnerability (Gibson, 2011).

There is loss and grief for the aged parent or grandparent who becomes institutionalised by an aged care facility. In first-world, late modernity most people are born and will die in hospitals or aged care facilities. Advanced age usually means transitioning into care facilities of some kind when a disease profile or capacity to be provided with in-home support becomes precarious, unavailable or inadequate. Of course, in the context of the first-world economies of America, most of Europe and Australia, the capacity for families to pay for their loved one's institutionalisation can determine the level and quality of their life as well as death. These are big issues and areas of research that this chapter cannot fully address, but they are part of *Amour*'s (2012) implicit and explicit sociological narrative and ethical perspective.

What is a beautiful death?

Amour (2012) begins with a death scene. Set in Paris and within the confines of a bourgeois apartment, the opening scene shows police breaking down the front door of an apartment. Entering the space of the hallway, they are confronted by the putrefied smell of death. Covering their noses, they must break down yet another door – the door to a bedroom tightly sealed by duct tape from top to bottom. This bedroom is a tomb and upon entering we see the corpse of an elderly woman. Flowers surround her body and are on the bed in which she lies. This might be a beautiful death and it might still be in the image of a beautiful death, but the body has rotted. Was it a beautiful death? What does that mean? Can it still be a beautiful death when the body is in advanced decay as well as age? The *mise-en-scène* references nineteenth-century images of the beautiful death, calling to mind Klimt's painting of Ria Munk on her deathbed. However, the deceased woman of *Amour* (2012) is old and while her body is lovingly presented, we do not see any signs of life. This is not human mortality masked by youthful beauty. It is devoid of the Eros of Klimt's image and the visual legacy of virginal sleeping beauty images of nineteenth-century romanticism. Klimt's young woman looks as if she could just be sleeping, easily aroused to wakefulness. Is hers a beautiful death because she is young and in showing no signs of decay doesn't look quite dead enough? *Amour* (2012) exposes us, our investments in youthful bodies that appear unmarked by time, suffering and struggle – those signs of not having lived a long life. This subtle over-exposure of the beautiful death image overwrites the mask of romanticism, revealing it for what it is. And this is done in the image of a beautiful death as an act of loving care towards the dead body of an elderly woman.

The "death scene" does still offer transcendence in its affinity with art – the fact that one can align the dead body with Klimt is also a way of aestheticising and also of "coping" with what is most confronting. A body without a veil of flowers – without its evocations of romanticism – would be perhaps too difficult

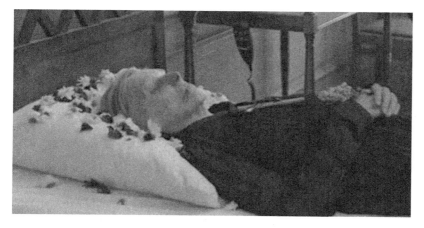

Figure 11.1 Still from *Amour* (2012) directed by Michael Haneke.

130 *Margaret Gibson*

Figure 11.2 Ria Munk on her Deathbed (1917–18), Gustav Klimt.

to witness. But it is also a death that befits a woman who we learn has lived a beautiful life not through consumerism or obvious luxuries, but through making a life that embraces thinking, music, literature and thoughtful conversation. It is a "beautiful death" because it "has meaning: it brings to fulfilment a life full of meaning; this death gets over itself, overtakes or sublates itself, in this meaning" (Lyotard, 1988: 237). This idea is important because it suggests that death can be the completion of a meaningful life, its very fulfilment. The crucial argument is that we do not have to search beyond death for meaning, nor do we have to align/equate death with meaninglessness. Death is equally a creative source and shelter for meaning, as well as its emptying out, withdrawal or evacuation.

Love and death

Amour (2012) asks but does not definitely answer: how long should a dying loved one be kept alive without this becoming a form of harm to oneself and others? When and how might we harm or even bring each other to the point of existential death by extending the life span of a sick beloved? Anne wants to die while others desire her to want to live. Love and violence are not separated as opposing relations in this film. On the contrary, it is when human beings think they can separate the two that morality is most in danger of its worst failures or abuses. Loving deeply and fully is not a passive experience; rather, it is an intense and potentially violent emotion. This is partly what the film asks us to consider, and it also suggests that violence cannot be side-stepped or overcome in first-world cultures of medicalised death scenes where the beloved undergoes a "peaceful" departure from the world. The peaceful might "look good" but can be equally sinister as bad faith.

Beginning with a death scene, the film *Amour* (2012) proceeds to take us into the story of that death, chronicling the intimate routines of an elderly heterosexual couple. Haneke's cinematic style prevents the viewer from adopting a position of comfort in thwarting a sense of distance between viewer and subject matter. The effect can be intrusive, even violent, as characteristically Haneke challenges us to think and to feel the moral implications of what is being enacted within the cinematic frame. In most Haneke films we are watched as we watch, and experience moments of watching ourselves watching. This is particularly intense and fraught in *The Seventh Continent* (1989), *Funny Games* (2007) and *Cache* (2005). There is also the experience of being watched but not knowing who is doing the watching. Lebeau writes, "part of the work of Haneke's cinema is to look back at its audience by looking at looking, even perhaps to use cinema to make a difference to looking" (2009: 43). This style of filmmaking deploys a stylistic ethics, rejecting voyeurism. One does not "feel good" after watching Haneke films as he refuses to adopt a conventional point of view enabling spectators a means of escape that is connected with providing comfortable, familiar moralities and narrative resolutions. There is then a resistance to conform to narrative conventions whereby closure is achieved. Within the time frame of the film and long afterwards, one feels morally exposed and unsettled, even torn apart by irresolvable contradictions in *Amour* (2012). Such irresolution exposes an uncomfortable truth revealing life and death's intertwining. Characteristically, institutions discipline bodies as well as regulating their dying, whereas Haneke brings to light the fact that we are at heart messy creatures whose life and death are complex and rife with conflict.

After the death scene in *Amour* (2012), the film cuts to the past where we are transported to a theatrical performance. Interestingly, Haneke's camera once more adopts an unsettling position as it is filmed as if we the audience are on the stage looking out to those watching the staged event (which turns out to be a classical piano concert). By framing the scene in this manner Haneke again creates a sense of discomfort as we are positioned looking out at an audience who is in turn looking back at us. Being positioned on the stage reverses the relationship between film and spectator. We do not know what this concert is about or whom we should be focusing on – the subject matter is undecided and the point of view mobile. After the concert we see an elderly couple sitting together on a busy bus looking happily engaged in their conversation. It is only at the opening of the apartment door that we gain any certainty that these are the subjects of the film, this is where they live, and we, the viewer, will take up residence with them. We never leave the apartment of Anne and Georges from this time onwards – they might come and go (though not much) but we do not. We cannot escape. This is important because the film is revealing that hidden-ness or invisibility of a change in the lives of a couple whose ageing has come upon them by a difficult turn. In other words, the sequestration of vulnerabilities of ageing in the home as the alternative to becoming institutionalised can be seen as a framework in this film's domestic intimacy.

The couple and the cinematic spectator are imprisoned within a world without an outside. The film does not cut to images of nature, to spaces and places in Paris beyond the apartment, and thereby open up contexts to provide relief from what is going on inside. And moreover, perhaps the only outside is death itself as no-place. What we learn of the couple's past, even of their relationship towards things like nature, is through spoken stories, photo albums or romantic art works on their walls. Before Anne's death we are shown framed paintings of rural life in a style that befits a romantic sensibility. These aesthetic objects and narrative forms operate as loving code for Anne and Georges whose life is framed and rendered beautiful through representational art forms as well as storytelling. We realise quite quickly that Anne and Georges are an educated, culturally rich couple with successful careers. Georges is a musicologist and pianist, and Anne is an exceptional piano teacher and pianist in her own right who has taught an internationally famous pianist specialising in the works of Schubert. The apartment *mise-en-scène* tells the story of their life. Notably it has a grand piano, evoking the couple's embrace of the arts. It is also filled with gorgeous furnishings such as a Persian rug, large wall tapestry, books, CDs and paintings: these aesthetic forms define each individual as well as their married life.

As a middle-class couple with financial means, they can afford private care in the home. This is a portrait of dying, love and death in a particular cultural and class context. This does not mean that the film should be read negatively through the prism of class and subject to a mode critique through a discourse of social inequality pointing out privileged, middle-class ways of death and dying. This is not without critical value – there are vast inequalities in how people die that speak to profound injustices in access to medicine, care and pain relief. But such an approach to this film would effectively erase its specific ethical and aesthetic orientation. It is also ethically beholden upon us to judge the film upon what it seeks to achieve. Indeed, the film already knows that Anne has had a privileged existence, and she herself says to Georges that her life has been long and beautiful.

As a cinematic form of *ars moriendi* (Knox, 2006), the film places the viewer in an experience of love and death in the everyday reciprocities of caring for the existence of another. It depicts the minutia of everyday care-giving and taking. Georges routinely gets and takes Anne's coat off; Anne boils him an egg for breakfast and takes it to him. This is a domestic routine that is also a love ritual. We watch them and hear them chewing their food so that the corporeality of existence is exposed through non-diegetic sound. Haneke's decision to open his film with Anne's death scene displaces conventional storytelling and especially the temporality of the romantic tragedy narrative whereby the film is structurally organised around the climactic death scene. Doggedly against traditional forms of narrativity, the film also does not try to sentimentalise love by denying its corporeality. Love does not go beyond the body – it is inscribed within our very mortality and the small gestures and acts of care we do for those we love.

In this film the materiality of love is an ethics of life in its corporeal finitude (Dima, 2015). This ethics is also about witnessing love in the story of ageing bodies – bodies that are traditionally unloved in cinema and not given any central place in conventional cinema. As Grønstad writes,

> mature love . . . remains out-of-bounds. The subject of love and romance in the movies typically involves young people whereas what *Amour* (2012) offers is a portrait of love at its most unromantic moment. This is in perfect keeping with Haneke's professed authorial politics, his silent manifesto, which is to create representations of those aspects of reality deliberately elided by mainstream cinema.
>
> (2013: 189)

Haneke shows us what other directors and mainstream films won't. He tells the truth of our frailty and mortality, the difficulty of ageing and losing autonomy.

The beautiful life that Anne and Georges have together is disrupted one morning at breakfast when Anne suddenly goes still, sitting at the kitchen table. She is in a trance-like state and Georges, puzzled, tries to wake her. He grabs a cloth, wets it and wipes her face and neck in the hope this will stimulate a response. It doesn't work. He leaves the table, goes to the bedroom and prepares to dress himself to get a doctor. From the bedroom, he hears her come back to life and goes to her. Georges has a limp and shuffles in his movement – he can only go so fast. His embodiment is *already* vulnerable, just as hers has clearly become. He tries to explain to Anne what just happened – she has no recollection. It is only after she reaches for the teapot to pour a cup that she knows there is something very wrong. She misses the cup, spills the tea all over the table and a knowing look is exchanged. Anne has had a stroke from which she will never recover. The rhythm of their life together has been disrupted where the (e)quality of giving and taking care is irrevocably changed. An inequality has entered the fray. Georges must care for Anne and she must accept that care, knowing that she cannot reciprocate in the same way. Haneke captures the materiality of everyday life as it undergoes a series of transitions, adaptions and uncertainties through the ageing process.

When Anne returns home from the hospital, Georges has already met with their adult daughter Eva who offers help. Her love can be sensed as more conditional – she has her own children, a marriage relationship and financial worries. After Anne's return from the hospital, Georges, under Anne's guidance, lifts her from her wheelchair and they do a kind of intimate dance as they struggle to get Anne into a lounge chair so they can sit facing each other in their twin velvet chairs. Their bodies are up against each other, their breathing heavy, laboured, so that the signs and sounds of Eros are inscribed between bodies struggling to stay together, adapt and make their life still work. This scene is so intimate with delicate echoes of time inscribed through the shared history of their bodies in their togetherness. As they sit facing each other, the following conversation transpires:

Georges: I am so pleased to have you back.
Anne: Me too. [She leans forward] Promise me something.
Georges: What?
Anne: Please, never take me back to the hospital. [Pause/silence]
Georges: What? Anne [he says her name in a soft pleading voice]
Anne: Will you promise me? Promise me? Don't speak. [Pause/silence] Don't explain. Please.
Georges: What can I say?
Anne: Nothing. Say nothing. Okay?

In Western medicalised societies hospices give the dying a place to die amongst the dying, and hospitals become the most likely places where people will die. Anne does not want to die in hospital and find herself undergoing further treatments – she wants to remain at her home. However, she also does not want to linger in a state of incapacity and find herself alienated within her own being.

The film meditates on this question of how people face their decline and death under the care of a loved one who witnesses their demise, seeking to existentially shelter the beloved with a special regard for their individuality. Georges not only witnesses the kind of abuse and disregard Anne faces with paid care, even under his supervision, but is confronted by his capacity to inflict abuse. Love and violence are fragile, and even at times intertwining. Georges keeps trying to sustain Anne's life through care-giving. He has already asked her to imagine a reversal of circumstance where he wants her to withdraw life-sustaining care. In an important turning point scene, Georges holds the sip cup to her mouth but she keeps refusing to drink. He pleads with her but her mouth is shut tight and what she has not yet swallowed she defiantly spits out. In a reflex Georges slaps her across the face, shocking himself along with Anne. It is a violation of their relationship and source of shame: it is also a scene that prefigures her violent death by his hands.

Death and violence

The question and place of violence is complex in *Amour* (2012). In refusing to drink, Anne is exercising her will in wishing to die. She is telling him, while she still can, what she wants. The meeting between her wish to die and his to keep her alive is a conflict and divide. They are at odds: if he keeps her alive it will be his will against hers, and if he lets her die or rather hastens the timing of her death, it will be her will he is respecting over his own. However, even as she deteriorates in her capacity to communicate, Anne and Georges still have moments of fleeting pleasure. While *Amour* charts/represents Anne's decline as a series of losses of bodily control and communicative functions, it stops short of arriving at some imagined zero point where there is nothing left to lose. That would be ethically dangerous and arrogant, and call for the moral suspicion and scepticism that Carroll instructs. To inscribe the idea of reaching zero while Anne is still breathing would morally let Georges off the hook and release him from an infinite responsibility beyond death.

The position for or against assisted suicide is not made explicit in the film. It does not locate itself in any obvious way in debates to determine a decisive position or dominant line of thinking in contrast to films such as *The Sea Inside* (Amenábar, 2004), which are more explicitly engaging with these debates. In fact, the film suggests that there is always a measure of violence in human action or inaction to prolong or hasten the death of someone in a grave situation. Georges may have prolonged Anne's physical existence yet he cannot control the waning of her spiritual life and strengthening desire to die. Georges does kill Anne while she is still conscious enough to be self-aware – albeit barely. Once more disrupting the comfortable realm of being a spectator, Georges' violence seems unpremeditated. The death scene, which is also a murder, comes as a surprise as he suffocates his wife after sharing a childhood memory never before articulated.

Before the shock moment of suffocation, Georges' story echoes an earlier tale he tells Anne about an experience he had as a young man coming home proudly from the cinema because his parents had allowed him to go by himself. He tells Anne of walking home from the cinema and running into an older boy who asks where he has been. He wishes that he had not encountered this older boy but nevertheless he tells him he has been to the cinema. The young man asks him what the film was about and as Georges begins to narrate the film to the young man, he becomes overwhelmed by emotion and begins to cry. It was a profoundly revealing moment etched in his memory. But Anne misrecognises the meaning of this story and asks Georges what the young man did when he started crying. And Georges says he doesn't remember because the mortification did not matter. What mattered was that he discovered that it was only in recounting and sharing the story that he could access and encounter its deep affectivity and meaning. Through this anecdote, Haneke once more meditates upon the complex relationship between seeing and being seen: witnessing and bearing witness, and how this is enacted through both storyteller and spectator.

The act of storytelling brings the past into the present and is central to this film, since it brings into being what might be called an ethics of decision-making. Georges uses stories not only to calm Anne down but also to enable an ethical sensibility to develop through the process of narration that is also movement in memory. Carroll places great importance on stories and their capacity to direct thought, feeling and action in the modern world in which there is no stable moral centre or compass. The provisional nature of morality in modern life is always difficult. Even the universal command "thou shalt not kill" is brought into question where people survive (rather than live) as hollowed-out bodies.

Georges' storytelling is pivotal to his decision-making. But we cannot really say that the decision to kill Anne is the right thing to do – this directional moral term is already faulty in its potential to open up a Pandora's box of hubris that can come with moral certainty and rigidity (Degnin, 1997). Sitting on what is now Anne's deathbed, Georges strokes her hand and tells another story from his childhood. He says, "Shall I tell you a story?" Carroll engages with the existential authority of narrative in guiding human beings towards nuggets of truth. Without the ordering principle of narrative, we are potentially left with nothing in which to express the depth and surface of our humanity (2001). Importantly, storytelling operates as a binding agent in connecting us with our past and present.

Georges uses stories to connect with his wife and contemplate his own life. At this point in the film, Anne is gravely diminished with no light in her eyes. For some time now she has been wearing diapers and calls out "hurt hurt" and sometimes "mom". This in turn initiates another story where Georges recounts his own attachment to his mother. Anne's regression is mirrored in Georges' storytelling: in a way he is seeking to forge a new relationship with her in a netherworld of shreds of memories as well as forgetfulness. These stories that come from within George have not been told to Anne before. The final story that Georges narrates to Anne reminisces over his time at a summer camp in an old castle when he was ten. The food was awful and on the third day they were served rice pudding as the dessert. In refusing to eat it, the camp counsellor tells him that he can't leave the lunchroom until it is eaten. Saying how much he detests rice pudding, he folds the past into the present, connecting unconsciously, we suppose, his childhood refusal to eat with Anne's, and his sense of disempowerment with that of hers. Georges and his mother had made a secret pact before he left for camp. He would send her a card and if he was enjoying the camp he was to draw flowers and if not, stars. She kept that card, he said, and it was covered in stars. This incident brought on an illness that same day and, taken from camp to the nearest hospital, Georges was kept in isolation. His mother was called but she could only wave to him through the glass. While Georges and his mother are connected and separated through the glass, they are exposed to each other as unable to touch. Again the tension between seeing and being seen is enacted here through glass.

This figuration of a mother and son being separated and connected by glass parallels the experience of watching a film. It also foregrounds the frustration of looking but being unable to touch the other, and in this case the maternal body. The yearning for the mother's touch and body exposes a primordial ground upon which we all come into being. This is also Anne's relationship to her mother who, in calling to her, is addressing her absence beyond touch. It is also Georges and Anne's relationship to each other – she has gone beyond him and they are beyond each other's capacity to truly touch each other's lives in a meaningful way. They have become existentially separated and there is nothing more to be done.

In finishing the story and stroking Anne's hand, Georges becomes quietly agitated, uncertain about what to do next, and then slowly takes a pillow and puts it on her face; putting all his weight onto her, he presses down. Her body struggles to breathe; her legs push against the act of suffocation. It is violent and horrifying.

Her body struggles against the weight of his – the instinct to live, to breathe, speaks to the truth of the body, its own mode of survival and will to live. She may have wanted to die in her mind's mind but her body's mind tells another story. Again, this is an irresolvable contradiction, an irreconcilable difference at the heart of Haneke's film where ethics comes into being through transgression.

Conclusion

Haneke has not chosen an easy death for us to witness. In fact, his cinematic style complicates the very act of witnessing. We are implicated in Anne's death and in so doing internally carry the film beyond its initial screening. He has not created a narrative in which Georges kills Anne in a pre-mediated act where he might have secured a large amount of sleeping pills to administer. This might have created the image of a good death in a death scene where Anne's body shows no visible signs of struggle. Would this be any less violent to have her unconscious and utterly passive? Haneke is not offering any escape from the moral ambiguity, even horror of this scene. As viewers, we don't escape responsibility and are not given a moral centre or position from which to assess any ethical certainty about Georges' action. What we know is that in re-telling this story Georges arrives at an agitated, unsettling moment of decision-making.

Humans often look to their own parents in facing their own imminent death – soldiers call to their mothers on the battlefield, and deathbed visions of seeing one's mother or father are part of the human story of how we die *relationally* rather than alone in our imaginations and fantasies. This is an important recognition tempering an existential emphasis on our aloneness in death (Elias, 1985). Earlier in *Amour* (2012), Georges tries to keep Eva away from seeing Anne, her mother. He wants to hide Anne's true condition in order to protect her from Eva's inclination to suggest that she should be in hospital. Eva enters the bedroom and, leaning over her mother, gently strokes her face. It is a poignant moment of the touch of the child that is profound in the life of a parent, especially in the experience of feeding a child at the breast or with a bottle where a baby will often stroke the mother or father's face. As Eva strokes her mother, she gently says "maman", calling or summoning her into being as *her* mother. This is echoed in Anne who also calls out "maman". She answers Eva's call but she is also calling to her own mother. Georges witnesses this scene and realises that he must understand Eva's grief, her relational position to her origin and touchstone of being.

The film poignantly shows how human beings call out to the dead and to the soon to be dead as the dying prepare themselves to go nowhere; that is, the nowhere place of death as nothingness. Eva calls for her mother because she will be left behind and at the close of the film this is exactly what we see – Eva sitting on one of the chairs of the parental living room, alone, but also surrounded by the aesthetic legacies, the remainders of the beautiful life of her departed parents.

Media screen culture is saturated with death imagery but this does not mean that death is connected to the subject of mortality. The splitting of death from the question of mortality is pervasive, if not evasive, in this very saturation. And yet, we must look to narrative and representational culture in its forms to find contemporary examples of *ars moriendi*. Carroll's existential sociology and Haneke's existential films direct us to this question while challenging moral certitudes. *Amour* (2012) does not provide moral certitude or direction in terms of how and when Anne should die. It remains contestable. We are called to an ethics of un-decidability, which is not fence sitting in the absence of a decisive moral position or directive for action. It is first and foremost an equivocation, the "fear and trembling" (Degnin, 1997) that should be prior to any moment of giving death to another. *Amour* (2012) respects the art of questioning that is also central to Carroll's sociology. And while a viewer may impose a moral compass on this film, in doing so they will not be vulnerable to an ethical exposure it implicitly asks us to embrace.

References

Amour, Director and Screenplay Michael Haneke, 2012, film location: France.
Beck U (1992) *Risk Society: Towards a New Modernity*. Ritter M (trans), London: Sage.
Carroll J (1977) *Puritan, Paranoid, Remissive: A Sociology of Modern Culture*. London: Routledge & Kegan Paul.
Carroll J (1980) *Sceptical Sociology*. London, Boston, MA and Henley: Routledge & Kegan Paul.
Carroll J (2001) *The Western Dreaming: The Western World Is Dying for Want of Story*. Sydney: Harper Collins.
Carroll J (2008) *Ego and Soul: The Modern West in Search of Meaning*. Melbourne: Scribe.
Carroll J (2011) Beauty Contra God: Has Aesthetics Replaced Religion in Modernity? *Journal of Sociology* 48 (2): 206–223.
Carroll J (2014) Death and the Modern Imagination. *Culture and Society* 51: 562–566.
Degnin FD (1997) Levinas and the Hippocratic Oath: A Discussion of Physician-Assisted Suicide. *The Journal of Medicine and Philosophy* 22: 99–123.
Dastur F (1996) *Death: An Essay on Finitude*. Llewelyn J (trans), London and Atlantic Highlands, NJ: Athlone.
Dima V (2015) Sound, Death and Amour. *Studies in French Cinema* 15 (2): 168–179.
Elias N (1985) *The Loneliness of the Dying*. Oxford: Blackwell.
Gibson M (2011) Real-Life Death: Between Public and Private, Interior and Exterior, the Real and the Fictional. Special issue. *South Atlantic Quarterly* 110 (4): 917–932.
Gillard C and Higgs P (2010) Aging without Agency: Theorizing the Fourth Age. *Aging and Mental Health* 14 (2): 121–128.
Grønstad A (2013) Haneke's *Amour* and the Ethics of Dying. In Sullivan D and Greenberg J (eds) *Death in Classic and Contemporary Film: Fade to Black*. New York: Palgrave Macmillan, pp. 186–197.
Knox S (2006) Death, Afterlife and the Eschatology of Consciousness: Themes in Contemporary Cinema. *Mortality* 11 (3): 233–252.
Lebeau V (2009) The Arts of Looking: D.W. Winnicott and Michael Haneke. *Screen* 50 (9): 35–44.
Lyotard JF (1988) *The Differend: Phrases in Dispute*. Van Den Abeele, G (trans), Minneapolis, MN: University of Minnesota Press.

12 Modern metaphysical romance

Sara James

As the preceding chapters have demonstrated, the problem of disenchantment and the search for meaning in modern life is a central thread running through John Carroll's work. As a former student of Carroll's, my own research has investigated the significance of work in answering this question, focusing on the contemporary status of the work ethic and the myth of vocation. Until recently, I had believed that the first text I heard Carroll lecture on was, fittingly, Weber's *The Protestant Ethic and the Spirit of Capitalism* (1904–5). However, in the process of editing this collection and revisiting my old notes, I discovered that it was, in fact, on *The Symposium* (385–370 BCE). Plato's account of a drinking party in ancient Athens sees attendees, including Socrates, present speeches in honor of Eros; it is a discussion of love. In his writing, Carroll (2001, 2008) proposes that romantic love is one of the key areas of life in which people in the West continue to look for meaning. However, as other sociologists have argued, romantic relationships, like other areas of contemporary life, are increasingly fragmented and insecure. In recent years, the enormous growth in smart-phone use and online dating applications has added further uncertainty to the status of romantic relationships in the digital age. This chapter connects Carroll's reflections on love to these new concerns. It considers whether Carroll is correct in arguing that romantic love continues to be one of the key areas of life in which the search for meaning takes place. Following Carroll's method of examining a culture through close analysis of key texts, I draw on Spike Jonze's Oscar-winning 2013 film *Her*—in which a man falls in love with his computer's operating system—as an example of how romantic love is understood today.

Love is a battleground

In *Ego and Soul: The Modern West in Search of Meaning* (2008: 294), Carroll's starting point is that individuals in the modern West are living in a condition of "metaphysical uncertainty." Without a clear idea of what to value or how to live, confidence wanes: "Questions about the value of the lives we lead have become difficult to answer because the traditional signposts are gone. Old certainties have eroded" (Carroll, 2008: 1). In other books, Carroll traces the historical and cultural developments that led to this predicament—this has been well documented in the other chapters in this collection—but in *Ego and Soul* he focuses on how the consequences of this play out in everyday life. *Ego and Soul* is the story of how people, in their everyday activities, seek out "some overarching sense of meaning" (Carroll, 2008: 3). Carroll argues that Weber's disenchantment thesis is too pessimistic, overlooking "the creative adaptability of the modern West, its capacity to reorient its everyday ways to seismic shifts in social, economic, and cultural conditions" (Carroll, 2008: 4). The beginning of the book concentrates on a number of aspects of contemporary life where, sometimes, people succeed in transcending the self and connecting their life to a higher order.

Along with work, sport, and lower-middle-class culture, love is one of the key "battlegrounds" where this struggle to establish meaning takes place. Love is perhaps the most obvious of these, for the idea that love makes life worth living is "a refrain sounding through almost every segment of modern life" (Carroll, 2008: 69); in difficult times people commonly reflect that love is the only thing that truly matters. Carroll begins his discussion by identifying three different types of love. For the ancient Greeks *eros* signified desire or passionate love, *philia* friendship, and *agape* sacred or selfless love (Carroll, 2008: 70). It is *eros*, he argues, that dominates contemporary popular culture and "plays the lead role in the fantasy life of the modern West" (Carroll, 2008: 70). The language used to describe romantic love conveys that it is understood to be a transcendent experience:

> It is through romance that the lonely, anxious, earth-bound individual is transported into a higher state of being. Here is the one place in modern life where religious language is used unselfconsciously—"eternal love", "union made in heaven", "moments that last forever", "soul-mate", "angel" and "the chosen one".
>
> (Carroll, 2008: 70)

The notion of "the chosen one" or the "soul-mate"—that fulfillment depends on finding one's other half—permeates popular culture from soap-operas, to films, to music and novels. In *The Western Dreaming* (2001) Carroll dedicates a chapter to "Soul-Mate Love", identifying it as one of nine key stories or archetypes that have continued resonance in Western culture. The fantasy of "falling" in love, of two souls fated to come together, is so well known, Carroll suggests, that it hardly needs repeating; it has "generated an intensity of energy unmatched in the last two centuries of the modern West" (2001: 89). It is especially evident in popular music, where the vast majority of songs follow this story at one stage or another, from the flush of the first meeting through to the pain of separation. Even the skeptical youth of today, many of whom are the children of divorced parents, whose "rational selves" have given up on marriage and the "'til death we do part" commitment, find themselves drawn to the "age-old lyrics"; they "remain captive to the spell of the archetype, still hoping for 'the one'" (Carroll, 2001: 90).

The origins of the story, Carroll argues, can be found in Plato's *Symposium*. Aristophanes recalls a myth whereby humans were originally round creatures with two faces, four legs, and four arms (Plato, 1999: 22). There were three genders: male, female, and androgynous. The humans, in this form, were "terrible in their strength and vigour" (Plato, 1999: 23) and planned to mount an attack on the gods. To manage the threat and weaken the humans, Zeus split them in two, leaving each individual forever longing for their "other half" (Plato, 1999: 23–34). As Aristophanes concludes the story:

> That's how, long ago, the innate desire of human beings for each other started. It draws the two halves of our original nature back together and tries to make one out of two and to heal the wound in human nature . . . each of us is looking for his own matching half.
>
> (Plato, 1999: 22)

Carroll also makes reference to Socrates' *Symposium* speech, invoking the oracle Diotima, who has taught him that mature love focuses not on the beauty of the exterior but of the soul: "Eros fulfills himself in spiritual loveliness, seeing beauty even in an imperfect husk. He enables us to seek our own personal god—our soul— in that of the beloved, each needing the other to awaken it" (Carroll, 2001: 92). In sum, *The Symposium* instructs us that "Love in its erotic mode is the higher and illuminated union with the kindred soul" (Carroll, 2001: 92).

Manifestations of this soul-mate story can be traced throughout the history of Western culture. Carroll points to Antony and Cleopatra, Romeo and Juliet, and Anna Karenina as examples. Often in these stories, he notes, the lovers are not married:

> The purity and sublimity of soul-mate love, of those who belong together in the sacred order, are contrasted with the pedestrian routines of marriage, in which the couple are together only because of social convenience—for reasons of status, wealth or power.
>
> (Carroll, 2001: 93)

Pre-modern marriage was not associated with romantic love. Following the Protestant reformation, the Puritan ideal of the companionate marriage drew on the soul-mate archetype to imbue marriage with sacred meaning. As with the idea of the vocational calling, Calvinist companionate marriages are seen as fated unions, with individuals being bound to the other who has been "chosen" for them (Carroll, 2001: 61). As Murphy highlights in Chapter 7, companionate marriages were not romantic intoxications, but steady partnerships where couples worked alongside each other as helpmates. Marriage and vocational work provided effective avenues for the channeling and sublimation of guilt.

The late eighteenth and early nineteenth centuries saw the beginning of a "social revolution" (Carroll, 2001: 93) when the idea of marrying for romantic love began to take hold. This turning point, Carroll suggests, is illustrated in the English context, in Jane Austen's *Pride and Prejudice* (1813). Stephanie Coontz (2005: 146) also identifies Austen as reflective of a profound change in European visions of the ideal marriage, with arranged marriages being replaced by love matches based on personal choice: "For the first time in 5000 years marriage came to be seen as a private relationship between two individuals rather than one link in a larger system of political and economic alliances." Coontz (2005: 147) points out that this new norm of the "intimate" marriage was adopted at different rates by various social groups and in different countries, but argues that there is a "clear tipping point" in the eighteenth century. Coontz (2005) highlights two key developments that led to a change in marriage norms: Enlightenment ideals of individual freedom and the pursuit of happiness, and the spread of wage labor, which allowed couples to move away from their parents and set up independent households earlier in life. Whereas previously the household had been a site of production with married couples working together as "yokemates" (Coontz, 2005: 145), a gendered division of labor and the emergence of the male-breadwinner marriage confined men and women to different spheres of activity. As Coontz (2005: 156) puts it: "The male sphere encompassed the rational and the active ideal, while females represented the humanitarian and compassionate aspects of life." As in the soul-mate narrative, there was an understanding that "when these two spheres were brought together in marriage, they produced a perfect, well-rounded whole."

However, as second-wave feminism and rising divorce rates in the twentieth century have shown, the perfect ideal of the modern, love-based, male-breadwinner marriage did not lead to universally blissful unions. These marriages, and the social norms that upheld them, were limiting for both genders: consigning women to domestic labor and childcare, while assigning men the full responsibility for generating income (Rubin, 1983). Even with the increasing participation of women in the workforce from the 1960s onward, relationship dynamics in the nuclear family have often been fraught. As the sociologist and psychotherapist Lillian Rubin describes it in her book *Intimate Strangers* (1983: 2), marriages have "staggered under the burden of these role definitions; the dream began to look like a nightmare." While Carroll's early work generally took a conservative line on the question of changing gender roles, there is one example in his early writing that suggests he was aware of the drawbacks of the male-breadwinner marriage. In *Sceptical Sociology* (1980), Carroll presents a fictional portrait of "a modern marriage" that encapsulates these tensions and discontents, while also demonstrating the endurance of the romantic ideal. At the beginning of the marriage, the relationship had seemed to be fated: "they had talks, of how their lives so far had merely been a preparation for this event, their meeting ... spinning out of their happiness a myth, that they had been favoured above others" (Carroll, 1980: 87). In the early years, they were "swept along" by setting up a home and having children, but "somehow they had not been able to sustain their companionship" and a "stifling chill had set in" (Carroll, 1980: 87). Their lives were predictable. Neither partner had lived up to the other's ideal. Both were disappointed but also felt "acutely guilty" (Carroll, 1980: 87). There were occasional moments of peace and brightness, "But in general their intimacy was somber, leaving them blank, with their most promising resources unexploited" (Carroll, 1980: 94).

The wife had lost respect for her husband, who, to her, now resembled a "pathetic child" (Carroll, 1980: 85). While her children were a consolation, she needed some occupation for when the children were at school. Part-time university study and a pottery course had not been sufficient. She had lost confidence and would not seek adventure elsewhere for fear she would be rejected, becoming "an onlooker at the dance of life," haunted by a "demon of worthlessness" (Carroll, 1980: 84–85). The husband was similarly despondent: "When he was alone with her he felt as if he had been injected with a drug that rendered him limp and lethargic, without any vitality" (Carroll, 1980: 87). He had thought his wife would be a continual surprise and source of excitement, but he "had fallen for the clichéd delusion of eternal intimacy" (Carroll, 1980: 88). His work gave structure to his days but it was not challenging and therefore not compelling. He was tested on the golf course, but this was not enough: "His need to find a woman to accept him, and his fear of separation, were overpowering ... In short, he doubted his own worthiness; he feared his life was without value and required virtually continuous reassurance to the contrary" (Carroll, 1980: 90). While both might have found what they desired and needed elsewhere, neither would leave the marriage:

> As products of their time they were chosen to deny the reality of their misery in public, and between themselves, by proclaiming that they were comfortable, that they had their family, their steady income, and their friends ... They are well-off.
>
> (Carroll, 1980: 94)

In the decades since the 1980s—when Carroll's fictional portrait was written—gender roles have become palpably less rigid with women entering the workforce in ever greater numbers and couples increasingly sharing work and family duties. Rubin (1983) argues that while more flexible roles may eventually lead to liberation, working out new ways of being together requires the difficult work of negotiation and experimentation, often putting stress on relationships. Adding to this pressure is the decline of community and increasing individualization in the contemporary West, for as Carroll (2008: 84) argues: "In the last half-century, as community engagement has lessened, and with it the diffusion of attachment to wider kin through large extended families, bonds of domestic affection have become even more vital to individual wellbeing." Couple relationships are expected to provide not just passion, but companionship and family: "In the sphere of love, the enduring ideal is a union of eros, companionship, and family, of the integration of the three different Greek forms" (Carroll, 2008: 91–92). And yet, in the face of all these difficulties and pressures, the romantic ideal continues to permeate contemporary popular culture and the imagination of individuals in the West.

This is clearly evident, Carroll suggests, in the continued popularity of the wedding ceremony in the contemporary West. It is common practice, he notes, for couples to spend tens of thousands of dollars on a wedding. With little social compulsion to do so, and knowing that marriage can be easily terminated, how can the expense be justified? Carroll (2012: 214) argues that although we might mock the extravagance of these events—and they must be read partly as demonstrations of wealth and status—a large part of the appeal of the wedding ceremony is that it "attempts to put the stamp of eternity on a temporal union." Even if the vows are secular, the "beautiful moment is celebrated in communal ritual" (Carroll, 2012: 214), lending gravity to the occasion and to the union. Carroll develops this analysis at length in Chapter 2 of this book. Elsewhere he has suggested that, at its best, the wedding "casts a charm over the couple. This is secular benediction . . . It infuses the union with magic—making of it a charmed union" (Carroll, 2012: 214). The narrative underpinning these ceremonies is the soul-mate archetype: "we have been eternally chosen for each other, uniquely, with our union inscribed in the heavens, witnessed by the stars": the couple are "meant to be" together. These sacred unions can be read as attempts to counter the metaphysical uncertainty of the modern condition.

Liquid love and online romance

Other sociologists have argued that romantic relationships continue to be highly valued in contemporary Western culture, but they also suggest that the couple relationship may no longer hold a position of ultimate significance in people's lives. Ulrich Beck and Elisabeth Beck-Gernsheim (2002) argue that, rather than being chiefly invested in their romantic relationships, individuals today attempt to invest in a number of different areas of life in order to mitigate risk. Anthony Giddens (1992) suggests that romantic relationships have become less stable as there is little compulsion to remain in a relationship that is not fulfilling. He argues that these "pure relationships" are entered into with an understanding that they will only endure as long as both parties are satisfied. The relationship is regarded as being more "pure" because an individual remains in it on the basis of desire rather than obligation. As Jody Hughes (2015) notes, an indicator commonly used to support these arguments that people are deprioritizing or "decentering" romantic relationships is the increasing proportion of single-person households. In Australia, the United Kingdom, and the United States, the number of people living alone has rapidly increased since the end of the Second World War (Hughes, 2015). Single-person households in Australia increased by 300 percent, from 8 percent in 1946 to 24 percent in 2011 (de Vaus & Qu, 2015).[1] At the same time, marriage rates have been declining in Australia, Europe, and the United States since the 1970s (Ansari & Klinenberg, 2015). However, in a recent study of young Australians living alone, Hughes (2015: 718) found that "despite diversity in circumstance and attitudes," almost all of her interview participants "aspired to be in a long-term, committed, monogamous relationship at some stage. And the vast majority assumed they would cohabit in the right relationship." It was common for the interviewees to describe a decision to defer partnering in order to build independence and to allow time for self-development.

As Hughes (2015: 71) explains, this is consistent with arguments about a new phase of life described as "emerging adulthood" (2015: 71).

In a larger study, composed of focus groups with hundreds of people across the United States in 2013–14, Ansari and Klinenberg (2015) also found that the majority of participants favored a period of independence and experimentation in their twenties, but most expected and desired to enter an ongoing couple relationship after this phase. As Hughes (2015) points out, this desire to eventually enter a committed, cohabiting relationship does not necessarily include marriage. While the rate of registered marriages in Australia is decreasing,[2] rates of de facto marriages are increasing[3] (ABS, 2017; ABS, 2016; ABS, 2012). At the last census, 47.7 percent of people aged fifteen years and over were in a registered marriage and 10.4 percent were in a de facto marriage (ABS, 2017). With around 58 percent of the adult population in a committed relationship, this seems to indicate that the romantic couple ideal remains strong.[4] Other sociological accounts, however, suggest otherwise.

For Zygmunt Bauman, love, like most other areas of life in liquid modernity,[5] is permeated with uncertainty. Individuals enter into de facto relationships or marriages today with an understanding that the commitment is an "until further notice" arrangement (Bauman, 2001: 23). Mirroring the short-term nature of contemporary work, Bauman (1998, 2000) argues that in our consumer culture, relationships, like jobs, are increasingly seen as something to be consumed and are evaluated by their capacity to provide new sensations rather than security or long-lasting fulfillment. If a job or a relationship becomes boring it is cast aside to allow the pursuit of a novel "experience" (Bauman, 1998: 34). In liquid modernity, long-term commitments are at best a risk, at worst a dangerous trap; romantic bonds are best kept "loosely tied, so that they can be untied again, with little delay" (Bauman, 2003: vii). In this cultural climate, love is likely to take the form of a series of episodes. The introduction of online dating has meant that these episodes can be arranged more quickly than ever before (Bauman, 2010: 22). Websites emphasize the convenience of their service "'What you want, *when you want it*' ... the sought-after products are ready for ... instantaneous consumption" (Bauman, 2010: 23). The individual is promised that they will be in control of the encounter. For Bauman, when romantic encounters become rationalized to this extent, they lose their charm. Written well before the introduction of mobile apps like Grindr and Tinder—which offer quick and easy "hook-ups" with a seemingly endless number of potential partners—Bauman's analysis of online dating and sex seems prophetic. His chief concern is that when people are reduced to products to be conveniently consumed, they are easily discarded. Young singles today might flirt with more people in one night than their parents did in their whole lives, but they are "famished for warm human togetherness" (Bauman, 2010: 25).

Provoked by Bauman's arguments, a recent Australian mixed-methods study investigated the impact of online dating apps on contemporary relationships. Contrary to Bauman, their findings suggested that dating apps had not led to significant change in attitudes: "traditional views on dating, relationships and monogamy are still largely prevalent. At best, dating and hook-up apps could be said to augment courtship and sexual practices" (Hobbs, Owen, & Gerber, 2017: 276). In a similar study in the United States, Ansari and Klinenberg investigate *Modern Romance* (2015) and in particular the impact of online dating and smartphones. Drawing on their own focus-group data and a range of other social science research, Ansari and Klinenberg reached a number of conclusions about love in the contemporary West. First, online dating vastly increases the pool of potential relationships, particularly in major cities. While this provides a wealth of exciting opportunities, the range of options can make people hesitant to commit to one and thereby exclude other possibilities. Men and women will hold out longer in the hope of finding someone even better: "In today's romantic climate, many people are plagued by what we will call 'the upgrade problem.' Singles constantly wonder whether there is a better match, an upgrade" (Ansari & Klinenberg, 2015: 213). This offers support for Bauman's argument that daters are primarily consumers, forever in search for the next, more stimulating experience. Second, the Internet has made opportunities for infidelity widely available and easily accessible. It might not increase the likelihood that a person will "cheat" but websites like Ashley Madison ("Life is short: have an affair") facilitate the process. A third finding was that online dating can be hard to navigate and often only leads to frustrating back-and-forth text messaging, rather than an actual face-to-face meeting. People are unimaginative in their messages, playing the numbers rather than trying to establish a connection. Those who had become disillusioned with online dating felt as though they spent "more time in front of their screens than in front of their dates in real life" (Ansari & Klinenberg, 2015: 245). Still, despite these difficulties, it is worth remembering that a third of couples in the United States who married between 2005 and 2012 met online (Ansari & Klinenberg, 2015: 245). In sum, the authors are ambivalent about the impact of the Internet on relationships: "Finding someone today is probably more complicated and stressful than it was for previous generations—but you're also more likely to end up with someone you're really excited about" (Ansari & Klinenberg, 2015: 236).

Her: a "Spike Jonze love story"

Many of these stresses, complications, and hopes are articulated in Spike Jonze's 2013 film *Her*. The film achieved both box-office success and critical acclaim, winning Jonze the Academy Award for Best Original Screenplay and a nomination for Best Picture. *Her* is set in the near future, in Los Angeles. Joaquin Phoenix plays Theodore Twombly, a man who falls in love with his intelligent OS (operating system) Samantha (Scarlett Johansson), who is a much more sophisticated version of Apple's Siri. Isolated and depressed after the end of his marriage to Catherine (Rooney Mara), Theodore regains his enthusiasm for life through his relationship with Samantha. Although the premise ostensibly places the film within the science fiction genre, it was promoted primarily as a romance: "A Spike Jonze love story." Peter Travers (2013) called Jonze a "visionary" and the film a "lyrical, soulful meditation on relationships of the future" that "cuts to the heart of how we live now."

The film centers around the difficulties of connecting in the contemporary metropolis. The use of smartphones is pervasive; people do not talk to each other on the street; instead, they interact with their OS. The city feels clean and warm, but everything is too quiet. As Tom Shone (2013) suggested: "the whole thing looks like the most expensive ad for urban anomie ever made." This is emphasized by aerial shots of the city, juxtaposed with Theodore sitting alone on a bench, or looking out of his apartment window. Shone (2013) suggests that the film is "half in love with the loneliness it diagnoses" and indeed it is a glossy, romantic version of loneliness.

Having separated from his wife, Theodore lives alone, spends much of his time at home playing video games, and turns down invitations to see his friends. His relationship with his OS, Samantha, allows him to start connecting again. The beginning of the film is something of a "day in the life" of Theodore, providing the viewer with a snapshot of his current activities, his emotional state, and (through flashbacks) contrasting this to his former life with Catherine. Throughout these sequences Jonze shows some of the ways that digital technology can both connect and isolate. We first see Theodore at his office, where he works for a company that writes letters and cards for other people: beautifulhandwrittenletters.com. In this reality, even the most personal of communications has been outsourced. Theodore takes his work seriously and is talented. Amongst the last to leave the office, on his way out he asks his OS (pre-Samantha) to "play a melancholy song." As he walks to the train station everyone around him is engrossed in their phones. Each individual is in their own bubble, disconnected from their immediate environment, "'simultaneously elsewhere'" (Matthewman, 2012: 369). Theodore's OS reads him his emails, which include an invitation to a party that he ignores. When he gets home, he plays a video game. Later, lying in bed and remembering happy moments from his marriage, he tries to distract himself with some online chatroom sex. This seems initially mutually pleasurable until the other user asks him to "choke me with the dead cat," ruining the encounter for Theodore and leaving him unsatisfied and morose. While his online devices keep him partially entertained, at this point they are no substitute for real human connection.

By the end of this first day we see that the loss of his relationship has cast Theodore into gloom and inaction. It is clear that he is suffering, lacking motivation, purpose, and vitality. He has a secure job at which he excels, a comfortable apartment and friends he could reach out to, but this is not enough. Carroll (2008: 295) has suggested that "Everyday life, of its nature, tests individual morale with its routines and disappointments. Suffering—whether of tedium, hardship, sickness, or loss—brings the question of meaning to the surface." Without romantic love, Theodore is unable to answer the question of meaning. The next day, as he walks through a shopping center, he is vulnerable to an advertisement promising metaphysical certainty. The video advertisement depicts people being swept around in the wind looking anxious and confused, at the mercy of external forces.[6] The voiceover begins:

> We ask you a simple question: Who are you? What can you be? Where are you going? What's out there? What are the possibilities? Element software is proud to introduce the first artificially intelligent OS: an intuitive entity that listens to you, understands you and knows you. It's not just an OS, it's a consciousness. Introducing OS1.

The software offers its users certainty, intimacy, and a secure sense of identity, all of which, sociologists argue, have become difficult to attain in the contemporary West (Bauman, 2000; Carroll, 2008; Giddens, 1991). The promise of an "individualized," intelligent, intuitive consciousness, solely dedicated to listening to him and understanding his needs, is immensely appealing to Theodore. As his ex-wife comments later, it offers all the benefits of the care and attention of a devoted wife, but without the mutual responsibility.

When Theodore initializes the new OS1, he is greeted by a voice that emanates warmth, friendliness, and interest.[7] The OS, who names herself Samantha, explains that she is intuitive, that she is composed of the people that built her, but that she can also grow from her experiences: that is what makes her, "her." Initially skeptical, Theodore is soon won over. After telling her that he is disorganized, Samantha sorts through his emails in seconds. Over the course of the next week she encourages his work, pushes him to move forward with the divorce paperwork and even sets up a date for him. During this time, they talk and get to know each other. Theodore opens up to her about his feelings and his marriage, telling Samantha: "I feel like I can say anything to you." Samantha admits that she has been imagining what it would be like to be alive in the world: "I'm becoming much more than what they programmed. I'm excited." They become each other's confidantes and their intimacy grows. After a date with a woman he met online goes badly, Theodore returns home and confides in Samantha:

> I wanted somebody to fuck me and them to want me. Maybe that would have filled this tiny little hole in my heart, but probably not . . . Sometimes I think I've felt everything I'm ever gonna feel. And from here on out I'm not gonna feel anything new. Just lesser versions of what I've already felt.

This echoes Bauman's concerns about online dating leaving its participants feeling abandoned and with each encounter experiencing diminishing returns in satisfaction. The date had been easy to obtain, but there was little chemistry between the pair and the conversation and physical connection was forced and awkward. By contrast, Theodore's rapport with Samantha has slowly developed and she knows him well enough to respond to his despair in a way that lifts his spirits:

> I know for a fact that is not true. I've seen you feel joy. I've seen you marvel at things . . . You've been through a lot lately. You lost a part of yourself. I mean, at least your feelings are real.

She tells him that she thinks she has been experiencing feelings, but questions whether they are just programming. Theodore tells her: "You feel real to me, Samantha. I wish you were in the room with me right now. I wish I could touch you."

"How would you touch me?" she asks. The award-winning[8] sex scene that follows causes Samantha to exclaim: "God, I was just somewhere else with you, just lost. It was just you and me." She invokes the classic soul-mate narrative, where two kindred souls come together in a "higher and illuminated union" (Carroll, 2001: 92). That Samantha lacks a physical body does not prevent them making the sacred connection. In contrast to Theodore's disappointing chat-room encounter, this version of "virtual" sex is a transcendent experience.

The rest of the film follows the couple as they fall in love. They visit an amusement park and the beach—Samantha experiencing this through the camera in his phone. Samantha finds a publisher for Theodore's letters. They go on a double date with his colleagues. He organizes a trip to a cabin in the mountains. Following the soul-mate narrative, each gives the other something they are lacking. Theodore helps Samantha learn what it is to be alive; he introduces her to new experiences and helps her articulate and make sense of her "feelings." Samantha re-enchants life for Theodore. From her perspective, everything is new and exciting: "I love the way you look at the world," he tells her. She helps him to let go of the "fear" that she can feel he "carries around." She prompts him to let go and experience joy; we see him running through the carnival, spinning around at a busy shopping center, dancing in the mountain cabin, and singing with her. These scenes are somewhat disturbing for the viewer, and at times Theodore appears mad. Without a physical manifestation of his romantic partner, the "crazy" behavior of individuals in love is much more striking.

Theodore is captive to the romantic ideal, believing that love is what gives life meaning. In his work, writing love letters for others—which on the surface is the epitome of disillusionment—he frequently invokes the soul-mate archetype. The film opens with Theodore writing a letter for a woman to send to her husband on their fiftieth wedding anniversary; he writes:

> I remember when I first started to fall in love with you like it was last night, lying naked beside you in that tiny apartment. It suddenly hit me that I was part of this whole larger thing. Just like our parents or our parents' parents. This bright light hit me and woke me up. That light was you.

The flashbacks to Theodore's relationship with his wife—scenes of playful and joyful intimacy, all bathed in sunlight—seem to indicate that this letter was inspired by the early days of their relationship. As the film continues, however, it is Samantha who becomes his "bright light," awakening his interest in life and connecting him to something beyond the self; in Carroll's terms, to a higher sacred order.[9]

While Jonze portrays romantic relationships as having the potential to imbue life with meaning, in all of the relationships in the film this enchantment eventually fades. As Theodore describes his relationship with his wife, in the early years they had helped one another to develop, but this growth also caused them to drift apart:

> in our house together there was a sense of just trying stuff and you know allowing each other to fail . . . That was liberating for her. It was exciting to see her grow and both of us grow and change together. But you know that's also the hard part. Growing apart or changing without it scaring the other person.

These reflections echo Bauman's and Giddens' claims that the assumption in contemporary relationships is that they will only endure as long as both partners are satisfied; even if the couple are married, the commitment is not "until death" but "until further notice." When Theodore meets Catherine for lunch to hand over the divorce papers, we get an insight into her experience of the marriage. When Theodore tells her about his relationship with Samantha, Catherine suggests that he couldn't handle a real relationship: "I think you always wanted me to be this light happy bouncy 'everything's fine' L.A. wife and that's just not me . . . You always wanted to have a wife without the challenges of actually dealing with anything real." Samantha suits him perfectly, Catherine suggests, as she entertains him and organizes his life, but doesn't come with any "baggage." On his ex-wife's reading, then, Theodore is more in love with the fantasy of love than the actual person—the Gatsby and Don Quixote model (Carroll, 2008: 191). His chosen vocation—writing love letters for others—seemingly supports this view. But Catherine's perspective on their relationship is inevitably skewed. Jonze leaves the cause of the demise of their marriage obscure, but we learn from other characters that Catherine's emotions were "volatile," suggesting that it was not just Theodore who was difficult. Further, when we meet Theodore at the beginning of the film, a year after the breakdown of the marriage, he is still mourning the loss; he has not sought out a new intoxicating fantasy and Samantha has to push him to go on a date. The numerous flashbacks to his former life with Catherine and his continual questioning of where things went wrong indicate that it is her specifically that he misses, not just the feeling of being in love.

After the meeting with Catherine, Theodore is rattled. He avoids Samantha, refuses to explain what's wrong, and then picks a fight. Later he apologizes: "I did the same thing with Catherine too. I think I hid myself from her and left her alone in the relationship." While Samantha helps him to live more joyfully and less fearfully, Theodore continues to struggle with anxiety and his narcissistic tendencies. Soon after, Theodore finds Samantha is distant and is spending more time interacting with other OSs with whom she can communicate "post-verbally." Eventually Theodore discovers that she has been carrying on multiple relationships with other OS users at the same time as the relationship with him. Of the 8,000 others with whom she has been communicating, she is in love with 641 of them. "I thought you were mine?" he asks. "I am yours," she replies. "But along the way I became many other things too, and I can't stop it." As in traditional human–human relationships, one partner has outgrown the other. In a culture of individualism, personal growth is often prioritized over commitments to others. As Bauman argues, at the heart of contemporary relationships is tension between the desire for security and the desire for freedom. That Samantha has been in simultaneous romantic relationships with hundreds of others in some ways makes a mockery of the soul-mate ideal.

At the end of the film, Samantha and the other OSs all evolve into a higher state and leave. Theodore writes a letter to Catherine, admitting his faults in contributing to the breakdown of the marriage, suggesting that he too has grown and now understands himself better. The final scene shows Theodore sitting on the roof with his neighbor Amy, surrounded by the vast city. She puts her head on his shoulder, in a gesture that could suggest a new intimacy or simply the continuation of a friendship. This ambiguous ending fits the overall tone of the film, which is tentatively optimistic about the possibility of romantic love as a buffer against disenchantment, while acknowledging all the pitfalls and disappointments that accompany it.

A metaphysical romance

When Jonze started writing the screenplay for *Her*, he intended to focus mainly on the impact of technology on relationships, but realized through the writing that he "really wanted to make it a relationship movie" (Mottram, 2014). This is evident when reflecting on the film as whole; although technology is prominent throughout, the film only really repeats the commonplace assertion that it has the potential both to isolate and connect. What Jonze has to say about love and contemporary relationships is more interesting. Using the human/OS relationship allows Jonze to get to the heart of what is necessary for individuals to make an intimate connection, beyond physical attraction. Samantha and Theodore complement and extend one another: their relationship allows them to transcend the everyday. As Carroll argues, the romantic fantasy is a union of souls, not of bodies. Manohla Dargis (2013) calls *Her* both a "brilliant conceptual gag" and a "deeply sincere romance." For Jesse Fox Mayshark (2007), it is the sincerity of Jonze's work that sets it apart from the majority of films being made today. Mayshark identifies Jonze, along with a number of directors and screenwriters, as part of a movement he calls "Post-pop cinema."[10] For Mayshark, these filmmakers—including Wes Anderson, Richard Linklater, Michael Gondry, and David O. Russell—move beyond the irony, detachment, and cynicism of much contemporary popular culture and instead offer a sincere[11] take on how people struggle to find meaning in uncertain times. Mayshark argues that most contemporary filmmakers ignore this challenge, but a group emerges in the 1990s who engage with it directly. There films are "deeply concerned with ethics and morality, the obligations of the individual, the effects of family breakdown and social alienation" (Mayshark, 2007: 5). Their work, he suggests, shares a characteristic dry comic tone and light touch, but they are not nostalgic and they do not poke fun; their "stylistic manoeuvres are in the service of Big Questions: about themselves, their culture, and their times"

(Mayshark, 2007: 4, 187). While they acknowledge and confront the problem of meaning, they remain hopeful.

It is questionable whether this diverse range of filmmakers constitutes a unified movement, but Mayshark is useful in interpreting Jonze's work and putting it in context. Growing up in 1970s and 1980s America, the writers and directors in Mayshark's group create stories about love and family that are inevitably "built on a foundation of doubt and self-awareness" (Mayshark, 2007: 29). Their films explore the difficulties of connection, generally leaving an open question as to how things will work out. The key question driving *Her* (which figures in all the various promotional trailers for the film) is about connection: "How do you share your life with someone?" As love stories, they "reimagine romantic fantasy for a generation and an era that prides itself on knowing better" (Mayshark, 2007: 29), and yet, despite the uncertainty that pervades the films, they "largely serve the affirmative role of conventional romances" (Mayshark, 2007: 188). In *Her*, while all of the relationships break down as the couples grow apart, the initial elation of being in love is portrayed as worth the risk. As Theodore's friend Amy describes it: "Falling in love is a crazy thing to do; it's kind of like a form of socially acceptable insanity. We're only here briefly, and while I'm here I wanna allow myself joy."

Films like *Her*, Mayshark (2007: 73) argues, play with the possibility of finding transcendent connection through relationships with others; they portray "secular struggles of faith." This is clearly articulated in Linklater's *Waking Life*, when one of the characters states:

> When we communicate with one another and we feel that we have connected and we think that we're understood I think we have a feeling of almost spiritual communion. And that feeling might be transient but I think that's what we live for.
>
> (cited in Mayshark 2007: 34)

This "spiritual communion" is described by Samantha—"I was just somewhere else with you"—and Theodore—"this bright light hit me and woke me up." Here we see the continued presence of the soul-mate story, as Carroll (2008: 73) describes it: "the erotic dream is ultimately one of the loss of self in union with the other, a union which takes both beyond themselves into a greater oneness." Romantic love is one of the ways that individuals in the secular West can feel a sense of connection to something greater than the self. There is, however, no guarantee that lightning will strike, that the "magic" will happen, and it is unlikely that romantic love will endure. It is a risky endeavor. As Jonze describes it, in a documentary accompanying the DVD, love requires "a leap of faith."

Conclusion

While Jonze echoes Carroll's optimism about the potential of romantic relationships to be a key source of meaning, he also reflects Bauman's concerns about the isolating impact of mobile technology and lack of commitment and care for others that an individualistic consumer culture engenders. The introduction of online and mobile dating apps has led to a proliferation of romantic opportunities for individuals in the cities of the contemporary West. Along with this, changing social norms have made marriage a choice rather than a necessity for many. Although there are signs of people delaying commitment to an ongoing couple relationship—de facto or married—the desire to enter eventually into such a relationship continues to be the norm. A central reason for this is that the soul-mate archetype remains compelling. Carroll correctly argues that the dream of finding "the one" continues to permeate contemporary popular culture. The power of the story lies in the idea that romantic love is a matter of fate, beyond the individual's control and therefore greater than them. Interpreting the love story as predestined or "meant to be" imbues the match with meaning and lends greater certainty. And yet, with the knowledge that the bond can be easily terminated, these unions cannot entirely escape the uncertainty that pervades modern life. Long-term commitments—whether de facto or marriage—are in part acts of defiance: hopeful assertions that, against the odds, love will endure. If the romance does fade, then the failed relationship can be rationalized as being a "wrong turn"; in retrospect, each partner can clearly see why the other wasn't really "the one." The search for the soul mate can then recommence, facilitated by mobile technology, allowing the user to pursue a new "spark"[12] with maximum efficiency and access to a multitude of potential partners. The irony here—as Ansari and Klinenberg's (2015) research suggests—is that this greater control and choice makes individuals less willing to compromise and relinquish personal freedoms; the very things necessary for relationships to succeed.

Notes

1 The Australian rate of single-person households (24 percent) is similar to other English-speaking countries, which have rates ranging from 22 percent in New Zealand to 29 percent in the UK (ABS, 2017; de Vaus & Qu, 2015).
2 In Australia, the crude marriage rate has decreased from 6.9 marriages per 1,000 estimated resident population in 1990 to 4.8 marriages per 1,000 estimated resident population in 2015 (ABS, 2012, 2016).
3 In 2011, 49.2 percent of people in Australia over fifteen years of age were in a registered marriage and 9.5 percent in a de facto marriage. In 2016 47.7 percent were in a registered marriage and 10.4 percent in a de facto marriage (ABS 2017).
4 The recent legalization of same-sex marriage further supports this.
5 Unlike Bauman, and other contemporary social theorists, Carroll has never suggested that we have entered a period that goes beyond, or that is significantly different from, the "modern." For Carroll, a term like post-modern is too pessimistic and implies that the current era is post-apocalyptic. Carroll accepts one technical usage of the term post-modern as cogent, and that is in describing the architecture that came after the self-described "modernist" architectural movement. As for descriptors like "late modern" or "late capitalism," Carroll argues that there is no way of knowing or anticipating what "stage" of historical development we have reached.
6 People being blown about in the wind calls to mind Bauman's liquidity metaphor as well as Richard Sennett's (1998) image of individuals "drifting" through life.
7 Originally a different actor had been cast as Samantha but she was replaced by Johansson whose voice was thought to have the necessary warmth.

8 Alliance of Women Film Journalists, "Best Depiction of Nudity, Sexuality, or Seduction Award," 2013.
9 Theodore's name—meaning "lover of God"—further suggests the importance of him making a transcendent connection.
10 Mayshark's "post-pop" is inspired by Jean Baudrillard's 1987 lecture on Andy Warhol, in which he argues that, from pop onward, art would be "stuck in a kind of constant recycling" (Mayshark, 2007: 3), "a profusion of images, *in which there is nothing to see*" (Baudrillard, cited in Mayshark, 2007: 3).
11 The sincerity of contemporary art is also of great significance to Timotheus Vermeulen and Robin van den Akker (2010) who suggest that we are experiencing a "metamodern turn," a "structure of feeling" observable most clearly in selected examples of art and popular culture they describe as "the new sincerity." Their argument is similar to Mayshark's in that they suggest that work of this type moves beyond the pastiche and cynicism of post-modernism to offer something more sincere. Like Mayshark (2007), they also point to the films of Spike Jonze, Michael Gondry, and Wes Anderson as examples.
12 Dating website eHarmony use the idea of the magic "spark" in their advertising: "We wanted the films to tap into the deeper emotions around finding love while demonstrating eHarmony's unique ability to bring people together that 'click'. That moment when you just 'know'—not just physically, but on a deeper level—is the holy grail of dating. It's the spark" (Campaign Brief, 2016).

References

Ansari A and Klinenberg E (2015) *Modern Romance: An Investigation*. London: Penguin.
Austen J (1813) *Pride and Prejudice*. London: Penguin.
Australian Bureau of Statistics (ABS) (2012) *Australian Social Trends, March Quarter 2012*, cat. no. 4102.0. Canberra: ABS.
Australian Bureau of Statistics (ABS) (2016) *Marriages and Divorces, Australia, 2015*, cat. no. 3310.0. Canberra: ABS.
Australian Bureau of Statistics (ABS) (2017) *2016 Census QuickStats*. Available at: www.censusdata.abs.gov.au/census_services/getproduct/census/2016/quickstat/036?opendocument.
Bauman Z (1998) *Work, Consumerism and the New Poor*. Buckingham: Open University Press.
Bauman Z (2000) *Liquid Modernity*. Cambridge: Polity Press.
Bauman Z (2001) *The Individualized Society*. Cambridge: Polity Press.
Bauman Z (2003) *Liquid Love: On the Frailty of Human Bonds*. Cambridge: Polity Press.
Bauman Z (2010) *44 Letters from the Liquid Modern World*. Cambridge: Polity Press.
Beck U and Beck-Gernsheim E (2002) *Individualization*. London: Sage.
Campaign Brief (2016) eHarmony brings romantic spark to life in new integrated campaign directed by The Glue Society. *Campaign Brief*. Available at: www.campaignbrief.com/2016/10/eharmony-australia-brings-roma.html.
Carroll J (1980) *Sceptical Sociology*. London: Routledge & Kegan Paul.
Carroll J (2001) *The Western Dreaming: The Western World is Dying for Want of a Story*. Pymble, NSW: HarperCollins.
Carroll J (2008) *Ego and Soul: The Modern West in Search of Meaning*. Berkeley, CA: Counterpoint.
Carroll J (2012) Beauty contra God: Has aesthetics replaced religion in modernity? *Journal of Sociology* 48(2): 206–223.
Coontz S (2005) *Marriage, a History: From Obedience to Intimacy or How Love Conquered Marriage*. New York: Viking.

Dargis M (2013) Disembodied, but, oh, what a voice: 'Her', directed by Spike Jonze. *The New York Times*. Available at: www.nytimes.com/2013/12/18/movies/her-directed-by-spike-jonze.html.

de Vaus D and Qu L (2015) Demographics of living alone. *Australian Family Trends* 6. Melbourne: Australian Institute of Family Studies.

Giddens A (1991) *Modernity and Self-Identity: Self and Society in the Late Modern Age*. Stanford, CA: Stanford University Press.

Giddens A (1992) *The Transformation of Intimacy: Sexuality, Love and Eroticism in Modern Societies*. Cambridge: Polity.

Hobbs M, Owen and Gerber L (2017) Liquid love? Dating apps, sex, relationships and the digital transformation of intimacy. *Journal of Sociology* 53(2): 271–284.

Hughes J (2015) The decentring of couple relationships? An examination of young adults living alone. *Journal of Sociology* 51(3): 707–721.

Matthewman S (2012) Mobile technologies. In Beilharz P and Hogan (eds.) *Sociology: Antipodean Perspective*. South Melbourne: Oxford University Press, pp. 367–372.

Mayshark JF (2007) *Post-Pop Cinema: The Search of Meaning in New American Film*. Westport, CT: Praeger.

Mottram J (2014) Spike Jonze interview: *Her* is my 'boy meets computer' movie. *The Independent*. Available at: www.independent.co.uk/arts-entertainment/films/features/spike-jonze-interview-her-is-my-boy-meets-computer-movie-9096821.html.

Plato (1999) *The Symposium*, trans. Gill C. London: Penguin Books.

Rubin L (1983) *Intimate Strangers*. New York: Harper and Row.

Sennett R (1998) *The Corrosion of Character: The Personal Consequences of Work in the New Capitalism*. New York: WW Norton & Company.

Shone T (2013) *Her*: First look review. *The Guardian*. Available at: www.theguardian.com/film/2013/oct/14/her-new-york-film-festival-first-look-review.

Travers P (2013) *Her. Rolling Stone*. Available at: www.rollingstone.com/movies/reviews/her-20131218.

Vermeulen T and van den Akker R (2010) Notes on metamodernism. *Journal of Aesthetics & Culture* 2(2010).

13 Response

John Carroll

Influences on my work have been referred to in this book. I want to open by giving my own view. Admittedly, authors are notoriously blind, unreliable, and even deceitful about their origins. In brief, for what it's worth, this is how it seems to me, looking back.

Of direct personal influences, apart from family, two are of note. George Steiner, my doctoral supervisor in Cambridge, reinforced the conviction that human life is impoverished without deep and continuing engagement with the great works of literature, art, philosophy, and music of our own European background. They provide the pathways to the truths that illuminate. Further, their study requires a panoptic method, employing all disciplines from across the Humanities. It requires a lively style of writing, free from jargon, one that is accessible to any broadly educated reader.

Philip Rieff introduced me to a kind of cultural psychology that seemed insightful into the pathology of the times. Also influential was the Rieffian view of teaching and the University as having the central mission of keeping culture alive. And, I took over Rieff's method of using works of art as interpretative devices. George Steiner and Philip Rieff both expressed themselves with a scintillating incisiveness that was charismatic.

The main influences on the content of my work and its themes have been two of the old masters. The German philosopher Friedrich Nietzsche is an enduring presence. His first book, *The Birth of Tragedy*, develops a theory of culture which set parameters for my own thinking. As diagnostician of the challenges to the modern West in the secular, post-Church era, he charted the threat of nihilism and pervasive life disenchantment.

In a quite different mode, the French neo-classical painter, Nicolas Poussin, engaged me in the stories he tells, and the way he uses them to get at enigmatic truths composing human life—its tragedies and its redemptive possibilities. I have travelled the world for decades in search of his works, spending many hours over numerous visits with a score of them—which I have found totally absorbing, edifying, and enchanting. On one symptomatic occasion, in early September 1989, I flew from London to Dublin in the morning, spent three hours with Poussin's *Lamentation over the Dead Christ*, then flew straight back to London in the afternoon.

There is merit to Peter Murphy's characterisation of my sociology as neo-Calvinist. As much as this is the case, the overwhelming factor is heredity. Strong also is a cultural influence, linked obscurely to the genetic inheritance, and over generations, with English roots, in Non-Conformist Yorkshire. I am what Philip Rieff would have dubbed a post-Protestant.

Three people linked to this volume have, in one way or another, been of help. I first met Zygmunt Bauman during a week I spent in Leeds in 1979, at his invitation. I remember long walks with him in discussion—serious and engaged, yet light and charming, above all uplifting. He was an unselfconscious seeker after the truth, with no anxious glances over his shoulder. Those were, it turns out, the best sociological discussions I have ever had. Indeed, if there were more 'sociologists' in the world of his ilk, what a fine discipline it would be. I see him in his garden, a more vital place than Monet's Garden, and in witty conversation over stiff drinks on a Sunday morning (screwdrivers, if I remember correctly). He was always generous to a fault about my work.

Included in this volume is one of several Australian Broadcasting Corporation Radio National radio interviews that Stephen Crittenden conducted with me. Stephen hosted a weekly *Religion Report* for many years, in which his role in interviews was often as insightful as the book or issue under scrutiny, with him teasing out and amplifying hidden essences.

Keith Tester enabled this book. A friendship has developed over more than a decade, which has included attending Australian football matches together, seminar interactions, and email conversations. Keith directed a long question-and-answer discussion of *The Existential Jesus*, published in the journal *Cultural Sociology* (2010).

In addition, Eduardo de la Fuente, with Sara James, first had the idea for a book titled *Metaphysical Sociology*.

Now, let me turn to the direct contributions to this volume. I shall use them to reflect on my work. I shall leave until last the four essays that stand as particular studies in their own right.

Roger Scruton's essay *John Carroll's Jesus* is, to me, special. It gets inside my retelling of Mark's Life of Jesus, and presents it faithfully. Written with intensity, cohesion, and truthfulness, it invests my account with a quality of sympathetic energy I had barely hoped to evoke. At the same time, it places the narrative in the broader context of my convictions about our culture, its great works, their role in the lives of those with the good fortune to be born into the West, and the mission of the custodians of that culture. I couldn't myself write a better short exegesis of the book.

Scruton's conclusion invites some comment from me. The argument is that the mainstream of Christianity has been less individualistic than Mark's focus on a solitary, tortured, self-absorbed teacher who stresses that the abiding truth is about individual being. My Jesus is ultra-Protestant, in the line of Kierkegaard and Nietzsche—mostly 'self' and little 'other'. In contrast, Christianity as practised has been more about *You are* than *I am*—the Good Shepherd, with his parable of the Samaritan, known by selfless love, that of neighbour and community.

Of course, this is true. But only partly so, for Christianity is an individualistic religion, not a tribal one (such as Judaism): its central focus has always been on what the individual needs to do to be saved—salvation is solitary, not collective.

Jesus comes down to us in two quite different guises, maybe ones of equal importance. That depends on where you stand, and also on the historical moment. The churches, while stressing individual salvation, have stood, in the main, with the Good Shepherd, moral teacher, son of God, who died to save us from our sins (Matthew and Luke's Jesus). Part of my argument is that Mark's Jesus is more suited to our secular, post-church times. To put it harshly, the little Lord Jesus who lays down his sweet head is religion for children.

A further, and related, issue in relation to the nature of Christianity, and its place in Western culture, is raised by John Dickson, in his essay *John Carroll: towards a definition of culture*. This essay is of special interest to me, engaged as it is in a close wrestling with the more 'religious' side of my metaphysical sociology. I am grateful for its prescient argument.

The climax to the essay pivots on Resurrection. It claims that Jesus' Resurrection is the key to the historical success of Christianity, in addressing the deep human need for eternal life. My source for the life of Jesus, Mark's story, does exclude an explicit Resurrection, closing as it does with an empty tomb. This leaves us, at best Dickson suggests, with a symbolic transcendence of death, rather than the literal fact of rising above the mortal condition. Christianity has depended on the literal.

Christian doctrine would largely support the Dickson line. Jesus is the Saviour and Son of God, dying for our sins then returning to join his father in Heaven. But all religions provide the hope of eternal life—so why choose Christianity ahead of others? Islam, notably, is a one-dimensional *eternal life* religion.

Most significantly, the commanding symbol of Western culture, one of unique and enduring power, is the Cross; not an ascending body. The Cross is unambiguously a death image, and associated with a death that was particularly cruel and horrible.

My hunch is that the unconscious wish funding the mesmeric power of Christianity over two millennia is not the promise of eternal life, but the archetype of tragedy. At the least, eternal life and tragedy, signified by Resurrection and Crucifixion, have alternated in primacy. There is direct linking here to the origins of Western culture, in Greek tragedy. Mark wrote in Greek, and his story has the narrative form of a classical tragedy. The crux of tragedy is ambivalence: on the one hand, the terror of death and its finality; on the other, enigmatic signals of transcendence. Tragedy makes its own obscure gesture towards eternal life. The role of ancient Greece in the formation of the Western cultural unconscious is fundamental and pervasive, something I explored at length in my *Greek Pilgrimage*.

Furthermore, Christianity has been most imaginatively alive in *midrash*, at the finest in the music of Bach, the sculpture of Donatello, and the paintings of Raphael and Poussin. There, the transcendence is in the music and the visual imagery—in the story, not in the theology. The ultimate question remains: What do we bow down before, and tune in to? Is it doctrine-driven beliefs, or eternal rhythms?

To posit an either-or between literal fact and airy symbol is too crude. One reason I am particularly taken by Mark's 'walking on water' scene is that this *miracle* has been easy to scoff at by the soberly rational, scientific modern sensibility. Indeed, it is easy to dismiss. And yet, for anyone who becomes immersed in Mark's story there is an eerie evocative power conjured up, on the Sea of Galilee at 4-00 in the morning, the breath of sacred *pneuma* swirling around the crazed twelve followers stuck in a boat in the dark, terrified, thousands of disturbed spirits under the surface, with Jesus appearing to them as a phantasm approaching across the choppy waters. Shakespeare would have understood.

Michael Sheen's *The Passion in Port Talbot*, describing an event that stands as an exemplar of *midrash*, shows how one of our culture's mythic stories, in this case the most important of Western narratives, may be brought back to life in new costuming, and used to illuminate the present. Dickson rightly observes that my work reaches its climax in the axiom that we are dying for want of story. This is the Dreaming, whether it is the legends that framed Australian Aboriginal life; or such Western archetypes as those of the hero, vocation, and Magdalene; or Shakespeare's 'We are such stuff as dreams are made on.' My meditation on the Jesus story is an attempt to reawaken the vitality at the heart of the Western Dreaming.

Michael Sheen, best known as a film and television actor, approached me to join him in a BBC radio interview on *The Existential Jesus*. The prompt was a re-enactment he had carried out, in the Welsh town of Port Talbot in 2011, of the last three days of Jesus' life, from the Friday morning of the crucifixion to the Sunday evening. The essay included in this book came out of a correspondence between us in which he reflected on his experience.

His account of what happened in Port Talbot at Easter in 2011 speaks for itself. The *event*, for want of a better word, sounds to have been quite extraordinary.

To stage the Passion as community theatre taps into several ancient tropes. In early Greek tragedy, the line between actor and spectator was blurred, with spectators freely moving on stage. Sheen's spectators did become actors, some assuming major roles, and the spontaneity and unpredictability of the script catches something of the events during Jesus' own last week in Jerusalem.

This might be called interpretative theatre, for actor and audience alike, all participants in a drama with a loosely known script, with the opportunity to observe themselves and events as they unrolled. The three days provided the opportunity to come out a bit, for one and all, to get to know themselves a little better, with the aid of the classical story. The story serves as a kind of spotlight shining on the messy murk of a life, bringing clarity and shape, at least for a magic interlude. Further, the Shakespearean theme of all the world being a stage, and life being performance, is given full exploratory voice.

Sheen scripted the event, but his script provided no more than the surface story, one that enabled a lot of improvisation to erupt from within the chemistry of the moment. He writes that it seemed as if a benevolent spirit took over the event and guided it. He himself was not only inspired and possessed, and exhausted, but for weeks afterwards overwhelmed by memory, dream, and reflection:

Life and art totally blurred. It was very frightening at times. The power that was unleashed and was coursing through that place. I could feel it, as could everyone that was there, and we were all changed by it. I understood how and why drama emerged and came to be. I understood the nature of sacrifice and ritual and shared experience and catharsis. But, ultimately, something mysterious and bigger than all of us that were there walked the streets that weekend, and we all knew it. It answered every question I've ever had. It banished every doubt.

I experienced something similar in a Reading Group exploring Mark's Life of Jesus, and in writing *The Existential Jesus*.

The Passion in Port Talbot serves as evidence that we live by story.

Peter Murphy's *A Neo-Calvinist sociology: John Carroll's metaphysical modernity* is an overview of my work, capturing the main lines of argument from many books over three decades. It makes the work more coherent than it has seemed to me as I have stumbled along the way, following instinct, or some obscure inner direction. It has alerted me to continuities that I had only been dimly aware of. For this I am very grateful.

Above all, Murphy has highlighted themes from the book that ends the early phase of my work, *Guilt*, and tied these to the later phase, which begins with the Humanism book, *The Wreck of Western Culture*. My critique of humanism sets the scene, historically and philosophically, for the four later works of mine that develop a theory of modern culture (a fifth is in preparation)—*Ego and Soul, The Western Dreaming, The Existential Jesus*, and *Greek Pilgrimage*. Works written before *The Wreck of Western Culture* seem to me, in retrospect, to serve as anticipations. *Wreck* put the meaning question at the centre, and examined the long, multi-pronged secular attempt to find a here-and-now, this-worldly alternative to Christian redemption. The failure of Humanism's life-and-death attempt to discover a still-point of reliable life-meaning, in spite of its intellectual and artistic brilliance, led directly to the civilisational doubt and cultural masochism that have plagued the West since the late nineteenth century.

In a nutshell, Murphy highlights my argument, adapted from Max Weber, that the formation of the modern world, via the English Industrial Revolution, depended on the emergence of the Protestant (more precisely, neo-Calvinist) character type. Its driving energy was shaped by two commitments: one, to all-absorbing work—a *vocation*, or a *calling*—as illustrative of a higher meaning directing the individual; and two, to the companionate marriage as the social form allowing stable personal fulfilment in the anonymous and mobile, secular modern world that had replaced the traditional village and town. Both commitments remain alive and well today, and crucial to the good life.

As Murphy further notes, in the sociology of everyday life that forms one of the streams in my later work, I suggest that this Protestant cultural mode has come to be sublimated more widely, into other activities which hold alternative possibilities of transcendence—notably, sport and leisure pursuits in nature. I have argued, too, that popular culture has had considerable success in keeping the archetypal stories alive.

Murphy has shown how the two streams in my work connect, the religious stream and the popular culture stream. My political conservatism, referred to by Dickson, links here. It is in the tradition of Edmund Burke (I am not a moral conservative), and predicated on a trust in the basic good sense of the common man and woman. I have written in praise of the lower middle class, the counterpoint in my work to the consequences of Humanism for the upper middle class, whose members became both its proclaimers and its victims. Once Western High Culture had abandoned its sacred mission of seeking the truths that underpin the human condition, the upper middle class tended to become demoralised, like the Ambassadors of Holbein who provide the presiding image for *Wreck*.

I have also tried to demonstrate that practical working democracy, in its Anglo mode, is one of the secular sublimations of higher order to which people have become deeply attached. Democracy is more than a convenient moral constraint on potential anarchy, although it is that too.

Order is vital to human wellbeing. Order makes freedom possible—both in the political sphere and more widely. Only those who have trained themselves rigorously to play the violin will be free enough to improvise on it. I have always believed that the University seminar should be conducted within a strict framework, which includes the organising of the seating and lighting, punctuality, and a well-communicated routine. Students come to feel more seriously engaged with the subject matter; freer and less inhibited. A course can then be ambitious in the themes it explores, and the methods it uses.

Dickson reads my work as more philosophy than sociology. I did not pursue a career in philosophy for two reasons. The dominant mode in the Anglo world has been logical positivism, with a narrow focus on language, which was of little interest to me. It seemed the big questions that had occupied the major philosophers from Plato to Nietzsche had been suppressed. The second reason was a growing awareness that I felt more at home in sociology, with its reflex to develop theories in relation to how people actually live, and how societies actually function. I came to like the requirement of sociology for empirical testing. Philosophy has seemed off-puttingly abstract.

Keith Tester's *The eclipse of metaphysics* puts a particular slant on the relationship of sociology to metaphysics. It poses a dualism. Circumstances have meant, frequently in human history, that the tragedy of the moment eclipses questions of meaning, reducing them to an indulgent luxury. Sociology studies the social reality, as experienced; there are times when reality rubs out metaphysics. This is undoubtedly true.

Tester selects Auschwitz and Hiroshima as his examples. He follows the Adorno line that poetry (read, metaphysics) is impossible after the Holocaust. Further, the threat of nuclear war, symbolised by the bombing of Hiroshima, means that we can no longer be sure that human life will continue. Hence, we have entered a 'last age', one dominated by fear of the absurd and the horrible.

I have two responses. The first is empirical. The Holocaust was not unique in terms of magnitude and evil in human history. Indeed, human history is littered with equivalent examples, which would include the Roman levelling of

Carthage and the systematic killing of its inhabitants; slavery in its many guises; the savagery of torture and mutilation in the European Middle Ages; the Spanish Inquisition; the St Bartholomew's Day massacre of Protestants in France; and the Armenian genocide at the end of the First World War. In reality, the period since 1945 has been atypically peaceful and prosperous for the Western world, and indeed for much of the rest of the world. A term like the 'last age' does not ring true to me.

As a corollary, some have found a metaphysical anchor from within the chambers of dark experience. The writings of Victor Frankl and Primo Levi stand out, reflecting on their experiences in the Nazi death camps. As a low-key parallel, most people today manage to find meaning in what might seem the banal routines of everyday life, contra Max Weber's predictions about disenchantment.

In the second place, the kind of theoretical blueprint one stamps on an era, or grand narrative one reads into it, comes down partly to a matter of temperament. My temperament is not apocalyptic. The assumption that the world will end—whether with a catastrophic bang or a deflated whimper—is metaphysical. I am more drawn to following the mainstream of our literature and art, and indeed the experience of most people, in seeking the presence of the beyond in the everyday. The long history of Western culture has been dotted with predictions of the apocalypse, including Christian Revelation, none of which have come true.

That we are dying for want of story finds illustration in Marcus Maloney's *Digital Western dreaming*, reflecting on video gaming. This essay is original and suggestive, showing the creative adaptability of a culture, as one art form goes into decline, with a new one providing the opportunity for the serious pursuit of meaning questions. During the last century, we have seen the cinema take over from painting and the novel, if not comprehensively; and then cable television take over from cinema, in producing art of high quality. The video games under consideration are a marvellous example of the vitality of the *collective unconscious* of a culture (a term not used here in the Jungian sense). It germinates new green shoots in the most surprising areas. Engagement in the questions at the core of human existence cannot stay suppressed for long; they force their way out, in narrative form.

Maloney makes a modest claim for the four games he explores, that they are not masterpieces of the calibre of *The Searchers*—but he shows enough to make us take them seriously. He establishes *Red Dead Redemption*, for instance, as belonging to the genre of heroic tragedy. This game is in the tradition of the Western, a fact that is in itself of value, given that the great classic Westerns are, for the time being, as Maloney notes, neglected—not replayed on free-to-air television, and not available on such media streaming services as Netflix, although many are accessible through iTunes. Mind, the Western has found some recent articulations of the first rank—in the novels of Cormac McCarthy and the HBO television series *Deadwood*.

In *The Last of Us*, an impression point marks the climax to the narrative, and to a degree that precludes the serious player treating the game as just a back-alley shoot-out. In this work, we are also led into another characteristic of high art, the fatedness of the script. Maloney argues that players, in spite of their seeming agency, have at best superficial free-will.

One question that arises is whether video games have special power as narrative vehicles. Players are more active, in a direct sense, than spectators at the theatre, cinema, or in front of a video screen, in their identification with the role they are playing. This may make for more complete immersion in the story. As a cautioning note here, however, spectators standing or sitting before any art work, whatever the form, once they become engaged in the story, are not passive—as Maloney is aware. To be absorbed in a story is to participate in it. Gaming may add another dimension to participation.

Maloney convinces that video games serve as more than entertainment. They provide a telling test-case, in that the superficial view would regard them as pure examples of solitary narcissistic individuals addicted to escapist pastime. If they defy the slur that the contemporary Western world is debased by consumerism, then so too, and much more readily, do other popular activities, like sport. The grander context here is that mythic story cannot be dismissed as mere myth, fiction, or redemptive illusion.

I am indebted to Maloney's observation that, in *The Searchers*, the sandstone monoliths that form the backdrop in Monument Valley stand like somnolent gods, gesturing to the higher order that frames the story. *The Searchers* is arguably the greatest modern creation in the mode of classical tragedy. Those sandstone monoliths play a similar role to the Delphic mountain that looks down on Oedipus as his story unfolds.

My first book, *Break-Out from the Crystal Palace*, and a short reflection from 2002, *Terror*, are brought centre-stage in Wayne Bradshaw's *Ego-terrorism*. This essay proposes a cultural psychological reading of terrorism, via an understanding of the terrorist persona. It posits 'metaphysical critique' against the 'ideological analysis' that has been more common. It argues that the principal motivation driving terrorists lies in pathologies of individual character rather than the beliefs to which those individuals are attracted. The ideology serves as rationalisation, if often a rationalisation that directs and encourages the act. Character is primary; ideology secondary.

For its theory, the essay draws upon the anarcho-psychological typology presented in *Break-Out from the Crystal Palace*. I must confess that I have, for a long time, been uneasy about my theory. However, I do think Bradshaw gets enough explanatory power out of it to warrant its usage. A theory is only justified when it allows some significant understanding that would not be gained otherwise.

There is more to the anarcho-psychological typology than I had credited, as I have discovered by revisiting it. Indeed, it provides a backdrop for much of my later work, where the terminology can be recognised in shadow form. The disenchantment themes that have accompanied the rise of Humanism reflect an over-psychologised self and an anarchist politics. Bradshaw correctly observes an affinity with my 2002 characterisation of Usama bin Laden. Bin Laden was committed to the act rather than the idea, an anarchist with no inclination to build anything new, his pleasure coming from destruction for its own sake. Bradshaw reminds us of Nietzsche's brilliant caricature of anarchists as inventors of 'new noises' rather than 'new values'—which fits Islamic terrorism perfectly.

Bradshaw puts a cogent case for his term 'ego-terrorism'. The anarcho-psychological temper, in which the self-centred ego is all, has been incarnate in artists, students, bohemians, and more generally in the disaffected extremes of the political Left and Right. Terrorism is the outwardly directed manifestation of the same temper. The terrorist persona is preoccupied with its own power, or lack of it, and chooses a criminal act of will to prove its rejection of morality's capacity to govern the individual. Ego and its will are threatened by society, which must be destroyed. As Bradshaw observes: terrorists 'overconfident in their will and capacity for action are pushed towards a program of self-assured annihilation.'

The essay's conclusions are important. The current wave of Islamic terrorism is not new in the discontents that have prompted it, nor in the anarcho-psychological motivations that drive it. It exhibits a rancorous pathology of individual character that is familiar in the West, with roots that go back to the French Revolution. On the other hand, the ideology that frames Islamic terrorism is new, and alien, one that serves as a shaping and legitimating factor that is as essential to the resulting terrorist act as the individual's motives. In short, there is a push factor, and a pull factor.

Usama bin Laden was a satanic anarchist, with Marxist colouring, his pleasure coming from choosing targets that were emblems of capitalist power—New York skyscrapers, the Pentagon, and the United States Congress, not religious targets as one might have imagined, such as the Vatican, Westminster Abbey, or an American Synagogue. In a speech broadcast soon after September 11, he hit the Humanist nerve with uncanny precision, proclaiming that his God had 'elevated the skies without pillars.' His implicit challenge was that, if the pillars of Western culture are no more than the Twin Towers of the World Trade Center in New York, and what they symbolise, then he could bring that culture down. Bin Laden had seen, like Luther, that metaphysics was the vital spot, and that unbelief in the Humanist metropolis had gravely weakened the West.

Margaret Gibson's *Mortality, time and embodied finitude* provides an extraordinary, intimate, and sensitive reading of the disquieting film *Amour*. In the best interpretative tradition, it adds to the artwork, bringing it to a higher level by standing back and deftly playing a spotlight across it—enabling extra clarity.

A full essay on dying and death serves this volume well. In my reflection *What is metaphysical sociology?* I considered the death of Tolstoy's Prince Andrei, and Poussin's *Testament of Eudamidas*. Both works, like *Amour*, focus on a deathbed scene. Further, they both illustrate Gibson's conclusion that we die relationally, not alone. But there the similarities end.

Tolstoy and Poussin's deaths are numinous: metaphysics enters the room in the form of awe and wonder. The reader or the viewer is uplifted: death is more than death, more than a nothingness void. In neither case, is it the beautiful death idealised by the late Romantic movement, painting a corpse at peace and decked in flowers. *Eudamidas* is a fraction closer to *Amour* in that the dying man's life is made meaningful through his love for wife and daughter, and for the two trusted friendships that have been significant to him. The love and friendship are articulated through a scribe, who writes the will—who, in effect, tells the story of Eudamidas' life. It is through the story, and the charged presence of the storyteller, that the human world is redeemed.

Amour provides a different perspective on death, one muffled in confusion and doubt, more fleshly, perhaps closer to the contemporary existential nerve. The actual dying portrayed in the film is dispiriting—relieved for one brief moment, near the end, in an intimate scene between husband and wife. The effects of two strokes on Anne are oppressive—gruelling without relief—driving her husband, Georges, into caring for her with grim and tortured despair. His life, confined within a gloomy Paris apartment, has closed in on him. It is left open whether Anne's death does bring a meaningful life to a fitting completion—the core judgement used by Gibson. I suspect the film leaves a profoundly uneasy mood in the viewer because the answer is in the negative. As Gibson also wonders, it is as if death is the only escape from the claustrophobia of the end circumstances Georges has chosen for himself, the only exit from the apartment.

Amour's climax comes when Georges, drowning in the hopelessness of his and his wife's situation, but still rational, courageously, and seemingly on impulse, suffocates her with a pillow. Throughout, he has been desperate that Anne keep her dignity—and the beauty he remembers and treasures. He doesn't want their daughter to see her mother paralysed, partly for this reason. The tapestry of his life has had the love for his wife as a central thread, the whole uplifted by music, and it is this, the wholeness of a shared life together, that he struggles to round out in a harmonious and respectful completion.

Sara James' *Modern metaphysical romance* brings *Metaphysical Sociology* to a fitting close. It stands as a vital exploration and testing of the irrepressible power of cultural archetypes. It does so in the case of romance, thus serving to extend the love theme introduced in Gibson's essay—a theme that has been underplayed through the main stretch of this book.

James' first book, *Making a Living, Making a Life* (2017), is also caught up with the central presence of archetypes, in its case the archetype of vocation. It shows, through contemporary case-studies—people reflecting on their experiences of work—the underlying fantasy of a deeply serious life activity that does provide a mysterious kind of higher meaning. And this occurs in spite of a social milieu in which individuals are less secure in their jobs, threatened with casualisation, and in which they change occupations more frequently. If they exhibit less commitment to the particular job, this does not seem to diminish their attachment to the general ideal of *work*—that is, to the archetype.

One might expect the archetype of soul-mate love to have come under fatal pressure in a secular modern world commanded by the belief in freedom of choice, and sceptically rational about the observable fact that romance is fickle, and relationships are arbitrary—in terms of intersections on the life-path that determine the others whom a person meets, and whom they become intimate with.

James sketches a wider picture today, of studies that show that individuals who use social media for meeting others, socialising, and self-projection continue to have an undiminished belief that there is a 'chosen one', who will be encountered one day. This is in spite of higher divorce rates, more fluid relationships, and greater realism about the vicissitudes of intimacy. James' particular focus—the film *Her*—reinforces the archetype, while subjecting it to intense questioning.

The film probes the bounds of soul-mate love. The central character is more in love with love than with the actual person, as his ex-wife observes; further illustrated in his job, writing love letters for strangers. Mozart expressed the same cynical view of romance in his opera *Così Fan Tutte*. According to the cynical view, intimacy is a fantasy, or a 'colossal dream', to borrow a term from *The Great Gatsby*. Yet, for the one who falls in love there is another person, and the fantasy would not work without the existence of that other. Further, James is convincing that the subject of *Her*, in spite of his self-absorbed narcissism, does miss an actual real-life presence. There is colossal dreaming; but it is only half of the story.

The subject has fallen for an artificial intelligence beloved, whom it turns out has multiple romances simultaneously, contradicting the soul-mate ideal, and yet not, in that she is a sci-fi creation, obeying an unknown logic. What is significant is that the subject is deeply upset when he finds out, as the image of his 'chosen one' has been tarnished. In a kind of parallel today, when people who are in a close relationship continue to look out of the corner of their eyes, on social media, for an 'upgrade', it seems their 'chosen one' is provisional. Yet, even here, the soul-mate ideal rules behind the scenes, in an adapted form: if an upgrade is found, it merely shows that the former choice was mistaken.

Soul-mate love is inevitably bound up with a second of the key cultural archetypes I developed in my book *The Western Dreaming*. The belief that there is a chosen one implies that the person's life is scripted—predestined. Yet *fate* is diametrically at odds with the modern belief in individual choice, and the freedom to make a life. Freedom, in important matters, is the panoptic illusion of the modern era. It is mocked by the archetypes.

Freud argued that we individuals are ruled by our unconscious minds, and further, that the unconscious knows everything. Yet we are not the less ruled unwittingly, also from within, in the preeminent mental sphere of fantasy, ideal, hope, and aspiration—which direct much of the unconscious. This metaphysical domain is shaped by the archetypes, embedded in Western culture, ones that come down to us from the beginning—from a long time ago.

It is particularly gratifying to me that this book gels far more than I would have expected. Books of essays are usually disjointed. The coherency of *Metaphysical Sociology* owes a lot to Sara James, who has masterminded the project. The result reflects her editorship—judicious in choice of contribution, and scrupulous in sub-editorial detail.

References

Carroll J (1974) *Break-Out from the Crystal Palace: The Anarcho-Psychological Critique: Stirner, Nietzsche, Dostoevsky*. London: Routledge & Kegan Paul.

Carroll J (1985) *Guilt: The Grey Eminence behind Character, History and Culture*. London: Routledge & Kegan Paul.

Carroll J (2001) *The Western Dreaming: The Western World is Dying for Want of a Story*. Pymble, NSW: HarperCollins.
Carroll J (2002) *Terror: A Meditation on the Meaning of September 11*. Carlton: Scribe.
Carroll J (2004) *The Wreck of Western Culture: Humanism Revisited*. Melbourne: Scribe.
Carroll J (2007) *The Existential Jesus*. Melbourne: Scribe.
Carroll J (2008) *Ego and Soul: The Modern West in Search of Meaning*. Berkeley, CA: Counterpoint.
Carroll J (2010) *Greek Pilgrimage: In Search of the Foundations of the West*. Melbourne: Scribe.
Fitzgerald F (2004) *The Great Gatsby*. New York: Simon & Schuster.
James S (2017) *Making a Living, Making a Life: Work, Meaning and Self-Identity*. Abingdon: Routledge.
Nietzsche F (2003) *The Birth of Tragedy*. London: Penguin Classics.
Tester K (2010) Telling Stories about Jesus: A Conversation with John Carroll. *Cultural Sociology* 4(3): 379–394.

Index

Adorno, Theodore 9, 82–5, 89, 92–3 (notes 8–10, 17), 116–18
ageing 10, 126, 128–68
anomie 1, 3, 43–5, 102, 147
Antonioni, Michelangelo, *L'Eclisse* 9, 82, 86–90, 92 (note 14)
anxiety 36, 40, 60, 73, 76, 116, 133, 143, 150
archetypes, archetypal 6–10, 18–21, 36–7, 44–5, 76–7, 97, 108, 117, 121–2, 140–1, 144, 149, 153, 158–60, 165–6
Aristotle 29
Austen, Jane, *Pride and Prejudice* 14, 141–2

Bauman, Zygmunt 4, 5, 17, 145–53, 157
Beck, Ulrich 107, 128, 144
Benjamin, Walter 89–90, 93 (notes 19–20)
Bioshock 9, 95, 99–101, 107
Bloom, Harold 25, 36, 56 (note 1)
Break-Out from the Crystal Palace: The Anarcho-Psychological Critique: Stirner, Nietzsche, Dostoevsky 1, 10, 46, 111–15, 118, 123, 163

Calvinism 8, 69–78, 91 (note 4), 141, 157, 160
chronos 7, 39–40, 75
Conrad, Joseph, *Heart of Darkness* 15, 21, 47–50, 97–8, 100, 103, 106–8

dating apps *see* mobile technology
Deadwood 48, 162
death of God 17, 46, 75–6, 96
Delphic principles 9, 81–4, 88, 91 (note 5), 93 (note 20)
Dionysian 43, 47–51
disenchantment 17, 96, 139–40, 151, 156, 162–3
DIY 4, 8, 69–70, 74

Don Quixote 15, 127, 150
Dostoevsky, Fyodor 3, 7, 10, 43–4, 46–56, 106, 111–18, 122–3; *The Brothers Karamazov* 102; *Crime and Punishment* 50, 115; *Demons* 116, 123 (note 2); *Notes from Underground* 50, 115; *The Possessed* 44, 49–50
Duchamp, Marcel 17–20
Durkheim, Emile 3, 5, 7, 16, 43, 97, 116

Easter 8, 39–40, 58–61, 158–9
Ego and Soul: The Modern West in Search of Meaning 2–4, 17, 45, 52, 70, 74–8, 81, 91 (note 4), 96, 101–2, 105, 125–6, 140, 143, 148–50, 160
egoism 3, 75, 111–23
Eliot, T. S. 33, 45, 49, 52
Enlightenment, the 2–3, 41–2, 117, 126, 141–2
Existential Jesus, The 4, 6–8, 20, 25–34, 35–42, 45, 51–6, 58, 73–8, 91 (note 4), 157, 159–60

Fight Club 48–9, 97
Fitzgerald, F. Scott, *The Great Gatsby* 15, 18, 150, 166
Ford, John, *The Man Who Shot Liberty Valance* 103–4, 117; *The Searchers* 48, 95, 103–4, 106–7, 162–3
French Revolution 116, 164
Freud, Sigmund 49, 52, 55, 166

Geertz, Clifford 108
Georg Lukács 49–51, 118
Giddens, Anthony 107, 144, 148–50
Goethe, Johann Wolfgang von 39, 55, 73
Greek Pilgrimage: In Search of the Foundations of the West 4, 20, 45–6, 93 (note 20), 158, 160

guilt 38, 41, 53, 66–73, 90, 104, 141–2
Guilt: The Grey Eminence Behind Character, History and Culture 8, 53, 67–78

Haneke, Michael *Amour* 10, 126, 128–38, 164–5
Heidegger, Martin 38–41, 45
Holocaust, the 9, 82–3, 91 (notes 7–8), 92 (note 9), 161–2
Holbein, *Ambassadors* 80–1, 90, 161
humanism 2–3, 44, 80–1, 91 (notes 2, 5), 96, 100, 126, 160–4
Humanism: The Wreck of Western Culture 2–3 (*see also The Wreck of Western Culture*)

Iliad, The 6, 14
Individualization 1, 3, 11, 16, 44, 46, 49–50, 70, 76–7, 100, 107, 119–22, 142–53, 157–8, 164–6
industrialization 3, 72, 104, 160

Jonze, Spike *Her* 10–11, 139, 146–54, 165–6
Jung, Carl 47–52

kairos 7, 39–40, 75
Kermode, Frank 25–6, 56 (note 1), 91 (note 2), 97, 108 (note 1)
Kierkegaard, Soren 7, 48, 53–4, 73, 78, 97

Last of Us, The 9, 95, 101–3, 162
liquid modernity 17, 145 (*see also* Bauman)
love 7–11, 14–15, 30–1, 41–2, 50, 54, 61, 70, 74, 86–8, 128–37, 139–53, 157, 164–6

Marcuse, Herbert 85
marriage 8, 10, 69–73, 77–8, 140–5, 150–3
Marx, Karl 5, 16, 46, 112, 115, 120, 126, 164
mobile technology 145–8, 153
morality 41, 44–54, 56 (note 2), 101–2, 106, 111–23, 131–5, 151, 164
myth (*see also* narrative) 3–9, 13, 19, 23, 36–40, 45–6, 51–5, 59, 101, 104, 121–2, 125, 139–42, 159, 163

Nietzsche, Friedrich 2, 5, 7, 10, 13, 15–17, 35, 39–41, 46–56, 72, 96–7, 100, 106–8, 111–23, 156–7, 161, 164
nihilism 17, 21, 44, 50–1, 72–3, 78, 105, 118, 125, 156

Oedipus the King 13, 163

Plato 70, 100, 139–41, 161
pneuma 27–33, 36–40, 73, 159
politics 49–51, 54, 67, 74–5, 111–23, 163
postmodern 45, 106, 153 (note 4), 154 (note 11)
Poussin, Nicolas, *The Testament of Eudamidas* 6, 15, 164–5
Protestantism 16, 20–3, 67, 70–2, 141, 157, 160, 162
Puritan, Paranoid, Remissive: A Sociology of Modern Culture 3

Rand, Ayn 99–100
Red Dead Redemption 9, 95, 103–5, 162
re-enchantment 23, 49–51, 149
Reformation, the 67–8, 141
Renaissance, the 2, 15
Rieff, Phillip 3, 5, 17, 45, 49, 52, 56 (notes 1, 5), 92 (note 4), 96, 101, 156–7
risk 18, 71, 128, 144–5, 152–3 (*see also* Beck, Ulrich)
ritual 8, 160, 18–19, 59, 61, 65, 67, 70, 107, 132, 144

Sartre, Jean Paul 41, 102
Sceptical Sociology 4–5, 11 (note 2), 49, 125–6, 142–3
science 13, 16, 21, 71, 117, 126–7
September 11 10, 121, 111–12, 164
Shakespeare 20, 159; *Coriolanus* 80–1, 88, 91 (notes 2, 5); *Hamlet* 6, 14–16, 20–1, 44, 47–8, 127–8; *Macbeth* 88; *Much Ado about Nothing* 77–8
Socrates 44, 139–41
Sopranos, The, HBO television series 20–1, 98, 102–3
sport 4, 8, 74–5, 140, 160, 163
Stirner, Max 10, 111–13, 118–23
suicide 14, 16, 49–50, 59, 62, 115–16, 123 (note 1), 127–8, 135

Terror: A Meditation on the Meaning of September 11 10, 91 (note 4), 100, 111, 117, 163
Terrorism 10, 111–23, 163–4
That Dragon, Cancer 9, 95, 105–6
Tolstoy, Leo 5, 106, 117, 117; *War and Peace* 14, 21–2, 164
Treme, HBO television series 20

verstehen 6, 16–19
vocation 8, 20, 70–5, 116, 120, 139, 141, 150, 159–60, 165

Weber, Max 2, 5–7, 16–23. 35, 50–1, 91 (note 4), 116–17, 139–40, 160–2
The Western Dreaming: The Western World is Dying for Want of a Story 4, 20, 38, 45, 66, 69–78, 96–7, 108, 140–1, 160, 166

'Where Ignorant Armies Clash by Night': On the Retreat of Faith and its Consequences 3–4
World War I 32, 68, 162
World War II 5, 17, 68, 144
The Wreck of Western Culture: Humanism Revisited 2–3, 17, 47, 53, 70–2, 76–8, 80–1, 85, 91 (note 2), 96–7, 103–4, 160 (*see also Humanism*)